REMEMBRANCE TODAY

REMEMBRANCE TODAY

Poppies, Grief and Heroism

TED HARRISON

REAKTION BOOKS

Published by
Reaktion Books Ltd
33 Great Sutton Street
London EC1V 0DX, UK

www.reaktionbooks.co.uk

Printed and bound in Great Britain
by TJ International, Padstow, Cornwall

British Library Cataloguing in Publication Data
Harrison, Ted.
Remembrance today: poppies, grief and heroism.
1. War and society.
2. Memorial rites and ceremonies.
3. Collective memory.
I. Title
306.4-DC23

ISBN 978 1 78023 044 3

CONTENTS

INTRODUCTION

REMEMBRANCE IS ABOUT RECALLING AND HONOURING THOSE who have died as members of the armed services. Every nation has its own rituals and customs, shaped by culture and history. I am British and to me Remembrance is about the symbol of the poppy, the two minutes' silence, the annual service held at the Cenotaph in London and the thousands of smaller ceremonies held at war memorials around the country.

This book seeks, by looking afresh at the origins of Remembrance, to examine what the traditions really mean today to a generation that has never known a world war and never been under military discipline.

Once it could be assumed that Remembrance united the nation. There are signs now that Remembrance-tide is about to become a divisive issue. This book will therefore ask some awkward but necessary questions.

Do the ceremonies, resplendent as they are with uniformed troops and graced as they are with serving politicians, inadvertently provide armed conflict with a cloak of respectability?

What is the role of popular culture in the promotion of Remembrance? Did it trivialize war when the X Factor contestants' 'Hero' became the fastest-selling charity single of the decade? Or was any trivialization justified by the profile of the Poppy Appeal being raised, particular among younger people?

Does Remembrance reinforce myths which, far from warning against the horrors of war, serve to glorify conflict and make it more, rather than less, likely to happen in the future?

This book began as an essay, a short reflection on Remembrance in Britain. However, from a single article titled 'Refocusing Remembrance', published in January 2010,[1] the process of reflection grew and developed into a wider project asking some fundamental questions about the way nations remember and honour those who die as members of the armed services. What started out as a review of British tradition and practice has became one of wider international relevance.

Remembrance is not solely a community, or national, experience. It is a personal one as well, and as it is for everyone else, my perspective on the issues raised is shaped by who I am, my background, date and place of birth, what I have seen and known. I was born in Kent, some 50 miles from London, three years after the end of the Second World War. It was a time when memories of the fighting, the bombing, the rationing, the anxieties, the fear, the sorrow, the restrictions and privations, were still fresh in people's minds, including my parents. References to the war were frequently made during my childhood. If I put an over-generous helping of butter on my bread I would be reminded that that was the entire week's ration in the war. I remember going to London and seeing bomb sites, devastated patches of land where once a house or shop had stood before being wiped out by a German bomb. I saw the cathedral city of Canterbury being rebuilt after the wartime destruction of many of its ancient streets. I recall too that throughout my childhood some of the fears of war lingered. When I was eight years old, at the time of the Suez Crisis, the government distributed fuel-rationing books. Fortunately they were never needed, but I was told by my father that they were just like the ones that had been in use only a few years earlier during the war. And hanging over the world during my childhood was the constant threat of the nuclear bomb. At the age of fourteen I was well aware from news reports of how close, during the time of the Cuban Missile Crisis, the major powers came to launching attacks and precipitating the Third World War.

If the Second World War was my parents' war, then the First World War was my grandparents' war. Both of my grandfathers had served, one in the Army and the other in the Navy. Sadly they died before I was of an age to talk to them about their experiences, but I have documents from those days and have seen photographs of them in uniform. My mother had her own childhood memories of war-torn France in 1919. Her father, my grandfather, had been deployed there as an Army major to work on clearing the worst of the devastation. With the fighting over he was able to take his wife and daughter with him and they lived there in married quarters for several months. Today the fields of northern France look tranquil and peaceful. Back then there remained quagmires of debris littered with jagged metal, unexploded ordnance and fragments of human remains. This is where my grandfather worked while his family stayed in the relative normality of a northern French village.

In addition to my grandfathers, I knew many other veterans of the First World War. Most of them then were younger than I am today. One of my earliest memories is of going with my father, the local vicar, to a residential care home in his Kent parish where some of the most severely injured and traumatized survivors lived. I took the visit in my stride, and maybe the rare presence of a child in the place brought some colour to the day, but my enduring, snapshot recollections are of a grim scene. There were men with limbs missing; some were blind; one, as far as I recall, moaned and made strange involuntary actions. They had been that way for over 30 years, since the day when, as young men, their war injuries abruptly killed their hopes for the future.

Despite war seeming very close at hand when I was a child, I am very thankful that when I became an adult I never myself had to wear a military uniform. I was relieved when the government announced that National Service, compulsory peacetime military training, was to be abolished and I realized I would not have to join up on reaching the age of conscription. From what I heard about service life, it did not appeal to me. I certainly had no intention of volunteering and making a career as a member of one of the regular professional services. I have therefore never drilled, marched, polished boots or been trained to kill.

I did however, during my time as a BBC reporter, witness fighting and I saw the consequences of war at first hand. I have met many military and civilian victims of warfare who had endured unspeakable deprivations and who were destined to carry the physical and mental scars through life. I came to know many members of The Guinea Pig Club, the injured British airmen who had received pioneering plastic surgery, when I co-authored a book about them.[2]

As a journalist I had many encounters with the military. I have flown with the Royal Air Force, visited warships and watched Army ceremonial and training. I also know from first-hand experience what it is like to be under fire. I have been both shelled from a distance by the American navy and threatened face-to-face by a man in uniform with a loaded gun.

For me, as a child, Remembrance Day was one of the landmark days in the cycle of the year. It happened not long after the party games of Halloween had finished and just before the Christmas preparations began. It was a solemn day and one of familiar ritual. It felt a bit like Good Friday, but with more colour. It was the day when my father's medals came out of the drawer and everyone in the family had to make sure they were dressed smartly and had a poppy to wear.

When I was four years old, my father moved to a new parish where one of his duties was to serve as chaplain to a Royal Air Force station. RAF Hawkinge in Kent had been at the front line during the Battle of Britain and a decommissioned Spitfire stood at the entrance to the site as a reminder of the airfield's crucial role in the recent history of the country. Today the airfield is covered in houses and the war years are vividly and movingly recalled at a local museum. At the time RAF Hawkinge was still regularly used for training. For a small boy it was fascinating to watch the activity on the airfield opposite our house. Tethered balloons would take novice parachutists aloft and I would watch the trainees leap and descend. Flying was largely restricted to gliders, but occasionally a helicopter would be heard overhead or a propeller-powered plane would land on the grass runway.

There was also a war memorial and an RAF church. The memorial still stands although, some time after the RAF closed the station, the church was demolished. A recycling depot now stands on the site. The memorial and church were the focus of the events of Remembrance Day. Every year, on the appointed November Sunday morning, veterans joined with serving airmen and -women to lay wreaths of poppies and mark the two minutes' silence. I can still remember the pomp and spectacle of that day at a site which ten years earlier had been part of a fully operational combat base on a war footing. As a boy, in a home without a television, I was unaware of the annual ceremony at Whitehall's Cenotaph. To me Remembrance had a local focus.

From an early age I never questioned whether to recall and honour the men and women who had died while serving in the armed forces was the right and proper thing to do. I still hold that to be true. As I looked around me at the adults who had direct experience of war, I could see that for them Remembrance Day was a moving and emotional time. Their memories were vivid and their grief real. Yet as a youngster I had no such feelings. How could I? My father and his brother had served in the Second World War and survived. Two of my great uncles had died in the First World War, but to me they were no more than names: John Graham had died aged 23 in July 1916 and Richard Graham, known in the family as 'Dick', had died aged nineteen in January 1915. They had both been young officers in Scottish regiments. Both died in France, where they are buried. Not even my father could remember them, although my grandmother's sorrow at the loss of her two young brothers never left her.

My role on Remembrance Day was not to grieve, but to be respectful. I was expected, through taking part in the events of the day, to 'pay my respects'. In some ways the atmosphere was like that of a funeral, but the funeral of someone I had not known. I had been a choirboy when young, and attending the Remembrance Sunday service was a bit like singing at a stranger's memorial service.

I do not recall being expected overtly to show gratitude as children today are taught. The Remembrance Day message to the current generation of young people is that they should give thanks to the people they have never known who have sacrificed their lives so that they could live in a world free from tyranny. A modern-day children's book on the subject puts it this way:

On Poppy Day, we say thank you to the people who fought to protect our country. Poppy Day is a way to show that we are grateful. Remembering Poppy Day every year means that this sign of respect will continue in the future.[3]

From what my elders said, and from what I learned at school, there seemed no doubt that Britain would have been a very different place if the Second World War had not been fought and won. Without the victory of the RAF over the Luftwaffe, without the bulldog defiance of Churchill, without the Normandy landings, without the final capitulation of Germany and the death of Hitler, Britain would certainly have been under the control of an evil, foreign tyrant. Yet in the immediate post-Second World War period displays of gratitude were not expected. Those of my parents' generation did not boast about what they had done themselves. It was not in their character. They did not ask, nor did they expect, to be thanked for what they had done during the war. They had simply done what was expected of them and now looked to get on with their lives in peace.

As I grew older the age of post-war austerity gave way to the 'never had it so good' 1950s. Time heals and even to those of my parents' generation the war years began to slip into history. While the traditional Remembrance observances continued unaltered, I however was changing. I was growing into a questioning teenager, egged on no doubt by the spirit of the age. In the 1960s, as Bob Dylan reminded us, 'The Times They Are a-Changin'. I started to feel uneasy about the Remembrance Sunday rites, which I was still expected to attend. It occurred to me that amidst the tradition, sentiment and ritual of the day one of the key reasons for re-membering the war dead was being overlooked. The observances, surely, were not solely about honouring, showing respect to, or even expressing thanks to a past generation. The more I looked into the subject for myself, what seemed far more important was the idea that through remembering the victims of war, the living dedicated themselves to peace. This had been the prime purpose of the rituals when they were first established in 1919. Remem-brance, when it began in its present form, was first and foremost a declaration and public affirmation that war must never happen again. Somehow, over the years, the emphasis had drifted away from this.

This was not an original observation, though at the time I was unaware of others thinking that way or the history behind that viewpoint. I discovered later how in the 1930s there had been a strong feeling that Armistice Day, as it was then known, was too militaristic in tone. Many survivors of the First World War made their views known. It was during this time that the Peace Pledge Union thrived.

In the 1960s, when I became politically aware, the shape of Remembrance Day remained almost exactly as it had been in the 1930s. The ceremonies that had gone into abeyance during the Second World War were revived in 1945 in precisely the same form as before. The tone of the occasion remained overwhelmingly militaristic. What seemed especially puzzling to me, as a questioning teenager, was how, at one of the most dramatic and evocative highlights of the Remembrance rituals, no reference was made to the evils of war. The more I heard about the First World War, the more it seemed to me to have been one of utter pointlessness, and yet the focal words of Remembrance conveyed no impression of the reality of that conflict. The words said nothing about dedicating the nation and future generations to peace. Instead, in the traditional declamation by a veteran at the memorial addressed to his dead comrades, death in war was both applauded as glorious and yet simultaneously diminished in significance by the very words used. To me, as an argumentative youth, the war deaths appeared belittled and demeaned by the words of Remembrance. Surely the premature and horrible deaths of many hundreds of thousands of young men should not have been downgraded to a few lines of sentimental poetry?

> They shall grow not old, as we that are left grow old:
> Age shall not weary them, nor the years condemn.
> At the going down of the sun and in the morning
> We will remember them.[4]

It did not help that the words, when I heard them as a child, were generally declaimed by a brusque man of statuesque military bearing who has survived in my recollection as pompous and self-important. Perhaps I am being unfair to his memory, but he seemed to put so much effort into maintaining his posture and appearance that the words were further diminished by his performance.

The messenger aside, what was I expected to make of the words? Part of me was stirred and another part repulsed. The dead, as vivid as memories of them were in the minds of the veterans, appeared to have been consigned to a mawkish Valhalla where heroes lived in a state of eternal youth. The words may have brought comfort to the survivors of war. Certainly, if you have seen a companion blown to pieces alongside you and had to clean his blood and flesh from your clothes, it may be necessary to protect your mental wounds with gentle, stirring or colourful words. Yet, looking at the poem by Laurence Binyon from which the Remembrance declaration is taken, what image of war is being passed on to the younger generation?

It talks of England as a mother in proud thanksgiving for 'her dead across the sea'. It talks of those who have died in euphemistic terms, as the 'fallen' whose cause was freedom. The poem talks of the young going to war with songs. They were staunch to the end despite the odds against them and fell 'with their faces to the foe'.

What is being implied here? Is the poet seriously saying that a mother should be thankful that her son has died? That what mattered at the end was that the boys fell with their 'faces to the foe', whatever the odds against them? That having died in battle, the young gain an immortality denied to those who survive? That to have died in the First World War, an absurd fight to the death between two posturing Empires, could be described as having fallen in 'the cause of the free'? These are questionable notions that demand to be challenged.

Contrast Binyon's words with those of the war poet Wilfred Owen, who died in the final stages of the First World War:

What passing-bells for these who die as cattle?
Only the monstrous anger of the guns.
Only the stuttering rifles' rapid rattle
Can patter out their hasty orisons.
No mockeries now for them; no prayers nor bells;
Nor any voice of mourning save the choirs, –
The shrill, demented choirs of wailing shells;
And bugles calling for them from sad shires.
What candles may be held to speed them all?
Not in the hands of boys but in their eyes
Shall shine the holy glimmers of goodbyes.
The pallor of girls' brows shall be their pall;
Their flowers the tenderness of patient minds,
And each slow dusk a drawing-down of blinds.[5]

I did not know Owen's poem when, as a young person myself, I intuitively felt that the words selected from Binyon's poem at Remembrance-tide failed in their key purpose, assuming that to be an affirmation of peace. Binyon's words were arguably counter-productive. Together with the evocative sound of the bugle playing the 'Last Post', the presentation and synchronized dipping of flags, the marching and the uniforms, they did not serve as a warning against war. Rather, they sounded like an honouring of the profession of arms, expressed in a manner that could easily be misunderstood as a justification of the military option. There was even the danger that the words might become an encouragement to fight, if it was believed that to die in battle was a glorious thing to happen to a young man; that to volunteer to fight and seek the glory of the battlefield was a noble ambition.

What also alarmed me was that the words, and the whole theatre of Remembrance Day ceremonies, stirred me. I was repulsed in equal measure, not least by the realization that I too could be stirred. I too found my mind and emotions manipulated by the rituals, imagery, words and music.

Remembrance throws up questions which demand to be answered, but are too often ignored. What, in the context of military service, does glory mean? What does it mean to be heroic?

But most fundamental of all: what is the purpose of Remembrance? Yes, it is to honour and thank the fallen, those who gave their lives in wars. Yes, it is to give comfort to those who mourn their loss? But what is the primary function of Remembrance? If Remembrance does not serve as a warning against war, and if it is not a reminder to the nation to rededicate itself to peace, then it is futile.

1

THE MISTS AND MYTHS
OF WAR

THERE ARE THREE WORDS CARVED ON THE CENOTAPH IN Whitehall: 'The Glorious Dead'. Yet the more I heard about the wars my parents and grandparents had known, the more I realized that those who lost their lives had had their futures and potential denied. So many talented young men were killed in their prime: great writers, artists, physicians, scientists, mystics, craftsmen never fulfilled. What was glorious about that? The dead were missed, mourned, grieved over, regretted, but how did they lie gloriously in their graves? And what if young men of the future had their heads filled with the idea that glory, status and meaning could be attained through fighting? Might it encourage a new generation to go to war to earn a share of that glory for themselves?

Many young men in the past have certainly been lured into military service in this way. Richard Holmes, in his book *Soldiers*, wrote that 'we must never underestimate the appeal of uniform, ritual and reputation, especially to the young'.[6]

Linking glory with military action is found in cultures around the world. Sometimes both sides in a conflict, dedicated to the defeat of each other, talk of glory being theirs.

There is a sad passage in the report 'Voices of Girl Child Soldiers, Sri Lanka', produced by the Quaker United Nations Office:

> The ultimate achievement was to be honored at a 'Hero's Welcome.' A hero's welcome was a special honor granted to those who risked and/or sacrificed their life in battle by

killing and destroying the enemy. The supreme hero's welcome was celebrated and took place after the girl's death. If by some chance the girl was not killed in battle and had escaped capture and had not swallowed the cyanide capsule her 'Hero's Welcome' might include a visit from some member of her family. When someone goes out for a Hero's death, they are honored. I feel sorry for them. Many die and never come back. Some have come back after performing dangerous missions. They are then promoted and become respected.

To talk of the dead of war as glorious is surely to belittle the word. Glory is what is due to God, say Christians: 'Glory be to God on high and on earth peace to all men' was the Christmas message of the angels. To glorify is to offer the highest praise and honour. Is every victim of a war glorious? The brave and the cowardly, the tender and the cruel, the caring and the indifferent, can they all be described as deserving of glory? To endorse the idea at Remembrance-tide that death in war is always glorious is to peddle a dangerous lie.

Speaking recently to a young man in his late teens who is actively considering a career in the Army, I asked him what attracted him to the service life. He talked of comradeship and of the pride, and perhaps the glory, of wearing a uniform. He enjoyed the idea of a physical challenge, of pushing his body to its limits. Unlike me at his age, he appreciated discipline and organization. He was uplifted and stirred by military music and ritual.

Had he, I asked him, thought about how he would feel seeing a close friend killed? Or what if he were permanently injured himself? Had he contemplated having to kill another man face to face? Could he live with himself if he ever accidentally killed a child in the course of duty? And how would he feel if, in the heat of the moment or under pressure from his peers, he overstepped the boundaries of acceptable moral behaviour? These possibilities he put to one side, despite being aware of them.

Andy Fowler was seven years old when he watched the Festival of Remembrance on television. He described his memories of the evening in an article he wrote many years later after serving for 22 years in the British Army.

> We had the community singing, and then the service with the Bishop of Coventry, auntie telling me that he had been a POW of the Japanese in the Second World War.
> Then the poppies fell, dropping onto the heads and shoulders of the young servicemen and women. I was amazed by how many poppies there were and how long it seemed to take, and I was immensely moved. And I believe that something of the soldier entered my boyish soul that evening, one of the reasons why 11 years later I found myself in uniform.[7]

Did those who adopted the poppy as a symbol of peace, grief and remembrance at the end of what they sincerely hoped would be the war to end all wars ever think that the poppy would one day encourage a young man to join up?

Herein lies the confusion and contradiction of Remembrance-tide. There are occasions when wars can be justified. Unless one takes a consistent stand as a pacifist, a view I can respect but not accept, it is generally agreed that nations have the right to defend themselves by armed force *in extremis*, should their citizens and/or territory be threatened. Therefore armed forces need to be trained for this eventuality. They need to be at their peak physically, technically and psychologically to go to war to defend by force that which may justifiably be defended by force. To be prepared psychologically, the morale of individual combatants must be kept high. A proven and effective way of achieving this is through generating, in servicemen and -women, a pride in their professionalism. If they are to be effective in resisting evil, in defeating another tyrant like Hitler, should the circumstances arise, no one can be allowed to question orders or harbour doubt. Solemn militarized rituals, such as those associated with Remembrance-tide, contribute towards this state of mental preparedness. Concepts such as glory can motivate trained soldiers. Self-sacrifice in a righteous and just cause, they are told, is honourable and, possibly, glorious.

At Britain's festival of Remembrance in the Royal Albert Hall, a child comes forward to say 'thank you from children to those who gave their lives so that we can live and be free'. The same idea was expressed in more formal terms by President George W. Bush in 2001. Referring to American war veterans, he said:

> many of them willingly entered harm's way to fight for our freedoms . . . Our Nation will always be grateful for the noble sacrifices made by these veterans. We can never adequately repay them. But we can honor and respect them for their service. As we consider the sacrifices and efforts of our veterans, we must never forget that freedom comes at a cost. Our veterans have much to share with our young people about liberty, patriotism, democracy, and independence. They are living examples of the timeless truth that freedom is not free.[8]

Both the words of the child and those of the president, while superficially plausible, express a dangerous half-truth. Not all wars are fought to defend freedom. Sadly many nations, including those of the 'free' West, also go to war without adequate justification or for economic self-interest. The same troops that are ready and waiting to defend right against might may themselves be ordered by political leaders to take offensive action. The fact that they are ready, prepared and trained to defend means that they are also capable of going on the attack. That sense of pride and glory that galvanizes a fighting force to defend its country also prepares the same men to go on the offensive, if ordered to do so by politicians. There comes a point too in the life of many professional soldiers at which, after months of training, they yearn to see action to prove themselves. There is a sense of eagerness to see some 'real action'. Regrettably too, in the atmosphere of war moral boundaries are crossed and troops from civilized and free countries commit atrocities.

There can be little doubt that the Second World War, when viewed from a British perspective, was a sad necessity. Force was the only option available to counter the ambitions and abhorrent ideology of Nazi Germany. Yet the Second World War presents a more ambivalent set of moral choices when viewed from the perspective of the Soviet Union. There Nazism confronted Communism and the armies of the two tyrants, Hitler and Stalin, fought a bitter and costly war. And it was on the Eastern Front, it is suggested by some historians, that the outcome of the war was ultimately decided.

It can be reasonably argued that through recognizing the noble sacrifice of those who died defending their country against the territorial ambitions of an evil dictator, a new generation might feel inspired to make a similar sacrifice should the need, God forbid, ever arise again. That is a lesson commonly drawn from the history of the Second World War.

But the First World War presents a far more confusing set of moral choices to historians. Furthermore, the conflicts that Britain and the other Allies have been involved in since 1945 present several troubling moral issues. These more recent wars and engagements range from the morally permissible through to the downright illegal. In affording equal honour to all combatants, in every theatre of war, does one encourage and glorify military service irrespective of context?

This hymn, always associated in Britain with Remembrance Day church worship, was written by one-time Conservative politician Sir John Stanhope Arkwright and published shortly after the First World War:

> O valiant hearts who to your glory came
> Through dust of conflict and through battle flame;
> Tranquil you lie, your knightly virtue proved,
> Your memory hallowed in the land you loved.

The hymn continues, speaking of those who served as giving all they had and all they hoped for. Saving mankind was in their mind, not saving themselves.

The hymn was written in the aftermath of what future generations have come to view as a pointless bloodbath of unprecedented horror and futility. Yet the words elevate each one of the millions of victims in status. Each one is transformed from a decaying corpse buried in a foreign field to a martyr inspired by the supreme sacrifice of Christ, who died, Christians believe, to save the sins of the world. Each dead soldier may now lie in the dark, still earth awaiting the last trumpet of Judgment Day, but they can be eternally reassured that 'Christ, our Redeemer, passed the self same way'.

> Still stands His Cross from that dread hour to this . . .
> Look down to bless our lesser Calvaries.

This hymn describes none of the horrors of war. It does nothing to balance and explore the moral dilemmas involved in resorting to armed force. Instead it makes reference in the line 'tranquil you lie, your knightly virtue proved' to the medieval concepts of chivalry when war was fought with the idea of 'gentlemanly rules'. Indeed, some might argue that if it is a sad fact of the human condition that young men go to war, then this hymn sanctifies one of the human race's basest instincts. If viewed that way, it is a gross distortion of the Christian message.

And yet, take the words away from the context of the First World War and apply them to the Second World War, and in particular apply them to a man who goes to war reluctantly, with a heavy heart, determined to use only the minimum force necessary, and is killed performing his duties courageously in a righteous cause – might the words of the hymn in this context be justifiable? Is his death a lesser Calvary?

A poem more in tune with the twenty-first century might be this one, 'What Need I the Waving Flags' by the contemporary poet Bill Mitton:

> I watch these old men march
> bereted and badged
> as I was in years long gone.
> Though I understand
> and will honour their need.
> I will never join them.

I need no marching or medals
to do honour to comrades dead
the metal would lie heavy
upon my aging chest.
I find no honour in gravestones
the faces in my memory
are still happy and young
I would rather they were here
growing old, honoured by
their children's children.
I need no military band.
I keep alive within my soul
the music of my comrades' songs
They are my morning reveille
and my twilights taps
What need I the waving flags
of these patronising politicians,
and hindsight's patriots
when these self same,
cloaked in self interest,
barter and sell the peace
hard bought by young lives,
whilst their casual neglect
of our injured and our widows
do such dishonour to our dead.
What right have I of medals
For I am here, aging still.
I hold in trust the memories of
such youthful, selfless, sacrifice
their smiles will haunt me ever.
For as our young soldiers still do.
I have, in scaring grief, carried home,
brave men upon their shields.

The aim of this book is to explore the meaning behind the
solemn national acts of commemoration we perform. It is to ask
why we perform those rituals and for whose benefit. Is it to help

relatives come to terms with their grief? Is it to give meaning to the deaths of those killed, or to seek it? Is it to remind ourselves that wars should never be embarked upon lightly? Is it to glorify the ideals of militarism? Are we participating in an act of public thanksgiving? Are we acting from ancient, almost primeval tribal instinct? Has Remembrance become one of the few remaining expressions of national identity in an increasingly global culture?

In addition to asking those questions, similar issues will be raised from the opposite direction. Might the pomp and ceremony of Remembrance encourage young people to sign up for service life for the wrong reasons? What message do politicians take from Remembrance? Does it encourage them to commit troops in their charge to action, rather than deter them? Does the fact that nations continue to go to war suggest that remembrance has failed?

From the answers to these and other relevant questions, new ways of remembering the war dead might emerge. Rituals of remembrance might suggest themselves that, while showing no disrespect to the dead of the world wars, focus more on the future, their primary purpose being to serve as a reminder that wars, far from being anything glorious, are the consequence of human failure and weakness.

Millions of people every November take a poppy from a Royal British Legion representative and place a donation in the collecting tin. The poppy is pinned to an outer garment for a few days and then discarded after Remembrance Sunday. It is one of the familiar rituals of the British year. But how many people consider the true meaning of the gesture and note how the symbolism of the poppy has changed, in several subtle yet complex ways, over the years? Wearing a poppy today is not what it was 30, 60 or 90 years ago. Sales of poppies have never been higher, but this cannot be taken as evidence that Remembrance itself is in a healthy state. There are even early signs that it could soon become a divisive issue, revealing a political fault line in British society. It is time to take stock and consider changes to the practice of Remembrance before honouring the war dead becomes damaged by controversy and division.

2

LEST WE FORGET

AT THE CENTRE OF REMEMBRANCE IN BRITAIN IS A CEREMONY
that takes place in London every year, on the Sunday nearest to 11
November. The ritual that unfolds feels timeless, although it is less
than a century old. The normally busy thoroughfare of Whitehall,
the wide street of government buildings running from north to
south that links Trafalgar Square with Parliament Square, is closed
to traffic. Replacing the usual convoys of red buses and black cabs
are lines of meticulously drilled troops parading in immaculate ceremonial uniforms. It is an occasion for which they have rehearsed
and prepared with great dedication. Like being selected to guard a
royal palace, it is a special honour to be chosen for this duty.

A military band plays familiar martial and popular classical
music. The programme follows the same pattern every year. It
begins with such patriotic favourites as 'Rule, Britannia!', of Last
Night at the Proms fame, and 'Hearts of Oak', the rousing naval
march. Music by British composers is mostly featured, such as
Henry Purcell's 'Dido's Lament' and Edward Elgar's 'Nimrod'
from his *Enigma Variations*, although one familiar work by
Beethoven is played.

Politicians, service chiefs and members of the royal family
gather, plus hundreds of ex-servicemen and -women, their families
and members of the public. It is one of the few times in the year
when the tourists in Whitehall are outnumbered. At precisely
11 o'clock, as Big Ben chimes the hour, the street, the city and the
nation fall silent for two minutes. The silence is broken by the
boom of a cannon and the bugle-sound of the Last Post.

It is both a time when the British people act together and an opportunity for every individual to have his or her own personal, silent thoughts. So, what might go through people's minds during those two special and hallowed minutes?

The surviving soldiers, sailors and airmen of the Second World War, wearing medals and standing stiffly to attention, might bring to mind the young comrades they knew who died around 70 years ago. The memory of losing a colleague in action can often become fixed in the mind forever, especially if that colleague was someone who, over weeks or months, had shared the same intense experiences of training and preparing for action. Some veterans have nightmares into their old age of that single traumatic moment when death was so close. The question 'why him and not me?' can nag away for a lifetime.

The memories of the widow of a casualty of a recent military deployment will be more immediate and focused on just one other person, a husband and father taken in the prime of life. She will recall the many moments of pleasure, think of the hopes unrealized, sense again the final farewell. She will shudder once more at the recollection of the knock on the door when the news of death in action was confirmed.

The thoughts of the serving guardsman, standing immobile with precision correctness, may briefly stray from the carefully rehearsed choreography of the ceremonial, and focus on vivid recollections of his last tour of duty in Afghanistan. Perhaps he too saw a colleague killed. He will certainly note the contrast between his current role and that performed just a few weeks earlier, before he swapped combat kit for bearskin and greatcoat.

And the politicians, mostly members of a privileged and protected generation that has never experienced the pain, fear, grief and exhilaration of warfare, what must they be thinking? It is their policies, decisions and mistakes that will have sent or will in future send young men and women to their deaths. Is this the moment they search their consciences? Or do they stand there savouring their own self-importance, having achieved their political ambition to be right at the centre of national events?

Hopefully they at least follow the guidance offered in the order of service printed for the occasion. It has a section that reads:

> For all present, suggested subjects for thought and prayer during the Silence are:
>
> We remember those who made the great sacrifice during the two World Wars;
>
> We remember those who have given their lives in the service of their country in other conflicts;
>
> We pray for those who suffer at this time;
>
> We pray for those who have been bereaved;
>
> We pray for peace;
>
> We pray that we may be worthy of the sacrifice made on our behalf.

Every country with a Remembrance tradition has developed its own variations on the same Remembrance theme. These national differences tend to reflect the nations' characteristics. The ceremony at the Whitehall Cenotaph displays Britain's rigid sense of hierarchy and formality in public official life. The Queen takes precedence over everyone and after her everyone else has their place as set out by constitutional precedent, within the political system, or according to military tradition. The King's Troop, Royal Horse Artillery, has the right, or honour, to fire the ceremonial cannon. The buglers of the Royal Marines sound the Last Post. Senior members of the Royal Family wear military uniforms reflecting their own careers or honorary ranks. Prince Philip and the Prince of Wales both appear in uniforms of the Royal Navy. Prince Philip served with distinction in the Second World War and Prince Charles was a full-time naval officer and trained as a helicopter pilot, as did his brother the Duke of York, who served in the Falklands War. The most colourful member of the Royal Family on duty at the Cenotaph is the Queen's youngest son, the Earl of Wessex. He failed to complete his military training with the Marines, but nevertheless stands there resplendent in the scarlet cap and broad scarlet coat collar which comes with the post of Royal Honorary Colonel of the Royal Wessex Yeomanry. The royal spouses watch from a balcony at the Foreign and Commonwealth Office overlooking the ceremony. In 2011 the eyes of the media were on the newly married Duchess of Cambridge, who performed her first Remembrance Day function wearing a double poppy.

When the time comes each year to lay the first wreath of poppies, and it is all timed to the second, an equerry brings it forward to the Queen, who walks with it the final few yards to the steps of the Cenotaph. She knows exactly what to do. It is one of the poignant rites she has now performed dozens of times in her 60-year reign. In fact she laid her first wreath as Princess Elizabeth before ascending the throne. After laying her tribute she stands for a moment and bows. Normally her subjects bow to her, but in this instance she bows her head to her subjects, albeit those who have died for Queen (or King) and country. She is followed by Prince Philip, the Prince of Wales, the Duke of York and the Earl of Wessex, followed by the Princess Royal, who must defer in precedence to her younger brothers. Each in turn pauses in solemn respect. The wreaths are laid at the cenotaph in an official, correct and pre-ordained order.

The royal homage paid, it is the turn of the leaders of the major political parties from all parts of the United Kingdom. They have been standing to attention in a line to the Queen's right alongside the west side of the Cenotaph, each holding a wreath of poppies in front of him. Behind them stands a line of former prime ministers. The serving Prime Minister is the first politician to step forward, normally followed by the Leader of the Opposition. The Welsh and Scottish National Party members of the Westminster Parliament share a wreath which is inscribed in both Welsh and Gaelic. The Speaker of the House of Commons is also there. The Foreign Secretary lays a wreath on behalf of Britain's dependencies, the remnants of the Empire. The wreath is not made of poppies, but by tradition is fabricated from exotic plants from Kew Gardens.

The politicians are followed by the Commonwealth High Commissioners to London, who pay their tributes on behalf of their respective nations. They number around 50 and represent nations that range in size from large ones such as Australia and

Canada to the very smallest such as Fiji and Malta. They step forward together in lines and lay their wreaths on the west side of the cenotaph. The First Sea Lord, representing the Royal Navy, which claims to be the senior service, comes next; then it is the turn of the Chief of the General Staff; followed by the Chief of the Air Staff; after which comes the representatives of the merchant navy and Fishing Fleets and the merchant air service. Over several minutes a heap of poppy wreaths builds up.

The service is normally conducted, not by the Archbishop of Canterbury, but by the Bishop of London, in whose diocese White-hall is situated, and who is also Dean of the Chapel Royal. Since 1996 the office has been held by the imposing figure of the Right Reverend Dr Richard Chartres. The choir is drawn from the Children and Gentlemen of the Chapel Royal, including the young trebles in their eye-catching scarlet and gold-trimmed uniforms dating back over 350 years. They are led in by a cross-bearer whose shining processional cross is adorned with poppies. The ceremony concludes with a version of Beethoven's Funeral March No. 1, arranged by Johann Heinrich Walch; the hymn 'O God, Our Help in Ages Past'; and the bugle call Reveille. After the singing of the National Anthem, the Queen and the Royal Family and their attendant equerries leave.

As well as the Church of England, the established church, which takes the lead role, the other major Christian traditions and world faiths are represented, although it was only in 2000 that Hindu, Sikh, Muslim and Buddhist representatives were first invited to take part.

It is a very British occasion, full of precision pageantry and moving spectacle. It represents all that is best in the British gift for inventing heritage. No other nation can organize such good dis-plays of ceremony. Yet the occasion also shows up some of the worst aspects of national life. The stifling class system and official pomp on display obscures the true horror and grief being recalled. The British are said not to show emotion. The stiff upper lip is pre-ferred to tears. This attitude may be changing, but the clinically precise rituals of Remembrance Day in central London can serve as the mask behind which emotion and reality hide.

Once the Queen and the official party have left, it is time for the march past of veterans and uniformed organizations. This takes over three-quarters of an hour and is both a moving and curious sight. It is estimated that in 2011 over 7,000 people took part. There are men in berets and bowlers hats. Some march head aloft with arms swinging as they were taught on the parade ground. Others march stiffly, impaired and impeded by the infirmities of age. There are veterans in wheelchairs. There are Chelsea Pensioners in uniform and members of the Salvation Army, plus a few eccentrics with strange hats and jackets covered in badges.

In the early years the march was one exclusively of military veterans, but as all veterans from the First World War are now dead and many of those surviving from the Second World War are increasingly infirm, the march has been opened up to others. There is now a contingent of Bevin Boys, for instance, men whose service in the Second World War was to work in the coal mines.

At the same time as the Whitehall Cenotaph service is taking place and being broadcast nationwide, hundreds of smaller ceremonies are also taking place. Remembrance-tide is marked in November with the wearing of poppies and the solemn laying of wreaths, not just in the capital but in every city, town and village in the country. Each nation of the United Kingdom provides its own variation on the common theme. In Edinburgh the sound of bagpipes is heard along the Royal Mile. The Scottish version of the poppy is slightly different in design from the English one and the charity selling the poppies was until recently separate from the Royal British Legion, the organization that sells poppies in the rest of the United Kingdom. In Northern Ireland the sound of the fife keeps the marchers in step and remembrance is less of a unifying occasion than in other parts of the United Kingdom. In some areas the marchers are the same men who earlier in the year took to the streets in their own partisan parades. Looking at the variations in the ways the regions and nations of the United Kingdom mark the day gives a clue to another function of Remembrance: being an expression of British identity. This will be explored in more detail later.

But whatever local, regional and national variations there might be, the core ritual remains the same. Everywhere there are veterans marching and standard-bearers wearing large white gauntlets, civic officials in chains and robes, children from the uniformed organizations and serving members of local regiments.

Sometimes the streets are lined with spectators behind temporary metal barriers. In other places, especially if the weather is bleak and wet, the march past takes place along almost deserted streets, noticed by just a handful of members of the public.

In almost every town centre, for the two minutes' silence at 11 a.m. on Remembrance Sunday, the traffic stops. Some cars have large plastic poppies fixed to the front engine grille. Often motorists draw to the side of the road at the appropriate time and pause.

Something similar happens on 11 November when the actual anniversary of the ending of the First World War occurs midweek. In central London, at precisely 11 a.m., on railway stations, in shops, on busy pavements, thousands of people stop what they are doing and stand in silence. Those who continue to scurry about their business are the conspicuous ones. Six years in every seven, therefore, Britain observes the two minutes' silence twice. This tradition is relatively new and was only reinstated in 1995.

Almost all nations that have experienced modern warfare have created rituals to honour those who have died as members of the armed forces. Similar acts of Remembrance are held around Europe, with each country that has been involved in the major wars of the last 100 years, both victors and the defeated, recalling the victims of those conflicts in their own way. The French, for instance, traditionally wear the blue cornflower, le bleuet, as their flower of Remembrance.

At the same time of year the USA marks Veterans Day as a national holiday, in addition to Memorial Day in May. Australia and New Zealand commemorate Anzac Day, but in April; the autumn of the Southern Hemisphere. While on Anzac Day all Australian and New Zealand servicemen and -women who have died on duty are now recalled, the tradition started during the First World War to honour members of the Australian and New Zealand Army Corps (ANZAC) who fought and died in the bloody battle at

Gallipoli in Turkey. Thus Anzac Day predates Britain's Remembrance Day by three years.

In Britain and in Commonwealth countries the shape and form of these annual acts of Remembrance were established in the immediate aftermath of the First World War and continued little changed after the Second.

It took only three years, from 1918 to 1921, for the familiar British rituals to become established. Much of what seems today to be an integral part of our heritage was originally improvised or designed in haste. The familiar shape of the Cenotaph in Whitehall was sketched out on the back of a menu card and originally intended to be nothing more than a temporary wooden structure. The Cenotaph rituals were largely the invention of one man, a Conservative politician and former Viceroy of India, Lord Curzon, who as Lord President of the Council chaired the 1919 Peace Celebrations Committee. The committee was initially convened to discuss how best to celebrate victory and divert public attention away from political and economic problems. It had little inkling that it would be establishing a tradition of solemn remembrance that, almost 100 years later, would have survived largely unaltered. The symbolism of the poppy and the Tomb of the Unknown Warrior evolved from the inspiration and determination of just a few individuals. Yet what became established in just three years so caught the mood of the times that the rituals quickly became entrenched in the British psyche and calendar. They immediately felt as if they had a history behind them.

Similarly the acts of remembrance in many countries of Continental Europe are rooted in traditions dating back to the desolate days of the early post-war period of 1918–19. Previously nations had tended to commemorate war with triumphal arches and victory parades. The most celebrated triumphal arch is probably that raised by the French almost 200 years ago, which is now one of Paris's most celebrated landmarks. The Arc de Triomphe celebrates the French Revolutionary and Napoleonic Wars. It is inscribed however, not with the names of the ordinary soldiers who gave their lives, but with those of the generals. It also lists French victories and battle honours.

In the aftermath of the First World War, a war of horrors on an unprecedented scale, all countries had to find new ways of channelling collective grief. The French, like the citizens of all the countries that took part, knew that to celebrate generals and victories in the old way would be utterly inappropriate. The Arc de Triomphe was transformed into a memorial to all who died, both great and insignificant, by being chosen as the site for France's Tomb of the Unknown Soldier.

It might be supposed that after the Second World War, and the failure of the memories of the First World War to prevent a second military conflagration, there might have been a call for the ceremonies of remembrance to be revised. But this was not the case. The question of whether a new war memorial should be erected in London to supplement or replace the Cenotaph was briefly raised in the British Parliament in 1946. A question was put to Clement Attlee, the Prime Minister, in the House of Commons. Would he make a statement 'as to the date of Remembrance Day; and if it has been decided to add the dates 1939–45 to the Cenotaph in Whitehall?'

When Mr Attlee answered that he was not in a position to make a statement on either matter, his MP questioner, Captain Bullock, said that many people were 'most anxious to have a statement at an early date'.

After consultation with interested bodies in Britain, the Dominions and Empire, it was decided not to make any radical change. In 1947 Lord Chatfield, speaking in the House of Lords, expressed the general mood of the time.

As your Lordships all know, the decision was taken last year to rededicate our beautiful Cenotaph, so that it should commemorate the glorious dead of both wars. That was a natural step to take. After all, although the two wars were twenty-five years apart, time will close the gap until they will appear to posterity as one great struggle against evil.[9]

Cabinet papers of the time reveal that the Home Office had been lobbied by religious leaders not to mark the end of the Second World War separately from the Great War.

> Shortly after VE-day, my predecessor received a deputation, led by the Bishop of Winchester, representing the Church of England, and including representatives of the Roman Catholic Church, the Free Church Federal Council and the British Legion. The deputation raised the question of the future of Armistice Day and Remembrance Sunday.

The Home Secretary wrote in his cabinet memorandum

> The deputation expressed the view that it was undesirable that there should be more than one Remembrance Day after the end of the present war, and they suggested the desirability of adopting one day as Remembrance Day in commemoration of two national deliverances and of the fallen in both of the wars. The 11th November and the Sunday following it are already well established in the United Kingdom and to a large extent throughout the Commonwealth and Empire; and the British Legion have a special interest in the observance of Armistice Day. The British Legion was strongly in favour of the adoption of one national day as a day of remembrance in respect of both wars and of the maintenance of the Cenotaph as the national memorial for both wars. They were very anxious in particular that the two minutes' silence ceremonial should be resumed. My predecessor told the deputation that he favoured one national day of remembrance associated with a national service of remembrance at the Cenotaph.[10]

It was not until 60 years after the end of the Second World War that a monument specifically related to that conflict was raised in Whitehall. It was designed to honour the role of women between 1939 and 1945 and takes the form of a 22-foot-high bronze sculpture depicting women's uniforms and working clothes.

The former Speaker of the House of Commons, Baroness Betty Boothroyd, who raised much of the money to pay for the monument by appearing on a television quiz show, described it as being dedicated to all the women who 'served our country and the cause of freedom in uniform and on the home front'. Unlike other war memorials, the monument is not purely a military memorial. 'It depicts the uniforms of women in the forces alongside the working clothes of those who worked in the factories, the hospitals, the emergency services and the farms.'

There are three other sculptures in Whitehall relevant to the Second World War, but they follow the older tradition of honouring war leaders. They are portrait sculptures representing three of the war's best-known commanders. All three were Field Marshals who were raised to the peerage as Viscounts, namely Slim, Alanbrooke and Montgomery.

There are other pieces of artwork in Whitehall relevant to Remembrance, but they are little known and rather obscurely placed. They were conceived of as a themed set and can be seen high up on the large building of Portland stone at the corner of Whitehall and Horse Guards Avenue, to the north of the Cenotaph. The sculptured carvings are on the top of the old War Office and comprise four groups, each appearing twice at intervals around the buildings. The works are called War, Peace, Truth and Justice, and Victory and Fame. They are by Alfred Drury and date from 1905. Described as highly allegorical pairs of reclining female figures they represent the dichotomies of peace and war: the sorrow and joy of peace and the horror and dignity of war.

Remembrance too has its dichotomies and contractions and Drury's artwork appear pertinent to them, even though they predate the world wars and the artist would have had no idea of the devastation that was soon to engulf and devastate Europe – outstripping any previous war in sheer scale.

The two world wars of the twentieth century were conflicts of unprecedented trauma and mechanical brutality with casualties numbering millions. In the First World War 9.7 million combatants died and when the military and civilian victims are combined a total is reached of 37 million people killed or wounded. Over 1 million servicemen of the British Empire died and twice that number were wounded. On 1 July 1916 alone, the first day of the Battle of the Somme, 19,240 British troops were killed. The combined First World War casualty figures for the Russian armed forces approached 5 million. Germany and her allies recorded 4 million war dead and twice that number wounded.

The Second World War saw even greater military and civilian deaths. Massive bomb attacks against civilian populations, the dropping of two nuclear weapons and the evil, systematic genocide of the Holocaust took the total tally of those who lost their lives to a figure that could be as high as 60 million souls worldwide, although it is so great that it has never been accurately quantified. Over 25,000 people, on average, died for every day of the war.

Of the dead 384,000 were members of the British armed forces and 417,000 were American military personnel. The Soviet military death toll exceeded those numbers many times and is estimated to be a figure approaching 10 million. Some estimates suggest that as many as 300,000 Soviet troops were killed by their own side. Adding civilian deaths, it is said that one Soviet citizen in eight died between 1939 and 1945 as a result of the war. There were 5.5 million German military deaths.

It could be said that the Second World War would be better named the Great War (Part 2). It came about as a consequence of the failure of politicians in 1918 to construct a peace treaty fit for the purpose of ensuring long-term continental and world stability.

There was no talk of reconciliation. Instead the Treaty of Versailles in 1919 involved Germany accepting a 'war guilt' clause with the implication that it accepted responsibility for the loss and devastation of the conflict. Article 231 stated:

> The Allied and Associated Governments affirm and Germany accepts the responsibility of Germany and her allies for causing all the loss and damage to which the Allied and Associated Governments and their nationals have been subjected as a consequence of the war imposed upon them by the aggression of Germany and her allies.

It could be argued that the negotiations that led to the treaty had contradictory objectives. On the one hand there was the desire to punish Germany for starting the war and extract from her the maximum reparations. On the other there was the need to ensure that the same countries did not go to war again. The Allied victors, France, America and Britain, failed to strike the right balance. The monetary compensation demanded from Germany was so great that it was not until 3 October 2010 that the last instalment was paid. The economic collapse of Germany, the rise of Nazism and the Second World War were proof of the treaty's failure.

Acres of French countryside had been devastated by the war and France took a leading role in demanding compensation to pay for a programme of rebuilding and economic recovery. Article 232 of the treaty acknowledged that Germany's resources were not sufficient to make total compensation but stated:

The Allied and Associated Governments, however, require, and Germany undertakes, that she will make compensation for all damage done to the civilian population of the Allied and Associated Powers and to their property during the period of the belligerency of each as an Allied or Associated Power against Germany by such aggression by land, by sea and from the air, and in general all damage as defined in Annex L hereto.

In accordance with Germany's pledges, already given, as to complete restoration for Belgium, Germany undertakes, in addition to the compensation for damage elsewhere in this Part provided for, as a consequence of the violation of the Treaty of 1839, to make reimbursement of all sums which Belgium has borrowed from the Allied and Associated Governments up to November 11, 1918, together with interest at the rate of five per cent (5 per cent) per annum on such sums. This amount shall be determined by the Reparation Commission, and the German Government undertakes thereupon forthwith to make a special issue of bearer bonds to an equivalent amount payable in Marks gold, on 1 May 1926, or, at the option of the German Government, on the 1st of May in any year up to 1926.

The economist John Maynard Keynes, who attended the peace conference on behalf of the British government, protested that the demands were too harsh and risked provoking a future conflict. In the book that made his reputation, *The Economic Consequences of the Peace*, he criticized 'the exorbitant war reparations demanded from a defeated Germany and prophetically predicted that it would foster a desire for revenge among Germans'.[11] His warnings were vindicated when, following the world economic crash of 1929, the German Weimar Republic began printing money to fund itself and the war debt. This triggered a period of hyper-inflation. The image of parcels of banknotes being required to buy a loaf of bread has not faded from German public memory.

Germany was given no option but to agree to a treaty that stipulated that the defeated power would forfeit land, accept guilt and pay a huge financial price. By the final sub-clauses of the Treaty of Versailles (Annex II.12), which was handed to Germany's representatives as a fait accompli, the financial demands were very specific.

In order to facilitate and continue the immediate restoration of the economic life of the Allied and Associated countries, the Commission will . . . take from Germany by way of security for and acknowledgment of her debt a first installment of gold bearer bonds free of all taxes and charges of every description established or to be established by the Government of the German Empire or of the German States . . . These bonds will be delivered on account . . . 20,000,000,000 Marks gold bearer bonds, payable not later than May 1, 1921, without interest . . . a further 40,000,000,000 Marks gold bearer bonds, bearing interest at 2½ per cent. per annum between 1921 and 1926, and thereafter at 5 per cent. per annum with an additional 1 per cent. for amortisation beginning in 1926 on the whole amount of the issue; a further installment of 40,000,000,000 Marks gold 5 per cent. Bearer bonds, the time and mode of payment of principal and interest to be determined by the Commission.

In insisting on extracting reparations from the Germans, the politicians were not out of step with public opinion. The British government, the wartime coalition led by Lloyd George, had won a landslide election victory in 1918 on the dual promise that after the war Britain would become a nation 'fit for heroes to live in' and the 'German lemon' would be squeezed 'until the pips squeak'. Lloyd George said of reparations that the victors must have 'the uttermost farthing' and 'shall search their pockets for it'.

It was a punitive settlement which had tragic consequences. Even before the rise of Hitler, German public opinion was calling for a repudiation of the war-guilt clause of the treaty. In 1927 President von Hindenburg declared that Germany had

entered the war as a means of self-assertion against a world full of enemies. Pure in heart we set off to the defence of the fatherland, and with clean hands the German army carried the sword. Germany is prepared to prove this before impartial judges at any time.

In June 1940, when the German army entered and occupied France, Hitler chose to symbolically exorcize the shame of the defeat of 1918 and the humiliating Treaty of Versailles. He made the French sign the surrender documents in a railway carriage near Compiègne, in exactly the same place where the Germans had been forced to sign the Armistice 22 years earlier.

The two world wars are directly connected. Events and decisions following the first led directly to the second. Yet, in collective memory the two wars are remembered very differently.

'The victims during the First World War were chiefly, but not exclusively, men obliged to fight and die for what turned out, very soon after the peace treaty, to have been a very bad affair', wrote Pierre Sorlin in his essay in the book *War and Remembrance in the Twentieth Century*.

What people remembered was straightforward and very sad: five years spent on the front line had marked the end of civilized values which soldiers, in all countries, had mobilized to defend. In their memoirs, in their poems, novels, drawings and paintings, the survivors did not indulge in moral or patriotic reflections, they attempted to convey the rebarbative reality of the trenches and to produce stories likely to make everybody understand that they went through an ordeal that was like hell.

The Second World War, however, produced more complex and ambivalent memories. 'The unprecedented extent of casualties and destruction was seen as typical of a modernization process which was ruthlessly sweeping away the systems and societies of the past', Sorlin wrote.

By turning armed forces into machines for slaughter, modern warfare tended to annihilate, even in the societies which had successfully waged it, any sense that the combat had been fought, or should have been fought, for the defence of a community . . . Emphasis was put on the killing of harmless people, especially of children . . . However almost everybody, including innocent victims, realized there was a reason for fighting. Many people had a clear, even if mistaken, idea of why they had to endure what they were enduring. The Second World War did not mirror the senseless slaughter . . . of the first; it was an ideological war, fought for ideological aims.[12]

That summary by Sorlin applies to both sides. Millions of German people were motivated, and some inspired, by an ideology based on a set of national and racial myths. These prospered in a nation still feeling the shame and humiliation of defeat. This gave them their reason for fighting. On the other hand, their Allied opponents endured what they had to knowing that these motivational myths amounted to nothing more than a set of evil falsehoods that had to be resisted. The false ideology, which was met with force and ultimately defeated with force, was also defeated on moral grounds. The peoples of the Allied nations were inspired to resist by a belief that they were fighting a just war. The British war leader Sir Winston Churchill summed up the mood in 1941:

> The forces ranged against us are enormous. They are bitter, they are ruthless. The wicked men and their factions who have launched their peoples on the path of war and conquest know that they will be called to terrible account if they cannot beat down by force of arms the peoples they have assailed. They will stop at nothing. They have a vast accumulation of war weapons of all kinds. They have highly trained, disciplined armies, navies, and air services. They have plans and designs which have long been tried and matured. They will stop at nothing that violence or treachery can suggest.[13]

There was a strong and realistic fear in Britain that if Hitler were to triumph, the British people would be forced to live under the tyranny of Nazism and be forced to adopt his political beliefs as their own.

To British and Allied combatants, the Second World War presented a moral justification which few could argue against. Volunteers and conscripts were not motivated by jingoism, but by moral obligation. The war met the criteria of both Christian and secular versions of the 'just war' theory in that it was waged for a just cause and declared by a lawful authority, with all peaceful ways of resolving problems having been explored and exhausted. Many pacifists who in the First World War would have been conscientious objectors volunteered to fight. The post-war revelation of the Nazi's Final Solution policy and systematic programme of genocide confirmed that fighting the war had been right.

Yet it should be stated that this view of the war is not universally shared today. As time passes and the Second World War can be seen in longer perspective, it begins to look more and more like any other war of history; in moral terms, if not in scale. 'The west's dangerous delusion that war can be a decent and worthwhile activity is shaped by false memories of the Second World War', wrote Jonathan Jones in *The Guardian*. 'The good war was good only in self-congratulatory myth. In reality it was the most murderous conflict in history, destroying unimaginable numbers of civilian lives from Dresden to Auschwitz to Hiroshima.'[14] It is true that it spared Britain from Nazism, but it should not be forgotten that prior to the Second World War there was a strong body of support in Britain for the ideals of militarism, social discipline, anti-Semitism and right-wing politics that the Nazis and Fascists espoused. Sympathizers were not restricted to the Mosleyite gangs on the streets of London. They included members of the ruling classes at the highest levels, including the Duke of Windsor, the former Edward VIII.

There was no Armistice Day ritual at the Cenotaph in November 1939 and the traditional two minutes' silence was not officially observed during the war years. Poppies were sold to continue to fund the work of the British Legion which, as the war progressed, was continually having new, younger clients added to the lists of those it helped.

Putting Remembrance into abeyance for the war years was not a difficult decision. In the 1930s the annual observance was beginning to become an awkward political issue. There was an active peace movement in Britain and members felt that the military tone of Curzon's ceremony was increasingly inappropriate. The feelings of many at the time are expressed in the words of Siegfried Sassoon, the war poet whose 'At the Cenotaph' conjured up an image of the Prince of Darkness standing by the Cenotaph. There he prays that God will make the people and leaders forget the true meaning of the memorial.

> Breed new belief that War is purgatorial
> Proof of the pride and power of being alive.

Two lines later he prays, 'Lift up their hearts in large destructive lust.' Afterwards he bows to the Cenotaph and walks away laughing.

As the Second World War became more and more inevitable, it was felt that Remembrance itself had to bear some responsibility for the failure of the nations of Europe to maintain a peace won at huge expense. It had not served as an effective reminder of the true cost of war.

And yet in the minds of others, Remembrance during the 1930s had become too associated with peace and appeasement. There were still many whose view of Remembrance was unchanged from 1919. Despite the military overtones of the ceremonial, they viewed Armistice Day as a moral warning from the dead to the living never to go to war again. Neville Chamberlain's wife gave visual expression to this idea during the appeasement era by conspicuously placing flowers on the Tomb of the Unknown Warrior. By the time war was declared, the euphoria that had greeted Prime Minister Neville Chamberlain's declaration that he had secured 'peace in our time' had evaporated. His dramatic meeting with Hitler in 1938 was seen, with hindsight, as only an illusion of peace. War was accepted as a necessity and to honour those who had supposedly fought a war to end all wars only twenty years earlier seemed almost an insult to their memory. To have marked Remembrance in the traditional way between 1939 and 1945 would have seemed inappropriate.

Since 1945 Europe has experienced a period of relative peace. There have been conflicts, but the soldiers, sailors and aircrew of Western countries who have died for their countries in the last 50 years are numbered in thousands, not millions. Since the invasion of Iraq in 2003 some 5,000 American and allied troops have died there. The Falklands War of 1982 resulted in 900 British and Argentinian deaths. The Vietnam War, which ended with withdrawal in 1975, cost almost 60,000 American lives. The most costly war since 1945 involving America and the Western powers was that in Korea between 1950 and 1953. Official US battle deaths were estimated to be almost 45,000. The deaths of the civilians and soldiers of both North and South Korea are harder to quantify, but could be as high as 3 million.

When the traditional, and now familiar, acts of remembrance were first devised after the First World War, there were few taking part who did not bring to mind their own grief. 'An atmosphere of gloom, misery and deep unrelenting mourning settled on practically every house in the British Isles', wrote the young Barbara Cartland, whose father, an Army officer, died in May 1918, a few weeks before her eighteenth birthday.

The post-war world was in large part a world paralysed by grief, as Juliet Nicolson described the atmosphere of 1918–19. 'Grief is an iceberg of a word concealing beneath its innocent simplicity a dangerous mass of confusion and rage . . . Emotional effects can include at first shock, disbelief and denial, followed by guilt, self-reproach, numbness and yearning.'[15]

Grief is a private emotion. It can well up at unexpected moments, triggered by all kinds of reminders: anniversaries, objects, music, smells. But after the First World War grief was so widespread that it could not be contained as a private affair: it had a public facet. When the terms of the Armistice were announced to the House of Commons in November 1918 there was, in the words of *The Times History of the War*,

> no note of exultation . . . There was the joy of thanks-giving and with it an overmastering sense of compassion which made the sitting almost a solemn act of consecration'. Once the announcement had been made the House adjourned to St Margaret's Church for a religious service.

The armistice was followed by rejoicing in the streets of London as victory over Germany and her associates was celebrated. Much of it was drink-fuelled and simply a means of letting off steam after four years of tension and anxiety. Yet, those who had witnessed the carnage of the trenches first hand felt less able to participate in celebration. The Canadian Army chaplain Frederick Scott wrote of November 11th 1918:

> At 11 in the morning the bells of London rang out their joyous peals. . . . There was wild rejoicing in the city and the crowds went crazy with delight. But it seemed to me that behind the ringing of those peals of joy there was the tolling of a spectral bell for those who would return no more. The monstrous futility of war as a test of national

greatness, the wound in the world's heart, the empty homes, those were the thoughts which in me overmastered the feelings of rejoicing.[16]

A passage in Juliet Nicolson's *The Great Silence* gives two examples of a similar response to the victory, drawn from either end of Britain's social scale.

Duff Cooper, glamorous diplomat and grenadier, had returned from the battle lines a few days earlier. Back in London he felt overcome with despondency and unable to go down into the streets and join the Armistice party. As he watched the scene below him, with the coloured fairy lights threaded through the tricolour draperies, the cheering and the waving of flags, he was overcome with melancholy. He shuddered at the dancing and noise of celebration and could only think of friends who were dead.

Florence Younghusband . . . was travelling on the top of a London bus at the moment of the ceasefire. In front of her was a soldier, his face shattered by a shell. As Florence watched the soldier looked straight ahead and remained stonily silent. Suddenly the lady bus conductor collapsed into the seat beside her and, leaning her head on Florence's shoulder, she wept. Her husband, she confided to Florence, had died two months before and she felt incapable of celebrating.[17]

The suffering of the war did not immediately end with the ceasefire. For many weeks after 11 November telegrams continued to arrive at homes with the news of deaths from wounds. The war poet Wilfred Owen died one week before the Armistice and news of his death reached his parents just as the church bells of Shrewsbury were ringing to herald the peace. Once servicemen started to return home new problems arose. Many were physically wounded; almost all were mentally scarred, some profoundly. No one who had witnessed fighting was unaffected. Some men came home severely injured or disabled to a new existence as permanent dependents. What celebrations there were, were short-lived. As the months after the ceasefire passed, there was a general sense that some way had to be found to formally recognize the memories of those who had died. It was seen that through the public ritualization of Remembrance, the survivors of warfare could be given the opportunity to recall their own experiences, to make sense of the carnage they had witnessed, to receive public recognition for their service and to mourn. Some of the families of servicemen found in these public acts of Remembrance a substitute comfort for the funerals they had never had a chance to attend, or the graves they could not visit.

The merging of public ceremony and private grief was noted by Stefan Goebel in *The Great War and Medieval Memory*, 'This link became visible in the creation of the Empire Field of Remembrance on the old graveyard of St Margaret's Church opposite the Abbey.' The church described here is the parish church of the Houses of Parliament at Westminster. In November 1928 and in subsequent years the bereaved were invited to plant little crosses of poppies, provided by the British Legion's poppy factory, in remembrance of lost relatives and friends. Like the common act of touching a war memorial, and especially touching names inscribed on it (as can be seen in photographs of the period), putting tokens in the ground at St Margaret's constituted a ritual of mourning and separation. These crosses and poppies were public markers of private loss in a historic setting.'The Imperial war memorials in Westminster and Whitehall entwined intimate responses with cultural ones. Together they marked out a commemorative landscape transforming all of official London into an imagined cemetery.'

The custom of planting crosses in the ground by Westminster Abbey has continued. The Field of Remembrance, as it is now known, is planted annually and currently contains some 60,000 crosses. Many of those remembered by name are long dead and the tradition of planting a memorial cross is continued by their descendants. Each year the field has added to it the names of men killed in current conflicts. It is one of the few public places where Remembrance and grief remain linked.

When a serviceman or -woman today dies in action, the official response is markedly different from that of 1918–19. The current practice is for the body of a soldier killed on active service to be brought back to the family. An inquest is held at which the details of the death are described and explained. The death rate of the First World War made it impossible to repatriate remains, assuming that they could be identified. Thousands of men a day died during the major offensives. Some estimates have suggested that the bodies of 50 per cent of men killed in the First World War were so mutilated they could not be identified. Often a dog-tag found buried in the mud was all that remained of a comrade. Many families had no idea how a soldier met his end: heroically, accidentally, instantly, painfully or even ignominiously. Families of officers received a telegram. The deaths of other ranks were communicated via a pro-forma letter from the War Office, form B 104-82. Names were hand-written; the outcome 'killed in action' was often rubber-stamped. Enclosed with the letter was a leaflet with information about burial and a standard printed letter from the King and Queen.

Official communications informing families of a death were brief and to the point, although Rudyard Kipling was drafted in during the First World War to pen a standard letter that would appear less abrupt and curt. Only if a comrade or officer wrote a personal letter did a family receive any specific details. Thousands of families received no additional letter and this ignorance did nothing to assuage the overwhelming grief of the nation. It often happened too that the people of a single town, or even street, found themselves bereaved at the same time. This happened when a local, or 'pals' regiment had been in action and had suffered casualties. Many local regiments were made up of friends, brothers and neighbours who had joined up together. After the war was over their families mourned together. Today evidence of these local tragedies can be seen on war memorials. Where dates of death are also given, the same date will appear several times on one roll.

Following periods of intense fighting during the First World War, the War Office sent thousands of identical letters in a day. Each one, when it arrived, had a singular and devastating impact.

3

THE REMEMBRANCE DEBATE

TODAY, BY CONTRAST WITH THE IMMEDIATELY POST-FIRST
World War Britain, when the country pauses for the two minutes'
silence, the nation at large is no longer in a state of shock and
mourning. Only a small minority of those taking part have direct
experience of military service or of military bereavement. For the
parent of a young man killed in Afghanistan the moment is as
poignant as it would have been in 1919 for the parent of a victim
of the Somme, but for the overwhelming majority of members
of the modern generation the observance and experience of
Remembrance is not the same as it was for their grandparents. In
2009, 54 British service personnel died in Afghanistan. In the First
World War deaths averaged ten times that figure every day. For
most Western young people today what they know of war is
learned from history lessons, Hollywood and video games. Their
grandparents had war etched into their memories.

The purpose behind these acts of public Remembrance has
thus subtly changed. Where once they acknowledged and helped
ease widespread private grief, they have now refocused to pay a
more general tribute to the thousands of individuals who paid the
ultimate price, most of them in the historic past.

Although the rituals date from 1918–21, the ideological focus
of Remembrance is today on those who died in the Second World
War. The men and women who died in subsequent conflicts are of
course recalled, but the words used to explain the purpose behind
the ceremonies reflect the message and mood of neither 1918 nor
the twenty-first century. They are rooted in the 1940s, and summed

up in an oft-repeated mantra: 'They died that we might live in freedom.'

This is for two reasons. First, the survivors of the First World War are now all dead and there is no living link with that generation. Of the Second World War veterans, although now in their eighties or older, many are still alive and can testify as witnesses to the conflict. But second, and more significantly, it is because the ideological case and justification for the Second World War is far more simply stated than that for the First World War. Britain, America and the other Allied countries saw themselves as waging a war of reluctance to defeat an obvious evil. No one in 1939 went to war with enthusiasm, but they did so with a clear moral purpose. It is hard to argue against the assertion that those who gave their lives during the Second World War did so to ensure subsequent generations did not live under the tyranny of Nazism. Few if any of the lesser conflicts since have presented such a clear-cut case of right versus wrong, despite attempts by Western governments to present them as such.

The invasion of Iraq, the war in Afghanistan and the NATO military action in Libya were all presented by the American government as different theatres of an ongoing War on Terror. The official name used by the George W. Bush administration for American action in Afghanistan, and elsewhere, aimed at seeking and destroying al-Qaeda fighters was 'Operation Enduring Freedom'. Despite this and other attempts by both British and American political leaders to establish a moral link between current military engagements and the Second World War, large numbers of citizens of both countries have not been convinced.

Indeed the Iraq War of 2003 was such a divisive issue that in February of that year, in Britain, hundreds of thousands of people took to the streets of London to voice their opposition. The BBC reported the police as saying that it was the UK's biggest ever demonstration with at least 750,000 people taking part, although organisers put the figure closer to 2 million. Andy Todd, Assistant Deputy Commissioner of the Metropolitan Police, said the crowd had been tolerant and patient and 'the biggest I have experienced'. The police estimate of 750,000 people could be an underestimation', reported the BBC, 'due to people bypassing official routes or going straight to Hyde Park without joining the main march.' Protests took place in around 800 cities worldwide on 15 February that year. It was claimed to be the largest simultaneous protest in human history.

In America too the government failed to persuade the people of the war's justification. A 2009 Gallup poll found that 58 per cent of the American public believed then that the invasion of Iraq had been a mistake. Gallup has found this to be a generally rising trend since 2003, when three-quarters of the public supported the war. Opposition peaked at 63 per cent in the first half of 2008. It was also noted that opposition to the ongoing war in Afghanistan was growing.

During the Cold War era conflicts such as those in Korea and Vietnam were presented in terms of the defence of democratic freedoms in the face of the threat of communism. A commonly expressed line of moral justification was that of the 'domino effect'. If one country succumbed to communism, it would infect its neighbour. It too would turn to communism and in due course, one by one, all the countries in a region would follow.

Successive American presidents from Eisenhower to Nixon endorsed this view, believing that should South Vietnam turn to communism, then Laos, Cambodia, Thailand, Burma, Malaysia and Indonesia would follow. This was seen as a disastrous outcome by successive US administrations. But not everyone in the West agreed. For some in the West, communism did not appear to be an unappealing option. Left-wing idealists saw much good in communism, at least in theory, and much evil in the Western capitalist system that opposed it. The Vietnam War was widely opposed by the left. Opposition to the conflict broadened across the political spectrum as casualties mounted and high-profile opponents denounced the war and its methods. Many Americans of no particular left-wing persuasion opposed the Vietnam War as a foreign war in a far place. Muhammad Ali, the most high-profile objector of the day, famously said, 'I ain't got no quarrel with those Vietcong' and 'no Vietcong ever called me nigger'.

In the 1920s, in the aftermath of the First World War, it was not easy to justify the horrendous loss of life on moral grounds.

When Britain had first gone to war, men were inspired by calls to rally in support of the empire. Vesta Tilley, the music hall star of the day, sang this recruiting song to young men of Army age in 1914:

> We've watched you playing cricket and every kind of game,
> At football, golf and polo, you men have made your name.
> But now your country calls you to play your part in war.
> And no matter what befalls you
> We shall love you all the more.
> So come and join the forces
> As your fathers did before.[18]

It is the chorus to one version of the song that is still remembered: 'we don't want to lose you, but we think you ought to go.'

The young men of 1914 who volunteered with enthusiasm to fight for King and country were inspired by a sense of adventure, tribal loyalty to the British Empire, peer pressure and a sense of duty. They were often further motivated by stories of German atrocities. By the end of the war that spirit of euphoric jingoism had long since passed. With hindsight, the daily slaughter of the war and massive death toll seemed a disproportionate response to the supposed German crimes. By 1919, if the war had any justification, it was as the war that would end all wars. The suffering of the men in the trenches would be an abject lesson for future generations. From their suffering they would learn for all time that warfare was brutal and ultimately futile. Millions of British people came to associate the wearing of poppies not only with personal feelings of grief and regret, but with their dedication to peace.

The official line taken when the various acts of Remembrance were introduced in 1919–21 did not express this aspect. Just four days before Armistice Day in 1919, King George V announced that a two minutes' silence would be observed, with the words:

> Tuesday next is the first anniversary of the Armistice, which stayed the worldwide carnage of the four preceding years and marked the victory of Right and Freedom. I believe that my people in every part of the Empire

fervently wish to perpetuate the memory of the Great
Deliverance and of those who have laid down their lives
to achieve it.

The King of course could not admit publicly to the futility of the
conflict in which thousands had died in his name. That thought
did not have to be expressed out loud; it was what millions of
people knew in their hearts. Thus a period of silence and, later, the
wordless gesture of wearing a poppy enabled everyone to have
their own individual reflections. In the immediate post-First World
War period those reflections overwhelmingly focused on suffering,
loss and grief.

In the 1930s, when war again threatened Europe, the white
poppy was introduced by the Peace Pledge Union to reinforce the
red poppy's message of peace and sorrow. By that time Armistice
Day had become an established date in the British calendar. The
newly formed BBC broadcast an annual live radio transmission
from the Cenotaph and the nation could share in the sombre
military music and hear descriptions of the marching veterans and
drilled servicemen. The Peace Pledge Union wished to separate
the poppy from what they viewed as the military culture of the
Cenotaph rituals and allow people to wear the poppy both in grief
and as a statement of opposition to war. As will be explored in
detail later, this had been its original message when the flower
found on the First World War battlefields was first worn by the
families of those killed. In 1926 the British Legion had been
approached with the suggestion that the words imprinted on the
central black button at the heart of the red poppy should not be
'Haig Fund', but 'No More War'. To the disappointment of many
this idea was not taken up.

The Peace Pledge Union states that

The details of any discussion with the British Legion are
unknown . . . but as the centre of the red poppy displayed
the 'Haig Fund' imprint until 1994 it was clearly not successful. A few years later the idea was again discussed by
the Co-operative Women's Guild, who in 1933 produced

the first white poppies to be worn on Armistice Day. The Guild stressed that the white poppy was not intended as an insult to those who died in the First World War – a war in which many of the women lost husbands, brothers, sons and lovers – but a challenge to the continuing drive to war.[19]

Today the white poppy is still produced, but sales are small and vastly outnumbered by those of its red counterpart. It cannot compete with the high-profile marketing drive that accompanies Remembrance Day in the twenty-first century. In the 1930s the BBC had its own reservations about the militaristic tones of the Cenotaph service and sought to balance them with other broadcasts. Today the BBC endorses Remembrance Day, including the identical expressions of militarism, without reservation or question. In actively supporting the wearing of Royal British Legion poppies it also, by implication, endorses the legion's claim that it stands shoulder to shoulder with Britain's troops.

Along with so much in a consumer society, the red poppy is marketed as a commercial brand. Poppy merchandise is sold to raise money for the Royal British Legion charity, with the proceeds going to help former servicemen and -women and their families. Commercialism goes hand in hand with celebrity culture and at the annual Festival of Remembrance, held in the Royal Albert Hall, London, service personnel are joined by various celebrities to stage a show of what some view as mawkish patriotism, which climaxes in the release of thousands of red paper petals that flutter down from the ceiling. Throughout Britain, people of all generations, whether they have memories of war or not, are encouraged, in the words of the Royal British Legion, to wear their poppies 'with pride'. That pride is both in the professionalism and courage of service personnel and, by implication, in Britishness.

Of course grief can go hand in hand with pride and patriotism. A grieving widow can justifiably be proud of a dead husband's self-sacrifice for his country. When the widow of Staff Sgt Olaf Schmid, the British bomb disposal expert who was killed in Afghanistan in 2009, took part in the 2011 Remembrance observances, she said that she was still caught in 'an excruciating vortex of grief. There's a constant physical pain and a gnawing in your mind, intense panic as if something is lost. The mental and spiritual absence of him is massive.'

But what happens when pride and patriotism exist without grief? *In extremis*, acts of remembrance can then become celebrations of idealized militarism. Instead of regretting the need for fighting, the act of fighting is glorified. In 1934 the Nazis in Germany deliberately subverted the national day of mourning for the dead of 1914–18 by changing the country's Remembrance Day, Volkstrauertag, to Heldengedenktag, a day for the commemoration of heroes. The focus of the day was moved from sorrowful recollection to hero-worship, and in particular the glorification of those who had died for the Fatherland in the First World War. The masters of propaganda realized that Remembrance, by being linked with patriotism, could become an expression less of sorrow than of national regeneration. On the instructions of Joseph Goebbels even the practice of flying flags at half-mast was discontinued. This was an overtly political act. 'The cult of the fallen was at the centre of the Myth of the War Experience', wrote George Mosse in *Fallen Soldiers*,

> supplying it with symbols which refocused the memory of war. The enthusiasm which youth had once felt for war, as adventure or personal fulfilment, was difficult to sustain after experiencing the reality of war, but the nation, using the Myth of the War Experience, was able to keep the flame alight. The Nazis knew what they were doing when they made the cult of the war dead and the cult of their own martyrs central to their political liturgy. The cult of the fallen was of importance for most of the nation: almost every family had lost one of its members and most of the adult population had found in the war and lost a cherished friend. Yet it was the political Right and not the Left that was able to annex the cult and make the most of it . . . The Myth of the War Experience helped to transcend the horror of war and at the same time supported the

utopia which nationalism sought to project as an alternative to the reality of postwar Germany.[20]

In most nations of the Western world in the twenty-first century rites of Remembrance are seen as, and assumed to be, non-political. It would seem grossly inappropriate to turn them into political occasions. When, in the run up to a British general election, the Conservative party leader had his photograph taken outside Westminster Abbey, inspecting the wooden crosses of Remembrance planted there, he was roundly criticized. When his party political opponent, the Prime Minister, also had his photograph taken in the same pose, both were publicly taken to task by the Abbey's Dean.

As the *Daily Mail* reported,

> Gordon Brown and David Cameron have been forced to make grovelling apologies after they were accused of exploiting a Remembrance Day service attended by the Queen, turning it into a media 'turkey shoot' to win votes.
>
> The extraordinary and unprecedented apologies came after the Dean of Westminster Abbey rebuked them for competing for photo opportunities at the service to mark the passing of the First World War generation.
>
> Mr Brown was accused of a 'tit-for-tat' response on learning that Mr Cameron had had his picture taken in the Abbey's Field of Remembrance.

Yet is not Remembrance implicitly political? Not party political, but part of the wider political process by which nations acquire and maintain identity and order? Remembrance ceremonies involving the holders of the high offices of state cannot help but contain within them a political subtext. In Britain the focus of the nation's act of Remembrance takes place in Whitehall, at the heart of government. After the first wreaths of poppies are laid by the Queen and members of the Royal Family, others, as described earlier, are laid by the politicians of the day, led by the Prime Minister and the Leader of the Opposition. When in the final year of his premiership Tony Blair stepped forward to pay tribute to those killed in conflict, it did not escape the attention of many watching that he might himself have been responsible for some of the most recent of the deaths being honoured, by taking Britain into the Iraq War.

In 2010 a group calling themselves Muslims Against Crusades staged a demonstration, deliberately choosing Armistice Sunday to draw maximum attention to their cause. The event seen by the British people to be apolitical was to them overtly political. They decided to disrupt the traditional two minutes' silence by chanting, 'British troops burn in hell, British troops burn in hell . . .', and setting fire to a large poppy. They were three miles from Whitehall and well out of the view and earshot of the Cenotaph, but they ensured that cameras were on hand and gave the media the pictures required to enliven their reports of an otherwise uneventful, annual event.

When images of the Islamists' demonstration were later seen on television and in newspapers they provoked a torrent of rage. The *Daily Mail* ran a story contrasting the actions of the demonstrators with the dignity shown by a seven-year-old boy who was also in London that day, who proudly wore the medals of his great-uncle who had been killed in fierce fighting on the beaches of Greece in 1941 while serving with the Royal Engineers.

Jonny Osborne, said the paper, stood three feet tall in his shiny black shoes. He 'symbolised the face of a new generation yesterday as he marched shoulder to shoulder with servicemen and women to honour those killed by war.' However, the paper continued, another face of Britain was also on display.

It was contorted with hatred, poisoned by politics, and fuelled by flames from a giant, burning poppy. These were the Muslim extremists who brought shame to the memory of the dead yesterday by breaking the traditional two-minute silence . . . Ironically it was the freedom for which thousands fought that allowed them to stage their demonstration at the stroke of 11am – the exact moment the nation came to a halt.

'Jeering Muslim extremists burn a giant Remembrance Day poppy yesterday – and defile the commemoration of Britain's dead heroes', was how *The Sun* reported events. 'About 40 fanatics protested while millions of people across the nation honoured the men and women who died serving their country. Outraged senior Tory MP Patrick Mercer said: "They are beneath contempt."'

Vince Soodin from the Murdoch-owned *Sun*, claiming to be the only journalist 'to infiltrate the sick mob', filed an eyewitness account of events.

I was sickened as I witnessed the vile face of extremist Islam in the UK from the inside.

The mob chose one of the days most important to bereaved families to spew hatred, condemn Britain and damn our selfless servicemen as Nazis, terrorists and baby killers.

Then they excitedly sprayed lighter fluid on three large poppies and set them alight. One idiot even spat on the ashes.

The hatred in these men, who were mostly in their late teens to late twenties, was unlike any I have ever seen.

They brought shame on themselves and once again blackened the name of the religion that they claim to speak for.

Radio phone-in programmes, letters columns and opinion-based websites rapidly filled with condemnation of the protest. The demonstrators had achieved a scale of publicity beyond their expectations, even if their message, that British troops should not be involved in contentious action in Muslim countries, was somewhat obscured by the ensuing fury.

In many ways the demonstration was unhelpful to the cause. Not only did the poppy-burners match every media stereotype of fanaticism, but the reporting of their actions supported the impression that any misgivings about Remembrance-tide observations were confined to a handful of fanatics. However, in 2010, away from sensational media attention-seeking stunts, others were

asking pertinent questions. They were not Islamists or political extremists. They were British citizens who shared the consensus view
that sometimes a high price had to be paid to defend democracy
and the Western way of life. Some indeed were former servicemen and -women who had demonstrated their patriotism and
loyalty to Queen and country in uniform. At the core of their
concern was that in honouring those who had died in past wars in
defence of freedom, it might be inferred that they also supported
the ongoing use of troops in current controversial conflicts.

At the beginning of November a letter appeared in several
newspapers, including *The Guardian* and *The Independent*, from six
men who had served in the British forces in recent conflict areas
including Iraq, Afghanistan, Northern Ireland and the Falklands.

> The Poppy Appeal is once again subverting Armistice Day
> . . . A day that should be about peace and remembrance is
> turned into a month-long drum roll of support for current
> wars. This year's campaign has been launched with show-
> biz hype. The true horror and futility of war is forgotten
> and ignored.
>
> The public are being urged to wear a poppy in support
> of 'our Heroes'. There is nothing heroic about being
> blown up in a vehicle. There is nothing heroic about being
> shot in an ambush and there is nothing heroic about fight-
> ing in an unnecessary conflict.
>
> Remembrance should be marked with the sentiment
> 'Never Again'.

The letter was signed by Ben Griffin, Ben Hayden, Terry Wood,
Ken Lukowiak, Neil Polley and Steve Pratt. The six men were
military veterans with experience, between them, in Afghanistan,
the Falklands, Northern Ireland, Dhofar, Macedonia and Iraq. Ben
Griffin is a former member of the SAS who, after serving in Iraq,
left the Army after telling his commanding officer in March 2005
that he would not return to the country. He said he believed the
war to be morally wrong. Expecting to be placed under arrest and
court-martialled, Griffin was surprised to be allowed to leave the

service with an unblemished record. Indeed his commanding officer went on record describing him as a 'balanced and honest soldier who possesses the strength and character to genuinely have the courage of his convictions'.

Since leaving the Army Griffin has been highly and very publicly critical not only of the decision to go to war in Iraq, but of the conduct of Western forces in Iraq since the invasion. He has drawn attention to British connivance in the alleged immoral and illegal detention of civilians. 'The true meaning of the poppy is being forgotten as it becomes a political tool to support current wars', he told *Wales on Sunday* in November 2010. 'It has been turned into a "month-long drum roll of support for current wars."'

He was especially scathing about the Royal British Legion's involvement of celebrities in their campaign.

> This year's campaign was launched by inviting The Saturdays to frolic half naked in a sea of poppies. The judges on X Factor have taken to wearing grotesque poppy fashion items.
>
> The British Legion would say they are modernising and appealing to a younger generation. I disagree. I think that their stunts trivialise, normalise and sanitise war.

He also questioned the use of the word 'hero' in the contemporary context.

> The use of the word 'hero' glorifies war . . . and glosses over the ugly reality.
>
> War is nothing like a John Wayne movie . . . and there is nothing heroic about the deaths of countless civilians. Calling our soldiers heroes is an attempt to stifle criticism of the wars we are fighting in. It leads us to that most subtle piece of propaganda: You might not support the war but you must support our heroes, ergo you support the war.
>
> It is revealing that those who send our forces to war and those that spread war propaganda are the ones who

choose to wear poppies weeks in advance of Armistice Day.

Griffin believed his views about the war in Iraq were shared by many others in the British military who had opted to stay in the service rather than leave as he had done. In May 2006 he told BBC News, 'There's a lot of dissent in the Army about the legality of war.' At that time the BBC reported that 1,000 service personnel had absented themselves over the previous five years and been deemed absent without leave. John McDonnell, Labour MP for Hayes and Harlington, told Parliament that the number of absconders had trebled since the invasion, with more soldiers 'questioning the morality and legality of the occupation'. He also told the BBC that the numbers of British troops trying to absent themselves from service in Iraq were rising. 'My understanding is there are a lot more seeking to avoid service, through different mechanisms.'[21]

Five years on, morale in the services remains low, with a high number of experienced men and women seeking to return to civilian life. Not everyone wishing to leave the services does so on identical grounds to those advocated by Griffin. They may not go as far as to share his views on Remembrance. However, low morale in the forces is indicative of a lack of shared commitment to a righteous cause. There is no agreed need to counter a conspicuous evil, as there was during the Second World War. Yet Remembrance is not nuanced. The rituals imply that all service personnel who die do so in a good and righteous cause. This no longer applies. The world has changed since 1945.

The letter from Griffin and his co-signatories attracted considerable comment. This online comment was typical and received much support:

> It's the sheer stupidity of it all and the hijacking of the original sentiment, for political ends – to justifying today's crazy wars.
>
> It's pretty pointless to have a yearly remembrance to emphasise the 'never again' sentiment, when, in reality, no

such thing happens, and the remembrance is perverted by those in power to justify ongoing madness.

The comment finished with the observation that it should be the responsibility of the government to look after the needs of injured servicemen and women, rather than a charity. It added that it is immoral 'that said government is allowed to pervert that very cause, each and every year'.

Despite the reservations of many ex-service personnel and a feeling of unease that the welfare of injured troops is offloaded by government onto a charity, every year in Britain, whatever political party is in power, Remembrance follows the same unaltered pattern. In the two or three weeks before Remembrance Sunday poppy sellers are seen on the streets. Almost everyone in a public position is expected to wear a poppy. It is an unwritten rule, and should a public figure such as a politician or television newsreader neglect or opt not to wear a poppy, the act attracts comment and criticism. It is construed as a provocative, perhaps politically motivated, statement. Critics imply that the person in question is in someway unpatriotic or disrespectful.

Jon Snow, the presenter of Britain's Channel 4 news programmes, has consistently refused to wear a poppy on any other day than Remembrance Sunday. When accused by one viewer via the news presenter's blog of dishonouring the dead, Snow responded by saying that soldiers had died so that people had the freedom to choose when and where not to wear the symbol. He called the criticism of public figures who opted not to make a public display of wearing a poppy 'poppy fascism'. Few people in the media have the confidence to follow Snow's example. Wearing a poppy on air is a matter of individual choice, says the BBC, but no one steps out of line. During the period deemed Remembrance-tide by BBC diktat every presenter is expected to wear a poppy and producers have poppies ready to offer interviewees who turn up at the studios without one. MPs are almost always seen wearing poppies. When Conservative minister Ken Clarke forgot to wear a poppy when sitting alongside the Prime Minister during 'Question Time', his omission was quickly spotted by others and he was roundly criticized. There is not a single MP who would intentionally allow him- or herself to be seen without one in the chamber in the week leading up to 11 November. One political blogger noted that there was almost a competition amongst MPs to see who would be first to display a poppy. 'A few years ago the then Labour MP for Livingstone, Jim Devine, won chiding mockery from parliamentary sketch-writers for wearing his poppy from mid-October. One acid wit speculated he has simply left it on from the previous year.'[22]

One suggested explanation for this observes a growing tendency, as part of the subtle shift in the meaning of the poppy symbol, for the poppy to be worn not solely as a sign of Remembrance, but as evidence of the wearer's patriotism.

Wearing the poppy and observing the two minutes' silence has almost become part of the national identity. Some nations are united by football, but the United Kingdom has no unified national team. Other nations have unifying myths and national holidays celebrating the key moments of their history, such as Thanksgiving in America or Bastille Day in France. Britain just has Bank Holidays. Such celebrations as Britain does have are international. Halloween and Christmas have become Americanized. But Remembrance Day and the Cenotaph are British. And as if to emphasize this, the nations of the UK, while sharing a common theme, have their own variations on it. In Scotland, as noted earlier, the poppies sold are of a slightly different design to those sold in England. In Northern Ireland Remembrance Day is more vigourously observed by Unionists than by Republicans.

In 2006, while still Chancellor of the Exchequer, Gordon Brown suggested that Britain should have a special day to celebrate its national identity. He was making his first major speech of that year and attempting to position New Labour as a modern patriotic party. He also urged Labour supporters to 'embrace the Union flag'. Two years later a junior Labour minister quietly announced the idea had been dropped. Michael Wills MP, Minister of State for Constitutional Renewal, told Conservative MP Andrew Rosindell in a written parliamentary answer that 'there are no plans to introduce a national day at the present time'.

In fact by then there were no plans to introduce a national day at all. The government had come to realize the futility of imposing a sense of identity from the top. Identity comes from below.

British identity is a subtle construct, bound up 'in our institutions, culture and history', as one political commentator described it.

> It is easy to damage, but it is less easily repaired. How much more eloquent, for example, is Remembrance Sunday, in defining part of what it means to be British, in comparison to any number of reports or suggestions which the government might wish to instigate?[23]

The question arises: is a British citizen who, for conscientious, religious or ethnic reasons, feels uneasy about Remembrance less British as a result?

British Muslim Dr Abdul Wahid explored the issue in an essay published on 11 November 2011.[24] He noted the 'higher than usual profile' of the annual Poppy appeal in 2011 and how schools were 'being far more aggressive, some almost force feeding poppies to the kids'.

He quoted from the Royal British Legion's advice to schools on holding Remembrance Day assemblies. 'Remembrance Day is a day of reflection', allowing people 'to remember or think about all those people who are affected by wars, both in the past and now. It allows us to think about all those people who suffer in wars all around the world. And it reminds us how important it is to work for peace.' This statement, Dr Wahid said is, sadly, untrue.

> Poppy day is almost solely about remembering Britain's war dead and their families – and more recently those soldiers who have been injured in combat.
>
> You will never find anyone remembering, mourning or grieving for others killed in these conflicts – whether combatants from the opposing sides or civilians killed in collateral damage.

This is especially troubling for Muslims living in the UK. The British state – supported on all sides of the political divide but opposed by huge sections of the population – chose to invade two Muslim countries – Afghanistan and Iraq – within the space of 2 years.

While Remembrance Day is designed for people to recall those killed in those more recent conflicts, no thought is given, said Wahid, to the civilian victims of the wars. Neither is thought given to Muslims who fought against Britain in the First World War when the Ottoman Empire became involved. Anzac Day in Australia and New Zealand commemorates the thousands of men who died in Gallipoli. They died fighting Turkish Muslims.

Dr Wahid expressed his concern that there was no meaningful debate about Remembrance.

The conversation is usually emotive, patriotic, shallow and unchallengeable without provoking accusations of disrespect and disloyalty; and cries demanding everyone in the public eye should wear [a poppy]. Yet, a discourse is needed. There is nothing more distasteful than a selective use of history to generate 'patriotic unity' – except perhaps the manipulation of popular feeling so as to distract people from looking at the causes for the wars Britain has engaged in and to obscure the question of whether or not 'these people sacrificed their lives for us' as Prime Minister Cameron says.

Dr Wahid described the First World War, not as a war for the survival of Britain, but as

a war for the dominance of empires over each other . . . Just as in Iraq and Afghanistan, lies were fed to the population, and to their armed forces, to justify military conflict. Yet so few people examine these matters on the annual Remembrance day events.

Dr Wahid said that he would not himself wear a poppy, but that he had no disrespect for those who chose to do so. However,

> I will encourage people not to become intellectually inert over this issue, and to be bullied into silence by the oppressive climate that does as much to divide as to unite people.
>
> For all of this occurs against a background of a confused British identity. There are no coherent values to uniquely identify Britain; and the secular liberal capitalist values shared, with other European countries and the USA, are under serious question today.
>
> I believe the huge focus on the poppy this year is an attempt to generate some much-needed cohesion in British society.
>
> But patriotism – which thrives on the feeling that people are united because of some existential threat – is a very weak, temporary and shallow basis upon which to unify people.
>
> Moreover, I believe this is a deeply dishonest exercise. The First World War poet Wilfred Owen wrote: 'Dulce et decorum est pro patria mori' or 'How sweet and fitting it is to die for one's country' – except they are not dying for their country. Even if one shared this sentiment, the tragedy is that they kill and are killed for the sake of oil companies, defence contractors and firms involved in reconstruction.
>
> I mean no disrespect to those who have sincere memories of their family members killed or injured in war. But the more that people simply capitulate to this deeply political campaign by the politicians to promote Poppy day, the less they will scrutinize those who are pushing this agenda from Whitehall.[25]

If Dr Wahid was expressing views commonly held by British Muslims, then Remembrance Day presents Muslims with a conflict of loyalty: to their country of belonging and residence or to the wider Muslim *ummah*, the brotherhood, the nation of the faith.

Without allowing for this, Remembrance serves in a multicultural society not as a unifying event, but a divisive one – no bad thing, some will argue from the right of the political spectrum. These people say that in emphasizing the need for multiculturalism in Britain today, the essence of Britishness is being lost. Yet this response only substantiates the idea that Remembrance is implicitly political. It is not a politically neutral event. It reinforces a particular image of Britain's history, culture and self-identity.

In 2011 the far right-wing British National Party planned an all-night vigil and demonstration at the Royal Albert Hall to protest against 'Muslim fanatics who burned our Remembrance Poppy, defiling the memory of our Fallen Heroes, insulting the British nation and causing maximum distress to the British people'.

The supporting leaflet claimed,

Police, courts and Government did nothing, proving that we can no longer rely on them to protect the British people, our interests and our culture.

Defence groups are assembled across the country to defend against these Muslim Fanatics. It's up to us, and we will NOT allow Muslim Fanatics to defile the memory of our Fallen Heroes.

Interestingly in France in 2010 the defence minister, Hervé Morin, unveiled two plaques, one in French and the other in Arabic, at Paris's Grand Mosque. They commemorated the 100,000 Muslim soldiers who died for France. The mosque itself had been built at the request of French officers, in homage to Muslim soldiers who fell in the First World War.

The only other parts of the world that follow the British pattern of Remembrance are to be found in the Commonwealth. They are countries like Canada and New Zealand, which have a shared imperial past. It is easy, now that 60 years have passed since the end of the British Empire, to overlook the fact that the post-First World War Armistice Day rituals were devised not as national, but as imperial customs. Lord Curzon, who 'invented' the Cenotaph traditions, was also the man responsible for planning the Delhi Durbar in 1911, British India's jamboree to mark the coronation of King George V. Curzon was a man with a gift for organizing pageantry and his Remembrance Day rituals have stood the test of time.

Today, with the Empire long since gone, what was originally imperial has reverted to being simply national. Rather than setting the rules for the world, Britain now has to abide by them.

The poppy is revered by British people as a universal symbol of Remembrance. It is classless and devoid of party political allegiance. Yet that is not how the rest of the world can be relied upon to perceive it. Any national day of mourning or celebration, any national emblem of pride, will inevitably be viewed as political by someone who does not share the culture. This became apparent to football fans when in 2011 FIFA, the world football governing body, ruled that the England team should not wear poppies on their shirts for an international game at Remembrance-tide. FIFA expressed concern 'that other countries may demand to be allowed to wear emblems to mark significant national events'.

To an international body the poppy appeared to be one of many quasi-political symbols with which countries might opt to decorate their kit. After protests and the intervention of the Duke of Cambridge, FIFA reluctantly permitted the team players to place poppies on black armbands for their friendly match against Spain at Wembley.

Jim Boyce, a vice-president of FIFA, welcomed the compromise reached, but added:

> I can understand why FIFA do have this rule. Football and politics should not mix and, if you do give in to someone, it can create problems further down the line. It was sad that the issue was brought up in the first place . . . To me the poppy signifies the many, many people who gave their lives in two world wars. I do not think it is a political emblem and certainly should not be treated as such.

Nine members of the England team also had poppies embroidered on their boots when training and on 11 November the squad interrupted training to observe the two minutes' silence.

Controversy surrounding the wearing of the poppy is not restricted to those in the public eye. While some organizations, such as the main news broadcasters, expect their employees to wear a poppy, and to dissent provokes comment and criticism, employees in other organizations are explicitly told not to wear a poppy in the workplace. Some factories have cited health and safety as reasons for not permitting the wearing of a poppy at work. Companies with a carefully controlled corporate brand that extends to the way a uniform is worn prefer that badges and personal insignia, including the poppy, are not worn by employees. When in 2010 teenager Harriet Phipps was told by her employers, Hollister, not to wear a poppy with her working clothes, she organized an online petition demanding the right to wear a poppy at work. It attracted nearly 10,000 signatures. The company directive was later reversed, but not before the chain received a tranche of bad publicity. Harriet's grandfather 'Jack' Sidney Phipps, who served in the Second World War, was reported as saying, 'Wearing a poppy brings the whole nation together to honour those who have made the ultimate sacrifice. Poppies may not be cool enough for Hollister or Abercrombie & Fitch, but they suit the rest of us very well.'

Several other companies with strict dress codes also backtracked and allowed poppies to be worn. Mostly, however, companies compete with each other to show support for the poppy appeal and to identify with it. Most national newspapers in Britain add a poppy to their masthead during Remembrance-tide. The national broadcasters go one further and add a Remembrance theme to some of their regular programmes. In 2011 ITV broadcast a Remembrance edition of its popular quiz show *Who Wants to Be a Millionaire?* in which members of the armed services teamed up with celebrities to win prizes for charity. The BBC aired a Remembrance edition of the *Antiques Roadshow*, asking members of the public to show their war mementoes and have them valued. One man who showed his uncle's war medals had them valued at £100,000. 'The market is very buoyant at the moment', he was told by the expert. Admittedly the medals were exceptional and included both a George Cross and a George Medal.

Poppy sales in Britain are, it is claimed, at an all-time high. Between 40 and 50 million are sold each year and this is evidence, a Royal British Legion spokesman said in 2008, of the enduring covenant between the nation and the armed forces. 'Even though the war in Iraq may not be popular, people are quite capable of separating the politics behind the war from the forces themselves, and there is a great deal of sympathy for our men and women serving abroad.'[26] Three million poppies are sent abroad for expatriates to wear. They go to countries such as Spain, Germany and France where there are high concentrations of British full-time residents, and to embassies in over 100 countries.

Yet in Britain, despite the enthusiastic marketing of Remembrance by the mainstream media, support for the poppy appeal is not as universal as the BBC and Royal British Legion might suppose. That over 40 million poppies were sold in Britain does not necessarily mean that 40 million people wore a poppy. That figure could be much lower.

On 11 November 2011 a survey on the streets of London revealed that only one person in ten was wearing a poppy.[27] Similar observations in a Kent supermarket revealed one in three. In both cases an overwhelming majority of people were not wearing a poppy. There is no official data available on how many people in Britain wear a poppy, but there are several sources of anecdotal evidence. In November 2011 a number of online debating websites focused on the issue. 'I'm working in a Civil Service office employing 1000+ people; reckon I've seen 6 or 7 people wearing them all week. Considering the front desk has a donation pot and a box of poppies it's bloody sickening', reported one participant three days before 11 November.

Sales of poppies may recently have been artificially boosted by the tendency of many people to buy more than one. In 2011 the plastic mount and pin offered were ineffective and many people lost poppies and had to replace them. *The Daily Telegraph* columnist Vikki Woods is one multiple poppy buyer.

I buy not only a new poppy every year, but every week – or more, if I go into town more than once. There's a particularly charming and beautifully dressed lady who stands in the high street; though great in years she is high in endurance, facing the cold in a blouse and cardigan and fingerless mittens.

I'm constantly approached to buy poppies because I never wear them. Except on Remembrance Sunday. I never wear them because the stupid little plastic sticks are unusable on most female clothing. Women can't stick a poppy into anything now; certainly not my good black coat. We don't have buttonholes on our notched lapels.[28]

There are also people who buy a poppy but then refuse to wear it. How many of them there are is difficult to say, but their viewpoint was typified by David Woosnam of Grimsby, Lincolnshire, who wrote to the *Sunday Telegraph*.

The poppy fascists have won the day in Britain. I lost two uncles to German bullets. What did they die for? I suggest that they did not die so that the poppy could be used as a kind of reverse white feather – that the sheer absence of one would denote a lack of patriotism. I buy a poppy every year because the cause is a fine one, but I keep it firmly in my pocket. I blame some of our television companies for forcing poppies on staff and guests, as well as our politicians' bogus patriotism.[29]

The journalist Robert Fisk wrote in 2011 of how his father, a First World War veteran who had once worn his poppy with pride, decided towards the end of his life not to wear the red flower.

He was a soldier of the Great War, Battle of Arras 1918 – often called the Third Battle of the Somme – and the liberation of Cambrai, along with many troops from Canada. The Kaiser Wilhelm's army had charitably set the whole place on fire and he was appalled by the scorched earth policy of the retreating Germans. But of course, year after year, he would go along to the local cenotaph in Birkenhead, and later in Maidstone, where I was born 28 years after the end of his Great War, and he always wore his huge black coat, his regimental tie – 12th Battalion, the King's Liverpool Regiment – and his poppy.

My Dad gave me lots of books about the Great War, so I knew about the assassination of the Archduke Ferdinand at Sarajevo before I went to school – and 47 years before I stood, amid real shellfire, in the real Sarajevo and put my feet on the very pavement footprints where Gavrilo Princip fired the fatal shots.

But as the years passed, old Bill Fisk became very ruminative about the Great War. He learned that Haig had lied, that he himself had fought for a world that betrayed him, that 20,000 British dead on the first day of the Somme – which he mercifully avoided because his first regiment, the Cheshires, sent him to Dublin and Cork to deal with another 1916 'problem' – was a trashing of human life. In hospital and recovering from cancer, I asked him once why the Great War was fought. 'All I can tell you, fellah', he said, 'was that it was a great waste.' And he swept his hand from left to right. Then he stopped wearing his poppy. I asked him why, and he said that he didn't want to see 'so many damn fools' wearing it . . . What he meant was that all kinds of people who had no idea of the suffering of the Great War – or the Second, for that matter – were now ostentatiously wearing a poppy for social or work-related reasons, to look patriotic and British when it suited them, to keep in with their friends and betters and employers. These people, he said to me once, had no idea what the trenches of France were like, what it felt like to have your friends die beside you and then to confront their brothers and wives and lovers and parents. At home, I still have a box of photographs of his mates, all of them killed in 1918.

So like my Dad, I stopped wearing the poppy on the week before Remembrance Day, 11 November, when on the 11th hour of the 11 month of 1918, the armistice ended

the war called Great. I didn't feel I deserved to wear it and
I didn't think it represented my thoughts.

Bill Fisk was not alone in his disillusionment. Victor Gregg, who
wrote a candid and vivid description of the Second World War,
described how he threw his medals away, casting them out of a
train window. On Remembrance Sunday he goes to the Rifle
Brigade memorial at Victoria in London and joins the 'few who
are left from my time. It's a matter of respect. I won't go to Whitehall, though. I'm not interested in hearing some geezer spout on
about sacrifice.' Easter 2012 saw the launch of the organization
Veterans for Peace UK, made up of ex-service personnel dedicated
to 'counter militarism and educate on the true nature of war'.

Today some of the words used in connection with Remembrance do more than talk of past sacrifice. The slogan chosen by
the Royal British Legion in 2011, its ninetieth year, was 'shoulder to
shoulder with all who serve'. In choosing these words the organization was deliberately going beyond its prime remit, the welfare
of ex-service personnel in need. It was making a statement that it
supported all in the military, irrespective of the rights and wrongs
of the cause for which the politicians had sent them to fight. It was
going beyond its core dedication, 'When you go home, tell them
of us and say, for your tomorrow, we gave our today', which is to
do with remembering soldiers who have died in wars to defend
the nation. Standing shoulder to shoulder is implicitly a political
statement of support for the use of military support in any cir-
cumstance that the politicians of the day might sanction.

Several politicians quoted the slogan in publicity about themselves. Lilian Greenwood, the Labour MP for Nottingham South,
had her photograph taken holding the slogan, which she published
on her website. John Mann, MP for Bassetlaw, had an almost identical photograph taken for his website. Tory Mark Pawsey from
Rugby carried the headline 'Mark stands shoulder to shoulder with
those who served' on his website, as, like several MPs, he borrowed
the Royal British Legion slogan for his own political purposes.

If the slogan had been phrased in a different tense, say 'shoulder to shoulder with those who *have* served' it might have escaped

criticism. In that sense it would have been saying that we stand alongside those who have been in the forces who need our help. The fact that it performs this role is because over the years governments have not given full support to veterans in need. This was acknowledged tacitly by the British government in May 2011 when it was announced that the Military Covenant would be enshrined in law. Previously the covenant had existed as an unwritten social and moral commitment between the state and the armed forces. It had no legal basis and merely implied that in return for the sacrifices that service personnel make, the state has an obligation to recognize that contribution and retains a long-term duty of care toward them and their families.

Concerns that the covenant was being sidelined were expressed in a parliamentary briefing paper:

> Criticisms over the last few years that the Military Covenant was being steadily undermined, have prompted a series of welfare-related measures intended to improve the terms and conditions of Service personnel, their families and the treatment of veterans. Upon taking office in May 2010, the Government outlined a commitment to 'work to rebuild the Military Covenant', which would include the writing of a new Tri-Service Covenant. In June 2010 the Prime Minister also pledged to enshrine the principles of the Military Covenant in law.[30]

The Royal British Legion's decision in its ninetieth year to make its lead statement of purpose that it stood shoulder to shoulder with serving members of the armed forces was a significant one. It coincided with the government's declaration that it officially accepted its long-term responsibility of care towards those who had been in the armed services. At one time the British Legion provided care and the government supported those in active service. The two distinct responsibilities were clear. Now there is a blurring of purpose. In that the Royal British Legion is the custodian of Remembrance in Britain, this blurring of purpose might suggest that Remembrance is moving away from its initial purpose. It is now not so much an act of dedication to peace as a statement of support for the use of armed force. And in this it makes no distinction as to the circumstances in which those forces are deployed. The Royal British Legion does not generally express a view as to whether force sanctioned by government has an obvious, or agreed, moral justification. It did however, in the case of the Iraq War, provide information as to how members of the services might contribute to the Chilcot Inquiry.

One of the best-known soldiers from the First World War was Private Harry Patch, who died in 2009 at the age of 111. Not only was he at the time the oldest man in Europe, but he was also the last surviving British soldier of the First World War. He had joined up in 1916 as a conscript and served as a gunner. He fought at the notorious Battle of Passchendaele. He had little time for the pageantry and displays of national pride associated with remembrance. His memories were vivid, personal and forever disturbing.

In his book *The Last Fighting Tommy*, Patch wrote:

> We came across a lad from A company. He was ripped open from his shoulder to his waist by shrapnel and lying in a pool of blood . . . When we got to him, he said: 'Shoot me.' He was beyond human help and, before we could draw a revolver, he was dead. And the final word he uttered was 'Mother.' I remember that lad in particular. It's an image that has haunted me all my life, seared into my mind.

'When the war ended, I don't know if I was more relieved that we'd won or that I didn't have to go back', he said in a BBC television interview at the age of 109.

> Passchendaele was a disastrous battle – thousands and thousands of young lives were lost. It makes me angry. Earlier this year, I went back to Ypres to shake the hand of Herr Kuentz, Germany's only surviving veteran from the war. It was emotional. He is 107. We've had 87 years to think what war is. To me, it's a licence to go out and mur-

der. Why should the British government call me up and take me out to a battlefield to shoot a man I never knew, whose language I couldn't speak? All those lives lost for a war finished over a table. Now what is the sense in that?

Whether Passchendaele in 1917 or Afghanistan in 2011, the purpose of war remains the same. To achieve military objectives men must be trained to be able and willing to fight to the death. The scale may be different, but the reality is unchanged: armed men kill each other. Should Remembrance more accurately reflect what war is really like?

As previously discussed, few wars present a clear-cut moral choice. Some wars are fought to defend the economic interests of the powerful and to enable politicians to save face or bolster their popularity, as much as to defend freedom or maintain the peace. Well-intentioned wars designed as peacekeeping operations can have unintended consequences and lead to greater loss of life than ever intended. It ought to be recalled too that often both sides in a conflict believe they have right on their side.

Even the Second World War, fought by Britain and the Allies to defeat the evil ambitions of the Nazis, involved tactics which were morally questionable, in particular the bombing of civilian targets.

Most societies that resort to warfare have to endorse a myth of heroism. How would future warriors be recruited and motivated to defend their country if soldiering was seen as a profession that at best was one of shameful necessity? This book does not intend to walk on the sensibilities of those for whom Remembrance is a comfort. If the familiar rituals are to change, then it should be gradual and evolutionary. Nothing I write is intended to belittle the true courage of many. And true courage is most often to be found not in medal-winning heroics, but in the unsung actions of ordinary men and women who, despite being scared almost beyond endurance, are determined not to let down their colleagues, families and country.

And for their sakes, it must never be forgotten that Remembrance should be about peace. When the current rituals of

Remembrance took shape after the First World War, this was, in the minds of ordinary people who had survived, its overriding purpose. It was a searing obligation of many who had experienced the horrors of war to remind future generations that warfare should never happen again. The First World War could only be justified, with hindsight, if it truly had been the war to end all wars.

If the focus of Remembrance has so subtly changed over 90 years that it now serves to justify the use of arms, then it has failed. It is important for the preservation of peace that whatever form Remembrance takes in future it must serve to ensure that the sacrifices made by our forebears were not in vain.

4

THE SEASON OF THE DEAD

ALTHOUGH REMEMBRANCE IS NOW ASSOCIATED WITH RECALL-ing the war dead, autumn rituals recalling and honouring the dead can be traced back to pre-industrial days. It is impossible to understand the deeply embedded cultural significance of the rituals without placing Remembrance into its social and historical context. Remembrance contains within it resonating echoes of a pre-industrial age when mid-autumn was the season of the year for recalling, honouring and maybe even connecting with the dead.

The slaughter of the First World War, which ended in November 1918, was unprecedented. Hardly a family in Europe was spared the first-hand grief of a son, husband or father killed or maimed. Many families in America and the countries of the European empires also suffered a loss. The war ended at the eleventh hour of the eleventh day of the eleventh month, and although initially that day in 1918 was one of relief that the fighting was over, as time passed, and the anniversaries came to be marked, the day became one of solemn Remembrance and sorrowful reminder.

Despite the widespread extent of the grief following a war of unprecedented, industrial-scale killing, in the main, people did not look for new, modern ways of mourning. To find appropriate words and actions they looked back to times past, when life had seemed to make sense. As historian Stefan Goebel wrote, 'the ultimate challenge facing war remembrance was not to sanctify the collective slaughter, but to assign meaning to mass death'.[31] The aim of war commemoration, according to the architect Sir Herbert Baker, writing in 1919 only six weeks after the war's end, is 'to express the heritage of unbroken history and beauty of England which the sacrifices of our soldiers have kept inviolate'.[32] If any sense was to be made of the industrial-scale killing, it was to be found in the mythology of warfare dating from the pre-industrial past and an equally mythological image of an idyllic homeland.

In keeping with that preference to hark back, the November date undoubtedly felt like the most suitable time of year to recall the war and those who had died, for the month comes at the time of year when, in Europe and many parts of the Northern Hemisphere, the dead have traditionally been brought to mind. Recalling the dead is a practice common to all cultures and has been throughout history.

The anniversary of the First World War Armistice, 11 November, falls during the season of autumnal colours and dreary weather, of decay and dying back, when leaves fall from the trees and the natural world retrenches for the winter. Centuries ago it was a time when, as feed became scarce, animals were slaughtered and their meat salted and preserved for the winter. It was said that during this season of death the living could contact those who had departed and the spirits of ancestors could return to their old homes and familiar haunts. In the long dark evenings stories were often told of a parallel world inhabited by malevolent creatures of the night who lived on an unseen plane which existed halfway between that of the living and that of the dead.

Even in modern times, once summer time has ended and October abuts November, there is no escaping the fact that daylight hours shorten and outside temperatures fall. Often, especially in Europe, the world seems blanketed in grey weather of unrelenting gloom. It is a sombre time.

Knowing this to be the inescapable mood of the season, the Christian church sets aside the first two days of November to focus the minds of the living on recalling those who have departed. The first of the month is All Saints' Day and the second is All Souls' Day.

Many saints have their own festival days. The feast of St David is 1 March. That of St Michael is 29 September. St Peter and St Paul share 29 June. All Saints' Day is a special feast celebrated by the

Roman Catholic Church, Anglicans and several other traditions, to bring to mind all the departed saints and martyrs of history, both those who are widely celebrated on their own named day and the majority who are not. It is the day when their lives and deeds are both recalled and hallowed and is thus also known as All Hallows' Day or Hallowmas. 31 October, the day before, thus becomes All Hallows' Eve, or Halloween, as it is better known in its abbreviated form.

This special day set aside to honour all saints and martyrs can be traced back 1,600 years and its association with the approach of winter dates back at least 1,000 years. All Saints' Day is immediately followed by All Souls' Day, on which everyone who has died, be they saints or sinners, may be recalled and prayed for. The day is set aside for the living to bring to mind all the friends and family members separated from them by death.

In some churches a list is read of the names of all from the congregation or community who have died over the previous twelve months. In the Roman Catholic tradition the day is more than one simply of recollection. It is a day for prayers to be offered for the souls of those in the state of Purgatory, atoning for their sins before being allowed into heaven.

Catholics pray, said Pope John Paul II, for the souls in Purgatory who await their eternal happiness, but who in the meantime receive the punishment due to sin that separates them from God. It is where, he said, we are cleansed from every defilement of body and spirit, because the encounter with God requires absolute purity.

> Every trace of attachment to evil must be eliminated, every imperfection of the soul corrected. Purification must be complete, and indeed this is precisely what is meant by the Church's teaching on Purgatory. The term does not indicate a place, but a condition of existence. Those who, after death, exist in a state of purification, are already in the love of Christ who removes from them the remnants of imperfection.[33]

For the church to sanction prayers for those in Purgatory implies that the connection between the living and the dead is not irrevocably severed. The church does not condone clairvoyance and mediumship, but does accept that through prayer, God and his saints offer a link through their intercession between the living and the dead.

In some countries, in particular Mexico, people take the recollection of, and contact with, the dead to levels way beyond those approved of by the church hierarchy: 2 November is famously observed in Mexico as Día de los Muertos, the Day of the Dead. Though Mexico is a Catholic country, Mexicans blend pre-Christian indigenous traditions with the faith imported from Europe. The annual rituals involve producing special foods, eating meals by family graves and dressing up in macabre disguises. The traditions predate the arrival of Europeans and may be as old as 3,000 years. Attempts by Spanish missionaries to eradicate the heathen Aztec practices failed and a compromise was reached by which the indigenous traditions continued, but at a time that fitted the calendar of the Roman Catholic missionaries. The season allocated was that adopted from Europe.

Despite the attempt to Christianize the day, some practices completely defy church teaching. Wooden skulls are worn as masks, or are placed on altars dedicated to the departed. Sugar skulls are made with the names of deceased friends and relatives inscribed on them. The carnival atmosphere of many of the events contrasts with the solemnity of the church liturgy for the day.

Mary Andrade, an American researcher who has made a study of the phenomena, says that

> The Day of the Dead in Mexico is not a mournful commemoration . . . but a happy and colourful celebration where death takes a lively, friendly expression. Indigenous people believed that souls did not die, that they continued living in Mictlan, a special place to rest. In this place, the spirits rest until the day they could return to their homes to visit their relatives.

Presently, two celebrations honoring the memory of loved ones who have died take place: On November 1st, the souls of the children are honored with special designs in the altars, using color white on flowers and candles. On November 2nd the souls of the adults are remembered with a variety of rituals.[34]

Many Mexican families decorate their homes to welcome the spirits of their ancestors and talk vividly of sensing their presence.

Arguably the November dates themselves came about as a compromise that the Roman Catholic Church had to make many years earlier when its missionaries encountered the pagans of northern Europe and the British Isles. Honouring the dead at that time of year was an established pre-Christian tradition. It fitted a religion based on the natural cycles of the year. It was common for bonfires to be lit and in some places the bones of slaughtered cattle were ritually burned. Even when the Celts and Norsemen adopted Christianity, the rituals and myths of the approach of winter were so entrenched that missionaries found that nothing could be done to eliminate them.

So the church leaders adapted their calendar. Originally the first Sunday after Pentecost, in late spring, served as an all saints' day. In the eighth century this was changed to its current position in the calendar and 100 years later the feast was officially upgraded to one of obligation, requiring all church members to attend mass. For the old pagans, the season of death marked the end of the old year; for the last 1,300 years the Christian season for remembering the dead has come at the end of the church's annual cycle of prayer, just before the new year starts with Advent and the promise of the arrival of the Christ child at Christmas.

After the Reformation the tradition and the date for recalling the dead continued in many Protestant traditions, including the Church of England and many Lutheran churches. While the theological emphasis changed, with prayers explicitly for those in Purgatory being removed from the liturgy, a solemn day for recalling the departed retained a strong hold. In Lutheran Sweden it is common to see candles lit at family graves at the beginning of

November. Swedish journalist Po Tidholm has described All Saints' Day as

> a day of dignity and reflection. The custom of lighting candles on family graves is still widely practised, and anyone travelling through Sweden on this weekend is met by some beautiful scenes. With luck, the first snow has fallen over the country's cemeteries.
>
> The countless points of light from the candles and lanterns placed on graves form beautiful patterns in the snow and lend a special feel to the landscape. People also lay flowers and wreaths on graves on All Saints' Day. A jar of flowering heather stands up well to the cold.
>
> In southern Sweden, outdoor work is nearing completion, while in the north, All Saints' Day marks the first day of winter and the traditional start of the alpine ski season.
>
> Until recently, shops and stores were closed to mark the occasion. Although this is no longer the case everywhere, most Swedes take the day off, and those who don't visit cemeteries usually stay at home with the family and cook an ambitious meal of some kind. Many churches organise concerts to celebrate All Saints' Day.[35]

The last night of the month of October is the most important date in the contemporary pagan calendar, when modern adherents of the religions of the natural elements hold their festival of the dead, Samhain. Whether they are Wiccans or Druids, they share the belief that it is a time to remember those who have entered the spirit world. They may light fires, some cast spells and ghosts are summoned. Although many of the rituals are reinventions, they attempt to recreate the religion of the ancient, pre-Christian world in which traditional communities paid due homage to the dead in order to ensure the return of new life. November arrived as the harvest was complete. Grain had been stored, fruits picked and conserved, vegetable seeds for the next growing season separated out and kept back for planting.

To quote from Sinquanon's Journal,

This association of death with fertility provided the background for a great number of end-of-harvest festivals celebrated by many cultures across Eurasia . . . These festivals linked the successful resumption of the agricultural cycle (after a period of apparent winter 'death') to the propitiation of the human community's dead. The dead have passed away from the social concerns of this world to the primordial chaos of the Otherworld where all fertility has its roots, but they are still bound to the living by ties of kinship. It was hoped that, by strengthening these ties precisely when the natural cycle seemed to be passing through its own moment of death, the community of the living would be better able to profit from the energies of increase that lead out of death back to life. Dead kin were the Tribe's allies in the Otherworld, making it certain that the creative forces deep within the Land were being directed to serve the needs of the human community.[36]

Samhain, pagans believe, is the time when 'the veil between the physical world and the spirit world is at its thinnest and so the most likely time for spirits to be seen on earth'.[37] One Wiccan ritual contains the words, 'tonight as the barrier between the two realms grows thin, Spirits walk amongst us, once again.'[38] The same ritual puts the myths of the season into words. As a black votive candle is lit, a member of the coven says:

Dark Mother Your cauldron is a well of death and rebirth,
Dark Father Your sword both protects and annihilates.
Hear me now as the past year slowly dies, only to be reborn
 again.

The final prescribed words are addressed to the visiting spirits of the ancestors:

Watch over me, my loved ones, and all of my
Brothers and Sisters, here and departed,
Who, tonight are joined together again . . .

Bless us all as we light our bonfires, our hearth fires,
And the eternal fires in our hearts.
Guide us and protect us,
Tonight and throughout the coming year.

It is very odd to those unfamiliar with serious Wiccan practice and witchcraft. Yet in a more light-hearted form thousands of witches, ghosts and ghouls take to the streets on the same night of Samhain.

Halloween customs have spread in recent years from North America to Europe. Children dress up and play 'trick or treat' in what has become a highly commercialized festival. Shops are full of ghastly masks and pointed hats. Sales of pumpkins soar and incongruous banners are sold wishing everyone a 'Happy Halloween'. The popularity of the activities of the day perhaps serves a practical purpose to express, handle and placate the dark fears that many children naturally experience. Parents and teachers may take the opportunity offered by the dressing-up games to talk to children about their fears. Scary role-play in a safe environment may teach children how to face their natural worries and anxieties about the unknown.

In the Western world Halloween has expanded as a fun day as religious observance has decreased. Even in an age and culture supposedly based on science and rationality, the need to ritualize the coming of winter remains constant.

One branch of modern paganism seeks to incorporate the teaching of the ancient Norse faith that, in recalling the dead, focused in particular on those killed in battle. Asatru is recognized as an official religion in Iceland, even though it only dates back to the second half of the twentieth century in its modern form. Groups of followers are now found in several Western countries, including the United States.

Asatru has gained a reputation for being a militant form of paganism that seeks to emulate the Viking elevation of the warrior-dead. The reputation is not undeserved. In one court case involving prisoners in Ohio demanding the right to practice their religion, the judge heard that Asatru preached 'that the white race needs to use violence and terrorism to prevail over the "mud races".'[39]

The religion has three types of deity: those of the tribe, those of the earth and the Jotnar, the giant warriors of destruction and chaos. Believers who are killed in battle, it is said, are taken by the Valkyries to their reward in the eternal banqueting hall of Valhalla. The noble virtues taught by the modern-day version of the religion include such military values as physical courage, loyalty to tribe and colleagues, self-reliance and perseverance.

Mentioning this minority form of militant paganism might seem an irrelevance to a study of Remembrance if it were not for the experience of Germany in the years that followed the First World War. The Germanic war memorials adopted much of the same imagery and harked back to the past, to medievalism and Norse myth. Under the Nazis the symbolism became explicit. In 1933 a war memorial at a school in Bavaria showed a mounted Valkyrie with a slain warrior across the saddle of her horse being taken to Valhalla. The Nazi press, as Stefan Goebel noted, 'gave a very explicit interpretation of the school's memorial', calling it a 'symbol of the resurrection of the German spirit from the night of spiritual and political captivity'.[40]

Folk culture, when allied to Remembrance, is susceptible to political manipulation and while this can be starkly and dangerously demonstrated in the history of interwar Germany, Britain and her Allies have not been immune from acusations of having done so.

This tendency is nothing new, as a study of history quickly shows. Barely have Samhain, Halloween, All Saints' Day and All Souls' Day gone by when in Britain the major fire festival of the year takes place. Guy Fawkes or Bonfire Night is celebrated on 5 November and in its current guise originates in the political manipulation of established tradition. Bonfires are lit, the effigy of a man is burned and loud and spectacular fireworks are let off. The effigy is normally that of the seventeenth-century Roman Catholic terrorist Guy Fawkes, who was apprehended as he and his fellow conspirators planned to blow up the Houses of Parliament at Westminster and the Protestant King James. For many years the Book of Common Prayer published a special form of service to mark the deliverance of the King from his Papist enemies. But the traditions of Guy Fawkes Night appear to be much older than the date of the plot, 1605. Bonfires have been part of the pre-winter rituals for many centuries, as have the creation of loud and unexpected noises to scare the evil spirits.

When Parliament instigated the traditions and encouraged the people of Britain to commemorate the thwarting of the Gunpowder Plot, it was taking over and formalizing a set of traditions that already existed. Like the Roman Catholic Church in earlier times, those in authority find it more convenient to adopt and redirect old customs than create new ones. The firework displays that most communities in Britain organize for the beginning of November are today well disciplined with health and safety considerations to the fore, although in a few parts of Britain the ancient November fire traditions retain an almost shocking barbarity. In the normally staid town of Lewes in Sussex, Bonfire Night has a rough, sectarian edge. Effigies of the Pope are burned and the street procession is a wild exhibition of pyrotechnics.

Thus, in various ways, well before the Armistice of 11 November 1918, mid-autumn was established in Britain as the season for the commemoration of the dead. There were prescribed and traditional rituals to perform and words to recite, some of which have echoes in the present-day Remembrance observances. One specific example, All Souls' Day, was historically associated with charitable giving in many parts of Europe. It was a particular time of year when money was collected for those in need. The act of giving was believed to help ancestors in Purgatory to whom one owed a debt of thanks. Today money is given at the same time of year to help those in need to whom society owes a debt, as former members of the armed services. Another example is to be found in street processions. Northern Ireland aside, there are few places in modern Britain where the streets are annually closed to traffic for processions; except on Remembrance Day. These processions have an historic link with traditions going back centuries. November was a common time of year, despite the weather, for people to march or walk in line through the streets, The custom survives in a few places to this day, most famously when the Lord Mayor proceeds through London.

Remembrance has now become the modern, secular equivalent of the season of the dead. For several years after the First World War, many of the bereaved attempted to contact the dead, as well as recall and honour them. In the early years of the twentieth century interest in spiritualism waned, but the war years reversed that trend. Indeed, the 1920s was a boom time for spiritualism. The services of both those who were charlatans and those of honest intent were much in demand from widows and grieving mothers.

In 1922, four years after the First World War ended, Estelle Stead, who ran a Spiritualist church in London, received several spirit messages from her late father, W. T. Stead, instructing her to photograph the Cenotaph during the traditional two-minute silence.

Estelle commissioned spirit photographer Ada Emma Deane, and the results of the photographic plates she took that day were remarkable. In addition to showing the large crowd actually present, there hovered above them a milky fog through which could be seen, very faintly, the faces of dozens of men purported to have been killed in battle.

'The more one examines this result,' Estelle later wrote in her 'Faces of the Living Dead': a Straightforward Statement, 'the more interesting and bewildering it is.'

Rather than provoking alarm among bereaved families, the apparent evidence of such spirits was, for many, a great comfort. It was widely believed that this was scientific proof of an afterlife.[41]

Stefan Goebel observed that

The fact that the bloodshed came to an end on November 11th, St Martin's day and soon after the feasts of All Saints and All Souls, seemed a mere coincidence to the secular mind, but a divine providence to some believers ... In any case, the proximity of the events allowed Armistice and religious observances to mingle, especially in Catholic-orientated circles. For them, All Souls' Day in particular offered a conceptual framework for commemorative practices. In Germany, the Bavarian Catholics insisted on concentrating their activities in the period of All Souls, thus hindering the introduction of a national holiday, the Volkstrauertag, on the fifth or sixth Sunday before Easter.[42]

A suggestion after the Second World War from British MP Tom Skeffington-Lodge that Remembrance Sunday be brought forward to the first Sunday of the month to bring it into 'close proximity to All Souls' and All Saints' Day' was not taken up despite his suggestion that the idea had the strong endorsement of Christian opinion 'the world over'.

Neither was the suggestion that a new date be found for a combined First and Second World War Remembrance Day adopted. This possibility was raised in a cabinet memorandum from the Home Secretary in 1945. Sir Donald Somervell had reported that there was general agreement that the dead of the two wars should be remembered on a single day, but there was some doubt as to whether November was the right time of year. A deputation of religious leaders to the Home Office had suggested a day in May.

The objections to the adoption of the 11th November as Remembrance Day for both wars are the uncertainty of the weather at this time of the year and the fact that the November Sunday tends to collide with Civic Sunday, which follows the election of new Mayors. Furthermore, unless the end of the Japanese war takes place some time in November, it would be unreal to remember on the 11th November (a day hitherto associated with the defeat of Germany in 1918) the much greater and more widespread sacrifices made during the present war. The deputation accordingly suggested that a date should be fixed in some other part of the year, possibly in May.[43]

Deferring a final decision, Somervell suggested the matter be left until the end of the war in the Far East. His predecessor Herbert Morrison said that he felt Remembrance Day should be linked with some real historic event, following the precedent of 11 November; that, he suggested, might be either VE Day or V-J Day, the anniversaries of the end of the war in Europe and Asia respectively. Until the date of a new national day had been officially fixed, however, the observance of 11 November should, he thought, continue.

The Bishop of Winchester, who had led the Home Office deputation of religious leaders, suggested that at some time nearer November a public statement should be made that, 'for this year at any rate, the 11th November would be celebrated as Armistice Day, pending the choice of a new national day.'

Somervell's recorded advice to the cabinet was that there should not be separate days of remembrance for the two wars; that it would not be appropriate to appoint 11 November as the day of Remembrance for the two wars; that when the Japanese war was over a day should be appointed as the National Day of Remembrance; and that it would be desirable to make an announcement such as that suggested by the Bishop of Winchester.

> Accordingly, I recommend that, should The King approve the holding of the Armistice Day service at the Cenotaph on the 11th November next, the preliminary announcements should make it clear that, although Armistice Day will be celebrated on the usual lines this year as a day of remembrance for those who have fallen in both wars, consideration would be given, after the termination of the Japanese war, to the fixing of some other date as a national day of remembrance on which those who had fallen in the two wars would be honoured and remembered.[44]

Within days of the cabinet receiving the advice, the war against Japan was over, following the detonation of two American atomic bombs over Hiroshima and Nagasaki. On 15 August 1945 Japan surrendered and on 2 September the surrender documents were signed in a ceremony on board the American battleship USS *Missouri*.

Eleven days later, the cabinet discussed Remembrance Day. Finding a new date on which to agree was difficult. The anniversary of the end of the war with Japan was objected to as

> this would make the ceremony fall during a holiday period. Attention was called to the desirability, if it were possible, of fixing a day which the United States would also be willing to observe as Remembrance Day, and the suggestion was made that the possibility of relating the date selected to the date of the signature of the Atlantic Charter should be considered.

The cabinet decided to consult further with the other Allied nations, the Empire, its dominions and all interested parties, particularly the King. Two months later the nation gathered again at the Cenotaph for the first time in six years. Despite the huge challenge of reconstruction that lay ahead, life had returned to a semblance of normality.

There was a comfort in restoring the familiar tradition of Remembrance Day. November, despite its uncertain weather, again caught the mood of the occasion. There was no further talk of moving the commemoration of the dead of the two wars to any other day.

If there was any change, it was in the way Remembrance took on a more overtly religious tone. This sermon, preached at the end of the war, expresses several common threads.

> We meet in thankfulness. But we meet also in sorrow. Sorrow for all that is broken – the broken lives and homes and hopes, the broken happiness of children, the broken treasures of art, architecture and human memory, whether the memory be of Beethoven's home in Bonn or Dr Johnson's in London. Sorrow too – I think we cannot honestly avoid it – that we have been obliged to use evil to cast evil out. We know that this can be no more than a partial and temporary outcasting, unless we now give our hearts and minds to the more final and more blessed over-

coming of evil with good. Because we have had to depart from this Gospel, however sadly and unwillingly, we must meet here also in repentance. It is clear to us, and rightly clear, that Germany must repent before she can be re-admitted to the community of nations. But we should remember that it is much easier, spiritually, to win a war than to lose it. Pride is strong and humility is difficult.

There is yet another reason for repentance. I stand here this morning with an uninjured body, with eyes that can see, and with a precious freedom to say to you what seems to my conscience right to say, knowing that you who are listening, and our country, give me this freedom. Your fathers helped to win it; your sons have helped defend it. When I remember the price at which my uninjured body and my freedom of speech have been bought, I feel bound to ask myself if I am worth it? It is not, I find, a comfortable question. But I think we are all bound to ask it of ourselves.[45]

On the other side of the Channel, a defeated and demoralized Germany was faced with huge social, economic and political problems. Every family faced huge practical difficulties and millions were also in mourning. The state provided no comfort. There was no public celebration of heroes, just private grief for lost husbands, sons and fathers and a sense of public shame and remorse.

The Allied forces that had defeated and occupied Germany forbade the building of war memorials until 1952. In 1946 they also ordered the demolition of any monument built by the Nazis which might be seen to glorify militarism.

Local monuments that honoured the dead of the First World War were usually spared, but any inscription suggesting militarism was likely to be removed. The words 'Germany must live, even if we must die' vanished from the military cemetery at Langemarck. Terms such as 'our dead' replaced references to national martyrs. Sometimes ruins were left as reminders of the horrors of war. Still today in Berlin the ruined tower of the Kaiser-Wilhelm-Gedächtniskirche bears witness to the bombing.

George Mosse wrote

> When new memorials to the fallen were eventually built
> . . . heroic poses were no longer used: instead, men or
> women were shown mourning the dead . . . The concept
> of the fallen as victims replaced the earlier heroic ideal.
> If a few scenes of fighting soldiers remained, they were
> not portrayed realistically but abstractly, robot like and
> wounded.[46]

In East Germany all national honours to the fallen were rejected. When in 1960 the Neue Wache was rededicated, the inscription no longer honoured war heroes but instead the victims of fascism and militarism.

The victors of the Second World War clearly thought that to have memorials associated with militarism in Germany was not conducive to peace. Nevertheless official Remembrance of the war dead in both the allied West and the Soviet bloc continued to maintain a strong military ingredient.

The Labour MP Gisela Stuart was born in West Germany ten years after the end of the Second World War and raised as a Roman Catholic. She recalls Remembrance being focused on All Saints' and All Souls' Days.

> When I was a child in Bavaria in the fifties and sixties, we
> would sell Christmas tree candles [with a black ribbon] to
> collect money for the upkeep of soldiers' graves and ceme-
> teries. On 1st of November there would be a wreath-laying
> at the local war memorial. One year I was selected to recite
> a poem, it was about the fellowship of soldiers. I was prob-
> ably 9 years old.
>
> In the local church there were pictures kept perma-
> nently of those who had fallen in the First and Second
> World Wars. Two of my uncles died in 1944 and 1945 in
> Russia and my mother's sister died in a raid north of
> Prague.[47]

From 1918, when searching for ways to make sense of the catastrophic four-year international conflict, people did not reject their collections of cultural memories, but turned to them for inspiration and comfort. In particular medieval imagery was borrowed. A crusader's sword adorned the Tomb of the Unknown Warrior in Britain. In Germany the design of war memorials harked back to the age of European chivalry. As Stefan Goebel argues, Britons and Germans needed a sense of historical continuity and meaning in the shadow of an unprecedented human tragedy. In both countries the survivors pictured the conflict as the last crusade and sought consolation in imagery that connected the soldiers of the age of total war with the knights of the Middle Ages.

> Older lines of continuity were reasserted in an effort to turn history into a coherent narrative that overshadowed the rupture of 1914–18. Medievalism in war remembrance, recovering the fallen and the missing soldiers of the First World War and relocating them in the grammar of medieval history, entwined intimate responses with cultural ones . . . Here was hope of redemption through tradition.

This is a motive that arguably is not dissimilar from that found in the traditional European cultures which seek continuity in nature, believing that through celebrating death at the completion of harvest, new life might be assured come the new year. The symbolism at the National Memorial Arboretum in Staffordshire embraces the cycle of the natural world. Autumn is when the leaves fall; spring celebrates new growth. The Arboretum, which was planted from 1997, now attracts 300,000 visitors a year to the 150 acre site.

The slaughter on the battlefields of Europe was poetically likened to a harvest: the young men being 'mown down' and their souls 'gathered'. Famously the poppy motif reinforced this imagery when it was seen growing in the fields, the first new life emerging on the land where the carnage had taken place.

Another largely overlooked aspect of Remembrance is the sense of atonement. It is a complex concept involving making amends and offering reparation for wrongs done. In many traditions atonement has a public dimension; it is a community activity. In pre-Remembrance Catholic practice, All Souls' Day focused on the atonement expected of souls in Purgatory. For Jews Yom Kippur is their day of atonement. It is not on a fixed date according to the Western calendar, but falls in late September or early October once the summer is over and autumn has set in. For veterans at war memorials around the country, Remembrance brings to mind not only comrades who have fallen, but enemies too. A soldier who kills another human beings in the line of duty does not easily forget the first time he is required to end another man's life.

> Looking another human being in the eye, making an independent decision to kill him, and watching as he dies due to your action combine to form the single most basic, important and potentially traumatic occurrence of war. If we understand this, then we understand the magnitude of the horror of killing in combat.[48]

It is also an inevitable fact of life during a time of war that some combatants step over other normal moral boundaries and do not just kill, but are involved in acts of additional savagery such as rape, looting and pillaging. The soldier returning from war to civilian life may have a host of disturbing and guilt-laden memories. Some of these may come to the surface at Remembrance-tide. The tears on the faces of veterans may not solely be for lost comrades; sometimes they will be tears of shame and guilt.

Atonement rituals following warfare can be found in many cultures and many eras. Christian warriors in the Middle Ages were required to do penance for a year to expiate the sins they had committed on the battlefield, noted the philosopher and psychiatrist David Livingstone Smith. 'In ancient Rome, Vestal virgins ritualistically bathed Roman soldiers to symbolically wash away the moral stain of killing. Similar ablutions were performed in societies as far-flung as the Masai of East Africa and the Plain Indians of North America.'[49]

Livingstone Smith suggests that 98 per cent of combatants experience some degree of guilt, remorse or psychiatric damage after around twelve weeks of fighting. The 2 per cent who do not are those with psychopathic traits. As Livingstone Smith observed, this 2 per cent make the best soldiers and often come back as decorated heroes. 'They are unable to experience concern for others and enjoy the exercise of violence and cruelty.' Of the 98 per cent, he noted that 'soldiers and veterans often carry an immense burden of guilt because they may have done things in the course of duty that violate the primal taboo of killing one's own.'[50]

In recent times peace and reconciliation initiatives have sought to bring warring nations and factions together to find ways of atoning for past deeds. Sometimes the simple action of public confession suffices. It gives the former enemy the opportunity to forgive or be forgiven. Across Europe much progress has been made since the Second World War. Economic cooperation between old enemies has vastly reduced the danger of conflict. Some institutions have dedicated themselves to deeper reconciliation. Following its destruction by bombing in 1940, the restored and rebuilt Coventry Cathedral is now one of the world's leading religious-based centres for reconciliation. Its role dates from the war years when Provost Dick Howard made a commitment not to revenge, but to forgiveness and reconciliation with those responsible. Broadcasting from the cathedral's ruins on Christmas Day 1940, he declared that when the war was over he would work with those who had been enemies 'to build a kinder, more Christ-child-like world.'

Yet atonement also needs to work at an individual level. Faithfully taking part in Remembrance-tide observances can enable the normal 98 per cent to atone for their own wartime actions as a private, silent act. The Remembrance traditions that grew out of the First World War served several purposes, and giving veterans the opportunity to quietly atone for their own wartime deeds was one important purpose that today is largely forgotten. Indeed, the origins of the Royal British Legion and the initiatives taken by Earl Haig to raise money through the poppy appeal to help ex-service personnel may be seen as the atonement of a general who felt deep personal responsibility for the casualties of war.

After the First World War those who had not been combatants felt the need to atone for their contributions to the war. Rudyard Kipling, who had used his populist pen to whip up enthusiasm for the fight, had lost his son. He had good reason to seek to atone for the part he played. There were many others who would have felt a similar sense of guilt.

When peace came in November 1918, the nations involved in the conflict reacted according to their own perceived outcome. Everywhere there was relief that the fighting had ended and there were some victory 'celebrations' in Britain, but by the time the peace treaty was negotiated and the details of the Treaty of Versailles were agreed to, the mood was less euphoric. In July 1919 a victory parade was planned for London. The architect Edwin Lutyens was commissioned to design a temporary memorial in Whitehall for troops to march past. His instructions were to make the monument simple so that it neither glorified war nor appeared that the Allies were not magnanimous in victory. The monument was made of wood and plaster and became known as the Cenotaph, from the Greek word for 'empty tomb'. Within an hour of its unveiling there were mounds of flowers heaped around it. The laying of flowers had not been officially organized: it happened spontaneously. Flowers were, and still are, traditionally laid in this way on graves.

If the politicians had hoped for a celebration of victory that July, albeit a muted and magnanimous one, they had misread the mood of the nation: 'The victory parade in Whitehall, in the event, resembled a funeral march.'[51] After July the 'victory parade' was often referred to as 'the peace procession' in government statements.

The Cenotaph became such a potent focus of sombre remembrance that Lutyens's wood and plaster construction was, by popular demand, quickly replaced by a near-identical one made in permanent Portland stone.

Juliet Nicolson wrote:

Here at last was a place where mourning could begin . . .
Here at last was a tangible object on which to focus per-

sonal grief. Lacking any inner substance of its own, it seemed to be the silence of grief made visible, the absence of the missing men made real. For a Christian the emptiness of the Cenotaph held a symbolism like that of Christ's tomb after the Resurrection. Comfort came in many guises and for some the Cenotaph carried with it the suggestion that the dead were perhaps not finally dead, but had risen again to a better life.[52]

The Cenotaph provided the grave at which many could mourn by proxy. In normal, peaceful times, funeral rites and the burial of the dead are essential parts of the grieving process. In many cultures graves are tended as a way of keeping in touch with family members who have died. The vast majority of grieving families after the First World War had been denied a funeral. Many were even denied a grave to visit. Many battlefield bodies were so mutilated they could never be identified and given a resting place and headstone in a military cemetery.

'On November 11th 1920, I was with Mum and my brother at the Cenotaph when it was unveiled by the King', recalled Donald Overall, whose father had been killed in the war.

I remember that nobody dared move; nobody wanted to move. There was the Cenotaph: resplendent, spotless, clean. Mother stood there with her arms around us two kids and she cried, and I just stood there dumbfounded. I can't forget that day. I was feeling for my Mum and I'd never had to confront those feelings before.[53]

Initially the Cenotaph had its detractors. In 1919, before the stone version was raised, Viscount Wolmer asked Prime Minister Andrew Bonar Law when 'the article known as the Cenotaph will be removed from Whitehall; and whether in future a Christian design will be adopted in national memorials for our fallen soldiers and sailors.' He was told in response that the Cenotaph was erected in order that on the day of the peace procession the nation should visibly express the great debt which it owes to all those who, from all parts of the Empire, irrespective of their religious creeds, made the supreme sacrifice.

Another MP asked the First Commissioner of Works

> Why the cenotaph erected to our glorious dead in White-hall should have on it no prayer nor mention of God nor Cross or other symbol of Christianity, seeing that ours is a Christian country and not a heathen nation?[54]

In one light-hearted parliamentary exchange, on the same occasion, an MP noted that when passing the Cenotaph, 'quite a crowd of people fail to take off their hats and show respect to those who died for them'.

In 1919, as the first anniversary of the ceasefire approached, plans were hastily made to mark the occasion. Memories of the horrors of the war were fresh in people's minds. Many families were still in mourning. *The Times* still carried a regular column recording the recent deaths of those who, well after the ceasefire, had died of war wounds. Many of the survivors of the trenches were permanently scarred by their experiences, either mentally or physically.

Politicians were unsure as how to mark the anniversary in the most appropriate manner, sensitive at last to the nation's need to grieve rather than celebrate a military success. Returning veterans, especially those who had been wounded, were finding it increasingly difficult to adapt to peace. Promises that they would be returning to a land fit for heroes appeared to be unfulfilled. Many people were asking whether the struggle had been worthwhile.

The idea of holding an Empire-wide period of silence to remember those who had died in the war had been first made on 8 May 1919 by an Australian journalist, Edward George Honey. Initially the government considered it too impractical to organize. Five months later, and just two weeks before the anniversary, a more specific proposal for a silence was made by Sir Percy Fitz-patrick, a South African author, businessman and politician, and was referred to King George V. Fitzpatrick's suggestion was that the precise anniversary of the cessation of fighting, the eleventh hour of the eleventh day of the eleventh month, be marked with a silence lasting two minutes. All transportation, manufacturing, office work, street movements would halt in 'a complete suspension of all our normal activities'.

On 7 November a proclamation from King George V brought the tradition into being. 'All locomotion should cease, so that, in perfect stillness, the thoughts of everyone may be concentrated on reverent remembrance of the glorious dead.' The silence, which was very much a last-minute decision, and set at two rather than five minutes at the King's insistence, came into being.

By 1920 the summer anniversary of the signing of the peace treaty had been forgotten. The date that both government and public felt instinctively to be the most appropriate on which to recall the dead of the war was 11 November. Not only did it happen to be the date of the ceasefire, it also came by fortuitous coincidence at that traditional time of year when, in the northern hemisphere, the dead are recalled. In villages and towns around the United Kingdom local communities had started to collect subscriptions to raise war memorials on which all the names of those killed would be recorded. These memorials, many of which had been completed by November 1920, became the natural focus for ceremonies of Remembrance. The Imperial War Museum in London estimates that there are 100,000 war memorials throughout the country. They take many differing forms, from the frequently seen community crosses, statues of soldiers and plaques to memorial halls, lychgates, gardens, hospitals, organs, chapels and windows.

In 1920 they attracted mournful gatherings of new widows and grieving parents. Men who had served and seen the horrors of war at first hand also stood in silence as church and town hall clocks around the world struck eleven. Afterwards wreaths woven from the evergreen leaves of the season were placed on the new memorials. Often the list of names carved on the memorials were read aloud, echoing the established practice of All Souls' Day in which the names of the recently departed are read out.

Replicas of the London Cenotaph were built around the Empire and in the many Commonwealth countries today a two minutes' silence is observed on 11 November, or the nearest Sunday to it.

In Australia and New Zealand the focal day of Remembrance is 25 April, Anzac Day. It marks the anniversary of the start of tragic Gallipoli campaign of the First World War in which thousands of Australians and New Zealanders died. In the Southern Hemisphere April, like the month of October in the north, is when the days are shortening and the winter approaches.

The traditional Anzac ceremony starts at dawn. Veterans parade, poppies are worn and buglers sound the Last Post. In 2008 the speech of the Mayor of Auckland, John Banks, contained words which were full of echoes of the past and ancient elemental beliefs. Of those killed in action he said,

> we feel them still near us in spirit. We wish to be worthy of their great sacrifice. Let us therefore once again dedicate ourselves to the service of the ideals for which they died. As the dawn is even now about to pierce the night, so let their memory inspire us to work for the coming of the new light into the dark places of the world. We will remember them.

In 1919 *The Morning Post* had written of the first parade at the new Cenotaph:

> Near the memorial there were moments of silence when the dead seemed very near, when one almost heard the passage of countless wings – were not the fallen gathering in their hosts to receive their comrades' salute and take their share in the triumph they had died to win?

Initially in Britain there had been some official hesitation in confusing the holding of a national day of thanksgiving for victory with one which focused on the dead. As the historian Stefan Goebel wrote in his book *The Great War and Medieval Memory*, a cabinet committee had wanted to

> emphasise historical continuity rather than human catastrophe and transform private grief into public ritual. The

committee felt that as Armistice Day is not a day of National grief, but rather a commemoration of a great occasion in the National history, it is undesirable to lay stress upon the idea of mourning.[55]

On 11 November 1920 a ceremony took place that irrevocably linked the day with Remembrance of the dead of war: the burial in Westminster Abbey of the body of an unknown warrior. The first time the possibility was raised in Parliament, the government took some persuading. To quote from Hansard:

> Colonel Ashley asked the Prime Minister whether, in order to mark the deep and lasting gratitude of the nation to those who fell while serving in the ranks during the late War, the Government will transfer from overseas the body of an un-known private soldier and give it burial with due pomp and ceremony in Westminster Abbey?
>
> Mr Bonar Law: In my opinion the feeling expressed in the question, with which, not only the Government, but I am sure the whole nation deeply sympathise, is carried out in a more impressive way by the decision, already announced, to reproduce in a permanent form the Cenotaph in Whitehall, which, as its name implies, is intended to represent an Imperial grave of all those citizens of the Empire, of every creed and rank, who gave their lives in the War.
>
> Mr Bottomley: Does not the right hon. Gentleman think that such a function as is proposed would be a source of enormous comfort to the parents of every boy whose resting place is unknown to see someone who is the recipient of this honour?[56]

The idea of repatriating a body from the battlefields of France was strongly supported by the Dean of Westminster and, after some initial reluctance, the King. The burial of the unidentified remains of a war victim eventually took place in Westminster Abbey. The unnamed and unidentified body of a soldier that had been exhumed from a war grave was transported with dignity and honour from France to London. The reburial took place in the building that keeps the remains of many of the nation's celebrated monarchs and subjects.

The inscription on the Abbey's floor reads:

> Thus are commemorated the many multitudes who during the Great War of 1914–1918 gave the most that man can give, life itself, for God, King and Country, for loved ones, home and empire, for the sacred cause of justice and the freedom of the world . . . They buried him among the Kings because he had done good towards God and towards his house.

As the people of Britain came to terms with their grief through the invention of new ritual and symbolism, so do did the bereaved in the other countries that had participated in the conflict. In 1921 an unnamed American combatant, 'a soldier known but unto God', was interred in Arlington National Cemetery in Washington, DC. In France the Unknown Soldier lies beneath the Arc de Triomphe in Paris, and an eternal flame burns in remembrance of all who died in the world wars. When the flame was lit, it was the first time that that particular ancient custom, dating back to classical times, had been seen in Europe for 1,600 years. The inscription on the tomb reads 'ici repose un soldat français mort pour la patrie 1914–1918'. (Here lies a French soldier who died for the fatherland 1914–1918).

Forty-one nations worldwide have adopted the idea of honouring all by honouring just one unidentified fallen soldier. In Russia the tomb is found in the Alexander Garden in Moscow and contains the remains of a soldier killed in the Great Patriotic War (Second World War); other countries use the same symbolism to remember the dead of wars other than the two global conflicts of the twentieth century.

In the USA Armistice Day was first proclaimed a national day of observance by President Woodrow Wilson in 1919.

To us in America, the reflections of Armistice Day will be filled with solemn pride in the heroism of those who died in the country's service and with gratitude for the victory, both because of the thing from which it has freed us and because of the opportunity it has given America to show her sympathy with peace and justice in the councils of the nations.

The original idea was that the day would be one for parades, public events and a brief pause in the work day timed for 11 a.m.

In 1926 Congress added its endorsement:

Whereas the 11th of November 1918 marked the cessation of the most destructive, sanguinary, and far reaching war in human annals and the resumption by the people of the United States of peaceful relations with other nations, which we hope may never again be severed, and . . .

Whereas it is fitting that the recurring anniversary of this date should be commemorated with thanksgiving and prayer and exercises designed to perpetuate peace through good will and mutual understanding between nations; and . . .

Whereas legislatures of twenty-seven of our States have already declared November 11 to be a legal holiday: Therefore be it Resolved by the Senate (the House of Representatives concurring), that the President of the United States is requested to issue a proclamation calling upon the officials to display the flag of the United States on all Government buildings on November 11 and inviting the people of the United States to observe the day in schools and churches, or other suitable places, with appropriate ceremonies of friendly relations with all other peoples.

An Act of Congress in 1938 made the day an official holiday, declaring it 'a day to be dedicated to the cause of world peace and to be thereafter celebrated and known as "Armistice Day".'

It was not until nine years after the end of the Second World War that the focus of the day was extended. Congress enacted and

President Eisenhower agreed that the day become 'Veterans Day', when the sacrifices and contributions of all servicemen and women, both those who had died and those who had not, be honoured. The president's Veterans Day Proclamation stated: 'In order to ensure proper and widespread observance of this anniversary, all veterans, all veterans' organizations, and the entire citizenry will wish to join hands in the common purpose.'

At the end of the 1960s some thought the day needed refocusing as a holiday, rather than a day of Remembrance. The Uniform Holiday Bill was intended to ensure three-day weekends for federal employees by celebrating four national holidays, including Veterans Day, on Mondays. It was thought that these extended weekends would encourage travel, recreation and cultural activities and stimulate greater industrial and commercial production.

But turning Veterans Day into an ordinary national holiday did not seem right. It somehow flouted the sombre purpose of the occasion and the mood of the season. There was much resistance to the change.

The first Veterans Day under a new law was observed with much confusion on 25 October 1971. The Department of Veterans' Affairs website records that

> It was quite apparent that the commemoration of this day was a matter of historic and patriotic significance to a great number of our citizens . . . and so on September 20th, 1975, President Gerald R. Ford returned the annual observance of Veterans Day to its original date of November 11, beginning in 1978. This action supported the desires of the overwhelming majority of state legislatures, all major veterans service organizations and the American people.
>
> Veterans Day continues to be observed on November 11, regardless of what day of the week on which it falls. The restoration of the observance of Veterans Day to November 11 not only preserves the historical significance of the date, but helps focus attention on the important purpose of Veterans Day: A celebration to honor Amer-

ica's veterans for their patriotism, love of country, and willingness to serve and sacrifice for the common good.[57]

In France Bastille Day celebrates the nation and its past triumphs, but the dark days of November are reserved for remembering the dead. Armistice Day is a national holiday in France and Belgium, the two countries over which most of the bloodiest battles of the war were fought. Most towns and villages have a war memorial at which veterans and civic officials gather on the day. Poppies are not laid in France as in Britain, for there the blue cornflower is the flower of Remembrance.

In Holland it the country's liberation that is commemorated. Uniquely a double national holiday is celebrated in May: Remembrance Day, called Dodenherdenking, and Liberation Day, or Bevrijdingsdag. Recalling those who died is not separated from celebrating liberation by holding one day in autumn and the other in spring. The nation's ultimate liberation from German occupation is so closely tied in Dutch consciousness with the sacrifices of the war that the two days are linked. Linking sacrifice with liberty is given an international dimension in that 4 May is seen as an occasion to recall those who have died in all conflicts worldwide and 5 May is a celebration of the universal concept of freedom.

On 4 May the official, nationally televised commemoration begins in the evening with a service at a church in central Amsterdam, after which veterans and victims' relatives lay wreaths at the National War Memorial on nearby Dam square. Church bells ring for a quarter of an hour till 8 p.m., when there is a nationwide two minutes' silence. Dignitaries and other victims' groups then lay more wreaths and a child reads out a self-written poem, selected by a local jury. A ceremonial procession past the National War Memorial marks the end of proceedings.

On Liberation Day, 5 May, the Prime Minister launches the day's events, traditionally from a different province each year. There follow cultural readings and exhibitions reflecting that year's topical theme. The big event of the day in many Dutch towns is an open-air pop festival featuring top acts. These events are designed to get young people involved. In the evening, there is an official, televised concert at the Amstel Bridge in Amsterdam, attended by the Queen and government ministers.[58]

Because each country of Europe has its own distinct experience of the two global conflicts, their forms of Remembrance differ. Nations recall the war according to their own experience and national characteristics and traditions. This is perhaps why in some countries, Britain in particular, Remembrance is closely linked to expressions of patriotism.

However in 2009, for the first time, France and Germany came together on 11 November. The French President and the German Chancellor stood side-by-side at 11 a.m. at the foot of the Arc de Triomphe, where they laid a wreath and rekindled the flame at the Tomb of the Unknown Soldier.

Standing in Paris 91 years after the end of World War I, Angela Merkel described the relationship between France and Germany as 'something special, something unique,' and urged 'even closer' co-operation between the two countries.

As their national flags fluttered in the wind, the two leaders vowed that their countries would never again go to war against each other. Merkel said that although the past could not be erased, the power of reconciliation helped to bear the burden of what has gone before.

'We show other countries in the world that it is possible to rise above the pain of the past,' Merkel said.

The French president told the crowds that it was not an occasion to celebrate, but to remember.

'We are not commemorating the victory of one people over another but an ordeal that was equally terrible for each side,' Sarkozy said.

He said Germany and France had a duty to uphold. 'We owe it to the people of Europe, to the people of the world, to act together.'

Sarkozy has proposed making November 11 – which is already a national holiday in France – an official day of Franco-German reconciliation.[59]

As post-war Europe comes closer, whether through shared trade or economic interdependence, the question arises as to how best to remember the wars without reigniting old tensions. This account of Remembrance-tide, written from inside the European Union's institutions, appeared in *The Economist* and illustrates some of the practical problems.

Today is a public holiday in Belgium, so Brussels is quiet. But the European Union is at work; the long battle over the EU budget is likely to go late into the night. This is not evidence of a masochistic work ethic (the EU is not usually shy about taking holidays) but apparently a sign of deference to Germany, which does not formally mark the day of its defeat in 1918.

To many Germans the end of the war is associated with November 9th, the day when Kaiser Wilhelm II abdicated. The day is regarded as a German 'day of destiny' for several other reasons, both good and bad. November 9th was the night of Kristallnacht, the Nazi pogrom of 1938 that presaged the Holocaust of the Jews. And November 9th was also the night the Berlin Wall came down, leading to the eventual downfall of the Communist bloc.

In Berlin two days ago to commemorate the date, the president of the European Council, Herman Van Rompuy, delivered a speech about the enduring importance of the EU, and the need to preserve the single currency. He also issued a warning against the return of nationalism that, to many ears, will sound unduly shrill given the way he carelessly associated Euroscepticism with the danger of war.

We have together to fight the danger of a new Euroscepticism. This is no longer the monopoly of a few countries. In every member-state, there are people who believe their country can survive alone in the globalised world. It is more than an illusion: it is a lie! Franklin Roosevelt said: 'The only thing we have to fear is fear itself.' The biggest enemy of Europe today is fear. Fear leads to egoism, egoism leads to nationalism, and nationalism leads to war ('le nationalisme, c'est la guerre') Today's nationalism is often not a positive feeling of pride of one's own identity, but a negative feeling of apprehension of the others.

As a reminder of the importance of Franco-German reconciliation in creating the foundation of the European Union, Le Figaro has a touching story of German soldiers in the Franco-German brigade, stationed in Strasbourg, taking part in the French Armistice Day commemorations.

At a ceremony in Paris, meanwhile, President Nicolas Sarkozy unveiled a plaque at the Arc de Triomphe to honour Parisian students who risked their life on Armistice Day in 1940 to demonstrate against Nazi occupation in the second world war. This illustrates the long tradition of French student activism and makes an interesting counterpoint to Mr Sarkozy's criticism of the way modern-day high-school students have, more recently, taken to the streets to denounce his pension reforms.[60]

Although Russia suffered appallingly in the First World War, following the overthrow of the Tsar, the Communist government did not share the same view of victory as Britain. The major war memorials in the country date from the end of the Second World War and the dead from both the First and Second World Wars, and subsequent conflicts, are recalled and heroically celebrated in May. Under the Soviet government the nation did however still have an autumn commemoration. From 1917 the Orthodox Church's feast of Our Lady of Kazan, held on 4 November, was replaced by a day to mark the Communist Revolution. In 2005 this Communist 'feast' day was replaced by a Day of People's Unity.

In ancient times, when November became established as the month in which to recall the dead, people readily believed in the spirit world. Christian conversion did nothing to subdue those beliefs, only re-channelling them.

November in modern-day Europe remains a sombre month, even in a secular and multi-faith age. Not even the proliferation of artificial light in cities and Christmas decorations in shops quite succeeds in bringing cheer to the gloom.

No wonder our ancestors associated this time of year with death and dying. It was the exact opposite to May Day, the fertility feast, when new birth and growth was celebrated. Again by curious but appropriate coincidence, the nations that mark the liberation of Europe from Nazism do so in May.

James Frazer wrote in his classic nineteenth-century study of ritual and magic, *The Golden Bough*, that

> These dates coincide with none of the four great hinges on which the solar year revolves, to wit, the solstices and the equinoxes . . . Yet the first of May and the first of November mark turning-points of the year in Europe . . . The beginning of November dates from a time when the Celts were mainly a pastoral people, and when accordingly the great epochs of the year for them were the days on which the cattle went forth from the homestead in early summer and returned to it again in early winter. Hence we may conjecture that everywhere throughout Europe the celestial division of the year according to the solstices was preceded by what we may call a terrestrial division of the year according to the beginning of summer and the beginning of winter.
>
> The eves of the two great Celtic festivals of May Day and the first of November closely resemble each other in the manner of their celebration and in the superstitions associated with them, and alike, by the antique character impressed upon both, betray a remote and purely pagan origin.

November as the month to recall the dead has roots leading back to primeval times and pagan superstition. These roots are not consciously acknowledged, and need not be. For the families of those who have died serving in the armed forces in the course of modern-day conflicts, it is a time simply of sad memories. The sale of poppies and the national rituals of Remembrance become a poignant reminder of their own loss and grief. They are like the generations who survived the world wars, directly touched by grief.

But for those with no experience of war, the lucky generation that has never been conscripted, never known wartime restrictions, never dreaded the knock at the door bringing news of a death on the battlefield, what Remembrance message reaches them? Is it the one that talks of sorrow, suffering and pointless loss of life? Or the one that lauds the hero who has sacrificed himself in the defence of freedom?

5

THE REALITIES OF WAR

THE RITUALS OF REMEMBRANCE, IN ANY COUNTRY, SERVE TO make sense of the senselessness of war. They do this by creating myths, symbols and images that not only bring comfort to the living, but lend special status to those who died in battle. Death is inevitable. But not everyone dies young as some soldiers do, and not everyone can have stories told about them of self sacrifice and heroism.

But formal Remembrance ought to have another function: to remind the living of the evils of war. And it is here that an inherent contradiction is to be found. The evils of war are best demonstrated by emphasizing the realities of conflict. Many soldiers die horrible and unheroic deaths. As many Russians were killed in the Second World War by their own side as British troops died from all causes. Many soldiers who do die bravely, do so pointlessly. They are sent by incompetent leaders to perform impossible or irrelevant missions. These are some of the realities of war which remembrance disguises if it focuses on honouring and glorifying all those who die in conflict. And if Remembrance endorses an image of 'the glorious dead', might it ultimately serve to undermine the message of peace? This is a question raised as a concern that should be addressed, not to imply an opinion. And examining the question involves some honest searching of ourselves. Why do we human beings resort to war? When we call for troops to be employed, when we stand, albeit at a safe distance, shoulder to shoulder with our troops, do we really understand what we are doing?

It might be argued that for the rituals of Remembrance to be effective, for them to have power and influence and to bring comfort to the living, war itself has to be mythologized. No nation admits the truth about war too openly: talk of war, and what happens when men fight, is full of euphemism. The words that are employed are designed to deflect from the harsh reality. Men are not killed, but targets are 'taken out'. Civilians are not killed, there is 'collateral damage'. If the infantry make fatal mistakes, the victims may be said to be 'caught in the crossfire'. To be killed by one of one's own side is to die from 'friendly fire'. Human beings are 'soft targets'. In fact the word 'kill' is seldom used in military communication; terms such as 'neutralize' are substituted. Even weapons systems are not often mentioned by direct name and purpose. It is as if some superstition prevents straightforward and honest language being used. Thus mines are referred to as 'area denial munitions' and bombing raids become 'air campaigns'. And the phrase sometimes employed to describe an operation to lay waste and destroy is 'to pacify'.

In Remembrance-speak, there are references, not to deaths, but to 'sacrifices'. Those killed are 'the fallen'. Their bodies 'rest'.

If I should die, think only this of me:
That there's some corner of a foreign field
That is forever England.[61]

For any war to be waged, politicians have to distance themselves from the realities. If the American President in the Oval Office sanctions an air strike in a far-away territory, he cannot allow himself to agonize over each casualty. He has to be convinced of a greater purpose and not dwell on the pain he might be about to inflict, albeit unintentionally, on a defenceless child. Some dictators have revelled in their cruelty, but we assume that in everyday life no Western politician would deliberately commit an act that might endanger an innocent bystander. No politician of a 'civilized' democracy would consider killing an opponent or destroying his property. Yet war is not an ordinary state. It is exceptional and exceptional rules of morality apply, and as with all exceptional events, war requires a larger-than-life justification. The defence of freedom is one frequently cited justification. The War on Terror is a more recent example. The defeat of a tyrant is another, as is a pre-emptive strike to destroy weapons of mass destruction.

Sometimes the emotion that appeals most readily to public opinion is that of affront. Insulted nations feel they must be avenged. At the time of the Falklands War in 1982, there was an overwhelming view expressed in the British Parliament and the media that the pride of the nation was at stake. How dare a tin-pot dictator invade British territory? The fact that up until then few people bothered about the islanders, or even knew where the Falklands could be found on a map, mattered little. Within days of the invasion of the islands, a jingoistic mood dominated public debate. From leading politicians to the ordinary person in the street, going to war seemed the only fit response to what amounted to a loss of national pride.

'Britain has been humiliated', Tory MP Sir Nigel Fisher told the House of Commons on 3 April 1982, after hearing the Prime Minister, Margaret Thatcher, announce that 'for the first time for many years, British sovereign territory has been invaded by a foreign power.'

The Liberal MP Russell Johnston said: 'we must face the fact that this is without doubt a very shameful day for this country.' Tory Julian Amery described the invasion of the Falklands in terms of 'the third naval power in the world, and the second in NATO' having suffered a humiliating defeat.

In her memoirs of her years as prime minister, Thatcher described how her sense of outrage at the invasion of the Falklands turned to thoughts of war. She asked the Chief of the Naval Staff what could be done. Sir Henry Leach is described as being

> quiet, calm and confident: 'I can put together a task force of destroyers, frigates, landing craft, support vessels. It will be led by the aircraft carriers HMS *Hermes* and HMS *Invincible*. It can be ready to leave in forty-eight hours.' He believed such a force could retake the islands . . . Before

this, I had been outraged and determined. Now my outrage and determination was matched by a sense of relief
and confidence.[62]

She sanctioned the sending of the task force. She had the widespread support of the electorate. Her core supporters, decent
middle-class home-owners who would not dream of using force
on a neighbour, however much they were provoked, agreed that
killing Argentinian conscripts in the South Atlantic was acceptable
behaviour in these circumstances.

As the task force prepared to sail to the Southern Hemisphere,
those who stopped to think about the real consequences of the
action and expressed their concerns were not popular. The pre-
dominant mood of the nation was to cheer on the troops. When
the warships set sail, thousands of well-wishers waved them off.
The mood did not change until the first British casualties were
reported. The government, however, kept the strictest control over
reporting of events. News was carefully managed. Embedded
journalists were not free to report as they wished. No television
pictures of action were allowed to be shown until the operation
was complete. The lessons of the Vietnam War had been assimi-
lated. It was the graphic reporting of suffering and the ability of
reporters to set their own agendas that had ultimately turned the
American public against the conflict. Dean Rusk, the US Secretary
of State, commented: 'This was the first struggle fought on television in everybody's living room every day . . . whether ordinary
people can sustain a war effort under that kind of daily hammer-
ing is a very large question.'

Despite the tight control over the media's reporting of the
Falklands War, the national mood inevitably became more sub-
dued as increasing numbers of British deaths were reported. In
some parts of the press, however, enemy losses were welcomed.
Notoriously *The Sun* announced the sinking of the Argentinian
warship ARA *General Belgrano*, and the loss of over 300 lives, with
the triumphant headline 'Gotcha'. War has a corrosive effect on
public morality. An airliner lost mid-Atlantic with hundreds killed
would have been reported as a tragedy. Enemy military personnel

killed by a nuclear submarine firing on a warship sailing away from the Falklands was a matter for patriotic rejoicing.

The British public's response to the Falklands War illustrated another common way by which the realities of war are blocked out. Those who watched events unfold from a safe distance became armchair tacticians. War being fought between armed men in inhospitable climes became reduced to a game of chess or Battleships. Television presenters explained the action using tables covered in model ships.

It is a sad fact that some onlookers get excited by war. The small boys who watched dogfights during the Battle of Britain and cheered as Germans were shot down in flames can be excused for their immature enthusiasms. Adults who cheer on their troops as if they were supporting a football team cannot be excused. The story in *The Sun* under the 'Gotcha' headline read like a sports report.

> The Navy had the Argies on their knees last night after a devastating double punch.
> WALLOP: They torpedoed the 14,000 ton cruiser General Belgrano and left it a useless wreck.
> WALLOP: Task Force helicopters sank one Argentine patrol boat and severely damaged another.[63]

It is essential to the successful prosecution of a war that the enemy is dehumanized. If this happens in the minds of the public at home, how much more does it happen amongst troops engaged in action? It is a common characteristic of war that the enemy is given animal attributes, even described as vermin. Metaphors drawn from hunting or vermin control are used to describe military operations in which ordinary, decent and normally morally upright men perform appalling acts of cruelty and destruction. 'Psychopathic thugs do not fight wars. Ordinary people do', wrote the psychiatrist and philosopher David Livingstone Smith in *The Most Dangerous Animal*.

> Although war is about killing, we do not like to think of our ordinary people – 'our boys' – as professional killers.

As Bertrand Russell once observed, 'we are quick to say that they gave their lives for their country but not that they take lives for their country'. To do so would be to upset the moral order of things. However we have no such reservations when it comes to the enemy. There are no heroes on the other side, no brave patriots making the ultimate sacrifice for their country. The enemy is ruthless and diabolical; his is a terrifying, cold-blooded killer.[64]

Chris Hedges, the award-winning *New York Times* war correspondent, wrote of this phenomenon.

While we venerate and mourn our own dead . . . we are curiously indifferent about those we kill. Thus killing is done in our name, killing that concerns us little, while those who kill our own are seen as having crawled out of the deepest recesses of the earth, lacking in our humanity and goodness. Our dead. Their dead. They are not the same.[65]

In order to demonize the enemy, and make it easier to kill opposing troops, they are described in non-human form. They might be likened to 'rats in a hole'. It is not unknown for victorious troops to take souvenirs of battle as they might take hunting trophies. During the Vietnam War, American and Australian soldiers collected Viet Cong body parts, in particular fingers and ears, although in some cases it was a penis or breasts.

As Livingstone Smith explains, 'psychologically speaking the victims are no longer human beings and cutting off their fingers or ears is of no greater moral consequence than taking the head of a bear to mount over the fireplace.'[66]

Dehumanising the enemy in warfare draws on ancient biological dispositions to overcome the problem posed by the taboo on killing members of our own species. To do this, particular mental modules are activated which cause the soldier to perceive his enemies as human in form but lacking a truly human essence . . . This is a form of self-deception. In a sense, the soldier must lie to himself about what he is doing. He is not spilling the blood of others, he is killing an evil beast, or shooting turkeys, or ridding the world of a terrible disease.[67]

It is soldiers who fail to lie to themselves in this manner, Livingtone Smith suggests, who fall prey to the psychiatric illnesses of service. A soldier's ability to deceive himself can make the difference between survival and extermination. In her book *An Intimate History of Killing*, Joanna Bourke commented that

> instead of focusing on mangled corpses, soldiers who could imagine themselves as movie heroes felt themselves to be effective warriors. Such forms of disassociation were psychologically useful. By imagining themselves as participating in a fantasy, men could find a language which avoided facing the unspeakable horror not only of dying but meting out death.[68]

Wilfred Owen was made aware through his own experience and observation that to survive, soldiers had to forfeit their moral feelings and dull their emotions.

> Merry it was to laugh there –
> Where death becomes absurd and life absurder.
> For power was on us as we slashed bones bare
> Not to feel sickness or remorse of murder.[69]

Those lines were written in the autumn of 1917. At the same time he was also working on his poem 'Insensibility', from which this extract is taken:

> Happy are men who yet before they are killed
> Can let their veins run cold.
> Whom no compassion fleers
> Or makes their feet
> Sore on the alleys cobbled with their brothers.

The front line withers,
But they are troops who fade, not flowers
For poets' tearful fooling:
Men, gaps for filling
Losses who might have fought
Longer; but no one bothers.

And some cease feeling
Even themselves or for themselves.
Dullness best solves
The tease and doubt of shelling,
And Chance's strange arithmetic
Comes simpler than the reckoning of their shilling.
They keep no check on Armies' decimation.

Happy are these who lose imagination:
They have enough to carry with ammunition.

Later in the poem come the lines:

Their senses in some scorching cautery of battle
Now long since ironed,
Can laugh among the dying unconcerned.

A very honest contemporary description of what it is like to be on active service can be found in an account written by a British Army officer, Patrick Hennessey, in his book *The Junior Officers' Reading Club*. He had joined the Army at university, partly, he admitted out of boredom and a sense of adventure; partly for the frisson of shocking liberal parents; and even a little bit out of an odd sense of duty.

He described what it was like being in armed combat in Afghanistan.

What nothing had prepared me for was the heady and dangerously addictive cocktail of adrenalin and dopamine that surges through the body, the dopey fixed grin of surviving a near miss and even something fulfilling in the delayed exhaustion that hits you like a train after the battle is won. Far from making me grow up, the initial experience of being shot at and shooting back was in danger of bringing out the child in me. The battle-hardened Afghan soldiers it was our job to fight alongside nodded knowingly along and gave us cheeky thumbs-up and refreshing chai during lulls in the fighting. They already knew what no one had warned us in all our training and preparation: 'war' was a terrible thing, but 'combat' – combat was worryingly exciting; counter intuitively, wrongly, immorally but undeniably fun.

It was a feeling that did not last, Hennessey wrote.

For two months we cruised around the Green Zone in Central Helmand riding our luck, rolling through ambushes and pushing back an obstinate and unimaginative enemy. Those were the 'good old days'.

The time came when the young soldier faced the reality of conflict when a close friend was badly wounded.

There was something too clichéd about the sight which greeted us – torn combats, dust and fearful eyes and blood, a Robert Capa photo come to life that I couldn't connect with reality even as we administered first aid and morphine to the injured. Kuks's voice, however, nearly knocked me flat. The deep, familiar voice of a friend was there somewhere, but buried beneath layers of pain and distress which cut through the detachment and made everything screamingly personal.

One of the young guardsmen impeccably tried to keep him awake as the morphine kicked in by trying to get him to count to 10 or recite the alphabet. 'Don't bother, Riddle,' we joked, 'he went to Harrow, he can't count or spell.' Weak humour, but what else was there, waiting for the life-saving Chinook to come, willing it to thunder over the horizon.

When it came, it wasn't the designated medical bird but one full of journalists returning from a stint in Camp Bastion, plunged suddenly into a noisy fight just as they thought they were heading home. The first girl I'd seen in weeks was sat in the prime viewing seat at the back, pretty even in blue helmet and body armour, but wide-eyed as four of us charged up the ramp with Kuks bloodied and half-naked on the stretcher. I screamed his vitals to the medic over the roar and then suddenly, with nothing more to do, felt a yawning emptiness inside. The rear-gunner must have seen it a hundred times and gave me a friendly shove as they took off and suddenly I was lying flat on my back, winded and feeling sick, in the middle of a field a long way from home.

It felt like hours had passed; it had been minutes. We pushed on with the patrol, but any lingering sense of adventure was gone. Other units had taken casualties, we'd inflicted casualties; this shouldn't have been any different, but it was. That night I tried talking to all the guys, tried exploring the range of my own responses – anger, sadness, guilt, maybe even guilty relief that it hadn't been me. No one slept. We knew there would be further losses on the tour and, sadly, there were.[70]

Letters home are an insight into life at the front. They act as a bridge between family home-life and the unrealities of daily life in which death, discomfort and uplifting camaraderie co-exist. Shortly before he died in Afghanistan, Cyrus Thatcher of the 2nd Battalion The Rifles wrote to his mother.

Unfortunately 3 blokes died 2 days ago in an IED[71] explosion in one of the FOBs[72] bout 2 kilometers away – we visited that FOB 2 days before the attack – fucking mental quite scary actually! We'v had a rest day so Im doing a bit of hand washing and fitness! God you'd be so proud Ha! Ha! Ha! We've still had spam, rice, beans and unflavoured noodles every day – promise me actually I promise you if

I see spam in the house ill fucking destroy it!! Im getting pretty good at making flat bread and we bout a goat of a local for 200 dollars and we slaughtered it. I got a good video. Its either catch it, kill it, or make it out here or else you go hungry LOL!! The showers are also freezing whilst Im on the subject of moaning?? Id'e best go again BUT ill keep writing when I get the time + ill be home in a couple of months. Love you'zzz all don't worry bout me to much. Theres only 3 things that kill people over hear BULLETS, BOMBS + EGOS so I might go down with a bad case of swollen head!! Ha Ha Ha Ha Ha. Love ya xxxxx[73]

What is seldom seen in a letter home is a description of how the enemy is killed. It is as if the serving soldier, while prepared to share much of his experience and some of his emotions, wishes to protect his family from the true purpose of his job.

In June 2011 a BBC Radio investigation asked a range of military veterans and serving soldiers what it was like to kill. Killing another man is, the BBC suggested, the most challenging and traumatic part of a soldier's job, but one which is often wholly overlooked. As Lt.-Col. Pete Kilner described it in the broadcast programme 'The Kill Factor':

a central part of what we do with our careers is, we kill the enemies of our country. So it's very important that we understand why, and under what conditions it's the morally right thing to do to kill another human being.

Lt.-Col. Kilner lectures at the West Point Military Academy. He calls himself a 'soldier ethicist' and has talked with countless fellow soldiers about their experience of 'intimate killing': taking the life of someone up close, whom they can see.

They don't like to talk about it. In general, if you're a soldier and you've killed in war, you lie and say no. It tends to be the secret we have that we're not proud of. We want to fight bravely, but it's hard to be proud of killing another person.

Learning to aim is one thing – learning to take aim at a person is quite another. Such acts are veiled by jargon, or not spoken about at all. We recruit people to kill. We train people to kill. We make the orders. Yet after the fact, we don't talk about killing.

We talk about destroying, engaging, dropping, bagging – you don't hear the word killing.[74]

The programme, broadcast on the BBC World Service, heard from several men who had killed in action about their first time. Andy Wilson, a soldier in the SAS (Special Air Service), Britain's elite special forces, joined the Army at the age of eighteen. Now 36, he still clearly remembers the first time he took someone's life in a kill-or-be-killed scenario.

He had an AK47 and he was going to kill me. I was cool, calm and collected the whole time. I knew I had a job to do. I knew I was going to do it, and I did. I was a soldier. That was my job. And that was war.

Ben Close of the Coldstream Guards first killed an enemy combatant in Basra when he was nineteen.

A vehicle came towards our checkpoint and didn't stop, so I fired a warning shot at him. He put his foot on the accelerator, towards me and the gate. I didn't have time to think, my heart was beating really quick.

Training took over. I just aimed up to his head, pulled the trigger. One round went through the windscreen – end of story. In that instant everything slowed down for me. I couldn't really hear much. The hardest time is doing it the first time. It got a lot easier after that.

The programme quoted a Second World War study that suggested that the fear of killing, rather than the fear of being killed, was the most common cause of battle failure. Lt.-Col. Kilner says the way to keep soldiers on an even keel psychologically is to reason with them, not to take away their choice and intellectual involvement with what happens in battle: 'If a soldier reasons that his or her cause is just, then killing sits more easily in the mind.'

The soldier's mind must be prepared for what he or she is called upon to do. Arguably it is the role of government propaganda to prepare the ground. Governments find that they need to put the case for war in such stark, black and white terms that they are impossible to reason against. Much of the recruiting propaganda of the First World War involved circulating stories concerning German atrocities. Claims involving the barbaric killing of innocent women and children by German troops were some of the most effective. Posters of the period show such images as a German soldier bayoneting a child and a savage ape-like monster ravaging a helpless maiden.

Governments, with the help of the media, create an image of war that both caricatures it and sanitizes it. In most Western countries there is a self-imposed restraint operated by the television news outlets on showing the mutilated corpses of victims of war. Those that are shown are the least gory and the camera does not usually linger. Jonathan Jones, art critic for *The Guardian*, stated that this was hypocritical when reviewing how the Western public and media reacted to the brutal death of Libya's Colonel Gaddafi shortly after his capture.

To get upset by photographs of the dead Gaddafi is to pretend we did not know we went to war at all. It is to fantasise that our own role is so just and proper and decent that it is not bloody at all.

In the 21st century we keep trying to re-enact some fantasy of a war that is utterly righteous, and from which we emerge with no guilt on our hands – not even the killing of a brutal dictator. We totally forget the fact that NATO planes blasted his Tripoli control centres with every chance of killing him. If a French or British raid just happened to have blown him to bits, would we be wringing our hands?

The stench of doublethink is more noxious than any vapour emerging from the meat store in Misrata. When I

look at this photograph what do I see? War. War and
nothing else. How many times do we need to be told that
war is hell? The phrase has lost all meaning for us. Think
about what hell is. Hell, in paintings by Bosch, is chaos. It
is meaningless, monstrous, and lacks any place of safety
or redemption. This picture of Gaddafi dead is a day in the
life of hell, also known as war: a corpse photographed for
souvenirs, displayed to satisfy the oppressed, in a moment
of violent gratification. When NATO intervened in Libya
what we see in this picture was probably the best – not the
worst – outcome on offer. And we should be grimly glad
of it. What fantasy makes us long for some impossibly
dignified and humane end to a bloody conflict?[75]

Sometimes based on fact, often based on fiction, wartime propaganda creates fantasy enemies and figures of hate. Once under military orders, the soldier steps into a world where moral boundaries
have been shifted. He is trained to do the unspeakable: kill another
human being. Protected by fantasy and euphemism, the soldier
does his duty.

Remembrance rituals also involve protective fantasy. They
comfort the families of the dead, who are never required to ask
whether their much-loved husband or father killed anyone else and
if so, in what circumstances. They comfort the survivors, who create
a fantasy of war from which the horrors of killing have been excised.

Fantasies have greater power if they are not solely rooted in a
single person's imagination, but are connected to, and appear to be
sanctioned by, a greater power, a higher authority. Throughout
much of history, justifications for war have frequently been given
the ultimate support. God has been invoked to give authority to
conflicts and reassure those suffering, and those about to inflict
suffering, that he is their ultimate protector and supporter.

A well known Bob Dylan protest song made much and made
mock of this idea. Sung by a supposed nobody from nowhere of
importance in America's Midwest, the ironic refrain keeps repeat-
ing the view he has been brought up to believe: that the country
he lived in had God on its side. When the settlers killed the Native

Americans and took over their lands, that was fine as God was on their side. When American boys crossed over to Europe in 1917 to fight in a war they never quite understood, they were still expected to proudly accept that God was on their side there as well.

Sometimes stories were told of signs of God's presence being seen at times of war. The most celebrated case from history had far-reaching consequences. Shortly before the Battle of Milvian Bridge in AD 312, the Roman emperor Constantine had a vision. He looked up to the sun and saw a cross of light above it and the message that through this sign, that of the cross, he would conquer. The next night he had a dream in which Christ explained to him that he should use the sign against his enemies. The story goes that Constantine ordered his army to display the sign of the cross on their shields, and he went on to claim a significant victory. It was a turning point in the history of Christianity as, following the battle, the emperor ceased persecuting the church. Christianity was eventually to become the state religion.

A far more recent battlefield legend of divine intervention can be dated to August 1914. In the early stages of the First World War, the British Expeditionary Force, the first men to be sent across the Channel to join battle, were involved in an event which became legendary. Whether the event truly happened as described is open to much debate, but the reports of the Angel of Mons came to be widely believed and confirmed the British public perception that the heavenly powers were on their side.

What supposedly happened was this, according to the Western Front Association's account. The BEF had advanced overland from the Belgian coast, and whilst moving into position alongside the French 5th Army had unexpectedly met the Germans at the town of Soignes on 22 August 1914. It was decided to go into a defensive position overlooking the bridges of the Mons-Condé Canal.

On the morning of the 23rd August 1914, the Germans attacked. They suffered what was for the time enormous infantry casualties from the terrific rate of the rapid rifle fire of the British professional troops. The British volleys brought the Germans to a stall.

General French recognised that he faced a further attack by the rapidly concentrating German reserves.

Realising the increasingly unfavourable disparity between the two forces, and feeling compromised by the retirement of the Lanrezac's French Fifth Army, the BEF commander decided to make a fighting withdrawal.

The ferocity of the battle on the 23rd August 1914 and the apparent stunning British victory over a superior force (when compared with failure of the French at nearby Charleroi) immediately engendered a rumour that swept the British Homeland: some form of divine intervention must have occurred.[76]

Stories quickly spread that a vision of an angel dressed in white, brandishing a flaming sword and riding a white horse appeared in the sky at the height of the battle. The angel is said to have

> rallied the troops and enabled them to crush the enemy and halt their advance . . . It was seen as a divine indication that God was on the side of the Allies and, in the end, they would prevail over the Central Powers.[77]

What had the men seen, if anything? The myth is said to have its origin in a short story published in the *Evening News* a month after the battle, but before the rumours had taken root in popular imagination. The story told of the ghosts of the bowmen of Agincourt coming to the rescue of their hard-pressed countrymen. Although the story made no mention of an angel, the bowmen, according to Paul Fussell, were described as a

> long line of shapes, with a shining about them . . . 'It was the shining that did it.' Within a week the author's ghosts had been transformed into angels, and what he had written as palpable fiction was soon credited as fact.

As much as the author protested, 'he was assured, especially by clergy, that he was wrong: the angel, in some versions, angel bowmen, were real and had appeared in the sky near Mons. It became unpatriotic, almost treasonable, to doubt it.'[78]

Years later veterans retold the story, many claiming to be eye-witnesses. The BEF, or 'the Old Contemptibles' as they proudly called themselves after being referred to by the German Kaiser as a 'contemptible little army', became legends in their own right. They were, according to the Western Front Association, Army regulars who were familiar with Army superstition.

> Perhaps one factor in the mass illusion at Mons was the fact that many of the soldiers were well versed in legends such as the 'shower of arrows' that saved the grossly out-numbered British at Agincourt. 'From serving on the Northwest frontier of the Indian Empire they would have heard too of the Jinn, spirits in human form that . . . were said to presage many a silent assassination in the night. Such barrack-room stories may have engendered thoughts of miraculous events in the minds of the deeply super-stitious old sweats of Regular Army.[79]

However evidence for the story is claimed to be found in a letter sent to by Brigadier-General John Charteris to his wife in England on 5 September 1914:

> Then there is the story of the 'Angels of Mons' going strong through the 2nd Corps, of how the angel of the Lord on the traditional white horse, and clad all in white with flaming sword, faced the advancing Germans at Mons and forbade their further progress. Men's nerves and imagination play weird pranks in these strenuous times.

If the letter is genuine, it is the earliest documentary reference to the angel and predates the *Evening News* short story.

'But how authentic is the entry, and is Charteris, whose expertise lay in the shadowy fields of intelligence and counter-intelligence, a reliable source?' asked David Clarke in an article in *Fortean Times.*

The account appears in a book published in 1931 that was assembled from an enormous collection of letters describing his experiences during the campaign. These were gathered by his wife Noel after the war and edited and as such they cannot be claimed as original or untouched.[80]

Whatever the veracity of the tale, what cannot be disputed is that the British War Office did nothing to discourage the stories. The fact that rumours were spreading that British soldiers had received divine or supernatural support aided recruitment. The idea that the Army had received heavenly protection helped lift morale. A similar account spread that the French soldiers involved at Mons also witnessed supernatural intervention; not an angel, or, as some soldiers claimed, St George, but Joan of Arc!

Whether folk tale, urban myth, delusion or mass hallucination, the importance of the stories lies not in its truth, but in its effect. Even as late as 1963 the war historian A.J.P. Taylor wrote of his belief in the 'supernatural intervention' at Mons. The 'event' as it was reported was widely commented upon in the British press and several artists painted their own impressions of the vision for publication.

It was not the only supernatural event reported. In June 1916, it is said, a bright white cross was seen in the sky in Flanders, but the Angel of Mons stands out as the story that confirmed to the British that God favoured their cause.

Whose side God did favour was disputed and both sides produced sentimental imagery based on Christian ideas. In one work of fiction by Walter Flex, 'Weihnachtsmarche' (Christmas Tale), the story is told of a war widow who, in despair on Christmas Eve, drowns herself and her son. She is miraculously restored to life by the ghosts of fallen soldiers. The story likens the dead soldiers to the angels who brought the news of Christ's birth to the shepherds. On retelling the story George Mosse commented that 'the intimate connection between the fallen soldier and Christ himself is written large in the iconography of the war. From Germany to Poland postcards showed Christ or an angel touching a dead soldier.'[81]

One website of Christian art offers an image by the artist Danny Hahlbohm entitled 'Not Alone – soldier and Jesus'.[82] It shows a soldier in American combat kit kneeling as if on a battle-field with a ghostly figure of a winged Christ standing over him. Hahlbohm, who is an army veteran, specializes in producing sentimental 'comforting' images and is best known for his ubiquitous 'footprints in the sand' poster.

Walter Flex went far further in incorporating Christian theology into a justification of war. He compared the war to the Last Supper. 'Christ reveals himself in war, therefore war itself is a strategy through which Christ illuminates the world. The sacrificial death of the best of our people is only a repetition of the Passion of Christ.'[83]

The Canadian Army chaplain Frederick Scott would have winced at such a travesty of the Christian message, and yet he was not averse to finding wartime meaning in the story of the Passion. 'On Good Friday we had a voluntary service. It seemed very fitting that these men who had come in the spirit of self-sacrifice, should be invited to contemplate the great world sacrifice of Calvary . . . I remember specially the faces of several who were themselves called upon within a few weeks to make the supreme sacrifice.'[84]

British Remembrance traditions blend fantastical images of war with religious practice in an almost seamless way. At the Royal British Legion's annual Festival of Remembrance, what starts as a display of military drill and prowess then becomes a gathering, or muster, of servicemen and -women and finally takes shape as an Anglican act of worship. At one point military drums are carried solemnly into the centre of the Albert Hall and placed one upon another. The idea behind the imagery is to mimic the drum head service, a religious service held on the field of battle using drums as a temporary altar. The temporary Remembrance altar is where wreaths are laid and a child comes forward to give thanks to those who have died. Nothing is overtly said to suggest that God approves of the wars in which these servicemen and -women fought, yet neither is anything said to emphasize Christian teaching on peace and loving one's enemies. The ceremony is an implied endorsement of the role of the military based on an unquestioned, but highly doubtful, assumption that all wars are fought to defend freedom.

6

THE REASONS FOR WAR

THERE IS NO SIMPLE EXPLANATION AS TO WHY LEADERS TAKE nations to war. Sometimes there is no option in the face of a threat from a belligerent neighbour, but too often reasons tend to be a mix of several unedifying motives: individual or national greed, pride, ambition, delusions of grandeur, old grudges, insecurities, revenge. And once one power group arms itself and starts to make threats, other nations feel the need to protect themselves and their inhabitants, boundaries and economic interests. What motivates ordinary people to fight for their nation is again not a simple thing to explain.

Sometimes men join up out of economic necessity, like Herold Noel who joined up prior to the Second Gulf War.

At that time I was 19, I was going to New York City Technical College, I had two kids. And I was living with my mother. So what's the best thing for me to do? Join the military and have my own home, right? Did I ever think I would go to war? It was before 9/11, before all of that. It never crossed my mind.[85]

In 1926 *The Times* reported that 60 per cent of Army recruits from the London area were unemployed when they signed on. In *Soldiers* the historian Richard Holmes quotes the story of a certain Spike Mays arriving at the barracks to start his basic training. 'He was received with a cheery greeting from Mitch, a fellow recruit: "Wotcher mate. Ain't 'arf hungry. Could scoff a scabby-'eaded ape."'[86]

In 1880, Holmes reported, one private who joined up noted that 80 per cent of the Army was drawn from the unemployed. 'Empty pockets and hungry stomachs are the most eloquent and persuasive of recruiting sergeants.'[87]

The modern British Army has been accused of using unethical recruitment practices, especially in the way that it targets schools and presents an unrealistic picture of service life to susceptible young people. The accusation comes from the organization Forceswatch.

> The military fails to properly inform potential recruits of the risks, difficulties and legal obligations of an armed forces career. Research has shown that it targets vulnerable social groups, including young people under 18 and people from poorer backgrounds.
>
> Many activities that the armed forces make available to young people capitalise on their impressionability by presenting a glamorous view of armed forces life without the risks, legal obligations and ethical issues involved.
>
> The language and tools used are often those that young people are drawn towards – toys, computer games and military hardware – and full use is made of ideas of steady employment, getting an education, having experiences that other young people do not have, and 'self discovery powered by the army'.[88]

Conscripts, of course, have no choice. When nations run short of volunteers they can make military service compulsory. Often, however, when wars start there is such a rush of public enthusiasm for the fight that volunteers readily come forward. Britain's recruiting offices in 1914 were overrun with volunteers. Patriotic citizens feel that a slight aimed at their country is also a personal slight and volunteer in a passion to save honour and face. Sometimes young men join the forces for adventure and camaraderie. After intensive training in which their normal peacetime scruples are systematically replaced by military values, they eagerly look forward to fighting.

Yet once the first adrenaline-driven euphoria of military engagement is past, soldiers often have time to reflect. They may have lost colleagues in battle or been wounded themselves. To fight is to be near death and when in close proximity to death, people ask questions about meaning. They focus on the purpose of this life, and the possibility of a life to come. At this time there needs to be a story to turn to, a myth or explanation that makes sense of what is happening. The explanation is all the more powerful if it has an 'out of this world' dimension and reasserts purpose on not just the human, but the cosmic scale. And after a war, looking back on the destruction and random nature of death in battle, those stories become more powerful still, especially if they find expression within popular culture. In song, poetry, film and literature, powerful images can be created that reinforce these stories and allow veterans, widows and others to reassure themselves that all was not in vain. And if those stories also suggest an element of restoration, they are of even greater comfort. If they tell of lives rebuilt, of the dead being aware of the gratitude of the living, of peace won and an ideal world rising from the old, then those stories have added power.

The 2001 television series *Band of Brothers*, produced by Steven Spielberg and Tom Hanks, was a Second World War drama following the progress of a group of US Army Airborne Paratroopers from the moment they parachute into France on D-Day through to the conclusion of the war. It was gritty and realistic in content and a classic drama of its kind. But it was the music that accompanied it that made the greatest long-term impact, the memorable score and the sentimental words.

In one sense the words jarred with the action. The men whose deaths were depicted with realistic Hollywood gore were lauded in mythological and unreal terms as heroes who bravely paid the ultimate price of war on the battlefield of sacrifice. Their deaths helped uphold not just a dream, but a shining dream of liberty and love. In a line that would not have been out of place in ancient Nordic culture, the dead young men fighting old men's wars are said to have won themselves a place in Paradise.[89]

The title of the series can be found in Shakespeare's *Henry V*, in the words delivered by the King on the eve of battle to motivate his English troops.

> We few, we happy few, we band of brothers;
> For he today that sheds his blood with me
> Shall be my brother; be he ne'er so vile,
> This day shall gentle his condition:
> And gentlemen in England now a-bed
> Shall think themselves accursed they were not here,
> And hold their manhoods cheap whiles any speaks
> That fought with us upon Saint Crispin's day.[90]

Both the popular song and the popular oration make disparaging reference to those not taking part; the old men and those 'now a-bed'. Here is an echo of the white feather campaign of the First World War. Those who do not fight are seen as cowards and wimps. Those who opt to fight are the heroes destined, even if killed in horrible circumstances and buried ignominiously without military honours, to be remembered as heroes. To use the words of Shakespeare again:

> Many of our bodies shall no doubt
> Find native graves . . .
> And those that leave their valiant bones in France,
> Dying like men, though buried in your dunghills,
> They shall be famed; for there the sun shall greet them,
> And draw their honours reeking up to heaven;
> Leaving their earthly parts to choke your clime

So, even if the corpse is left to rot, the soul of the fallen soldier finds its heavenly reward. But what form, is it believed, does this reward take? Something spiritual rather than temporal, but exactly what is disputed. Contemporary folk culture has imagery, but no theology, and formal Christian teaching on the subject is far from agreed upon between the numerous churches and denominations. The soldiers will be judged, but whether selfless battlefield deeds win them an automatic place in Paradise is uncertain. Catholics might teach that heaven would be the ultimate destination after time spent in Purgatory, a time possibly shortened by their self-sacrificial willingness to die in a battle against evil. Many medieval crusaders waged holy war after living lives of cruelty and dubious morality. They believed that to fight, and die if necessary, in a battle to win back the Christian sites of Jerusalem from Muslim control would earn them eternal reward. Later, following the Reformation, Protestants would argue that this was a flawed bargain with God. They would say that an individual's place in heaven cannot be won by deeds, but is a gift of God through grace.

Both Reformation Protestants and medieval Catholics would be familiar with one image of the afterlife as revealed in the Bible. The Day of Judgment, on which all souls will be resurrected, is described both in the Gospels and the Book of Revelation.

And I saw the dead, small and great, stand before God; and the books were opened: and another book was opened, which is the book of life: and the dead were judged out of those things which were written in the books, according to their works.

And the sea gave up the dead which were in it; and death and hell delivered up the dead which were in them: and they were judged every man according to their works.

And death and hell were cast into the lake of fire. This is the second death.[91]

St Matthew writes,

the Son of man shall come in his glory, and all the holy angels with him, then shall he sit upon the throne of his glory:

And before him shall be gathered all nations: and he shall separate them one from another, as a shepherd divideth his sheep from the goats.[92]

Ten years after the end of the First World War, the British artist Stanley Spencer was commissioned to paint a series of wall paintings in a private chapel at Burghclere in Hampshire which was built as a private family war memorial dedicated to the memory of Lieutenant Henry Willoughby Sandham, who had died in 1919 as a result of an illness he had contracted during the Macedonian campaign. While the chapel originated as one family's act of remembrance, it is now in the care of the National Trust and open to the public as one of Britain's most remarkable war shrines.

Previously Spencer, who had served in the Army during the war, had painted a unique version of the resurrection of the dead, setting it in the graveyard of the parish church at Cookham in Berkshire. In 'The Resurrection at Cookham' the dead are literally seen rising from their graves. For the Sandham Memorial Chapel Spencer designed as the central panel, a work that came to be known as 'The Resurrection of the Soldiers'.

The chapel is entered through an old wooden door in the front of a wide brick building at the end of a garden path. It is surprisingly small inside and utterly dominated by the paintings. Down both side walls there is a collection of paintings inspired by Spencer's own war experiences. There are scenes of men eating and being treated for wounds, all in a distinctive matter-of-fact style. There is no killing. There are no depictions of battle.

On the end wall of the chapel is the painting for which it is best known. At first sight the work appears to be a jumble of white crosses, of the kind commonly placed on a soldier's grave after a battle. Then pattern seems to appear. The focal point, a Christ figure, is to be found in the middle distance. Yet it is only the focus theologically. He is the judge of the Last Days. Compositionally the eye seems to be continually drawn away from Christ to all the characterful faces represented.

'Both in its evocation of the entirely ordinary and unheroic world of military life, at home and abroad, and in its treatment of the resurrection, Spencer's work is unique in war art', wrote Jay Winter of the chapel.

A series of side panels takes us through scenes of Spencer's war, in the drab and dreary corridors of Beaufort War hospital, to the brown and dusty hillsides of Macedonia. In these paintings nobody fights, no one kills, no one dies. There are some wounded men portrayed, one being painted with iodine, and one whose apparently frostbitten legs we see protected from contact with his sheets. But there is no pain in them. Nor is there any joy in the faces of the soldiers carrying on their mundane lives. It is as if they are all in a trance, stuck in a dreamworld of onerous tasks, avoided where possible, or simply endured.

The image of the rising dead of the Great War . . . was in no sense simply a reflection of Spencer's eccentric religiosity. He spoke a spiritual language many contemporaries used and adapted . . . He testified both to the robustness of the English mystical tradition and to the capacity of the apocalyptic temperament to see transcendence even in the carnage of war.[93]

Spencer was placing the slaughter of the war not in its historical context, but in its eschatological context. The war was like the great battle between good and evil that would precede the Last Days. The dead were to be honoured, not by this generation alone, but by eternity.

The idea behind the picture is mystical. Although many people visit the chapel today, the art found there is not populist. Spencer's image and his response to the war are not mainstream. Nevertheless he expresses a spirituality that is not inconsistent with more familiar religious symbolism associated with war. It is part of that spectrum of response to war that sees life after death for the soldier giving meaning to his death on the battlefield. Whether it is Katherine Jenkins in the Royal Albert Hall singing of young men going to Paradise, in the words of a television musical hit, or an address given at the funeral of a soldier who has died in Afghanistan talking of him as 'looking down on us from heaven', the idea is much the same.

The poem 'Rouge Bouquet' by Joyce Kilmer commemorates the deaths of members of an Irish-American regiment in 1918. It begins:

In a wood they call Rouge Bouquet
There is a new-made grave today,
Built by never a spade nor pick
Yet covered with earth 10 meters thick.
There lie many fighting men,
Dead in their youthful prime,
Never to laugh nor love again
Nor taste the Summertime.

Another verse on, and the poet talks of the men at sleep under the
protection of heaven.

There is on earth no worthier grave
To hold the bodies of the brave
Than this place of pain and pride
Where they nobly fought and nobly died.
Never fear but in the skies
Saints and angels stand
Smiling with their holy eyes
On this new-come band.
St Michael's sword darts through the air and touches
the aureole on his hair
As he sees them stand saluting there,
His stalwart sons:
And Patrick, Brigid, Columkill
Rejoice that in veins of warriors still
The Gael's blood runs.
And up to Heaven's doorway floats,
From the wood called Rouge Bouquet,
A delicate cloud of bugle notes
That softly say: "Farewell! Farewell!
Comrades true, born anew, peace to you!
Your souls shall be where the heroes are
And your memory shine like the morning-star.
Brave and dear,
Shield us here.
Farewell!

But the notion of soldiers enjoying or being rewarded with an afterlife is not confined to contemporary Western postmodern culture. It is widespread in many cultures and through history. As Kilmer's poem shows, modern references to rewards in the afterlife draw on age-old imagery. As has been suggested earlier, the imagery of many forms of Remembrance after the First World War harks back to some mythical golden age when war was chivalrous and not barbaric. While this can be a source of comfort, it can also be a dangerous idea and one that, in extremes, incites young men to violence. It suggests not only that war is sanctioned by a higher authority, but also that those who fight and die may be specially rewarded.

A thousand years before the mechanized horrors of trench warfare, belief in an afterlife provided not just reassurance to those about to embark in mortal combat, but motivation. Fighting was viewed in Norse culture as a gateway to eternal glory. Norse legends telling of the heroes' destiny have survived in sagas and, thanks to the operas of Richard Wagner, have been widely retold in recent times.

In Norse legend Valhalla was the hall of the chosen slain who were carried there as reward for their valour by a Valkyrie. It was a palace of feasting with walls made of glittering spears and a roof of golden shields. It was a place of honour where those who had died in battle were rewarded. It was set with long tables where the heroes were waited upon by virgins clad in white robes. By day the warriors fought as the army of Odin; by night they indulged themselves at a heavenly banquet.

And all day long they were hacked and hewn
Mid dust and groans and limbs lopped off and blood;
But all at night returned to Odin's hall
Woundless and fresh: such lot is theirs in heaven.[94]

Fighting and feasting, the heroes were said to spend their days in perfect bliss, while Odin delighted in their strength and numbers. This bloodthirsty and hedonistic myth reflected the approach of Norse society towards warfare and conflict.

The ancient Northern nations, who deemed warfare the
most honourable of occupations, and considered courage
the greatest virtue, worshipped Odin principally as god of
battle and victory. They believed that whenever a fight was
impending he sent out his special attendants . . . the
Valkyrs who selected from the dead warriors one half of
their number, whom they bore on their fleet of steeds over
the quivering rainbow bridge into Valhalla.[95]

The idea that those who give their lives in battle receive rewards in
Paradise is not solely found in some Christian traditions. Islamist
suicide bombers are said to believe that their self-sacrifice will guar-
antee to them an afterlife of pleasure. Seventy-two virgins will
await them for their delight. This is a frequently quoted myth,
especially by Western opponents of Islamic militancy. It is not
based on the authority of the Qur'an.

Lauding violence and promising rewards in Paradise is an
infamous way of inciting warriors and takes a contemporary form
in the activities of some of the more extreme Islamist preachers.
In 2003 the jury trying the London-based cleric Abdullah el-Faisal
at the Old Bailey heard how he tried to recruit British schoolboys
for terrorist training camps by promising them that if they died
fighting a holy war they would be rewarded with 72 virgins and
allowed to eat from the fruits of Paradise.

The court was played a tape titled 'Rules of Jihad', in which
el-Faisal told his audience: 'You have to learn how to shoot. You
have to learn how to fly planes, drive tanks and you have to learn
how to load your guns and to use missiles.' It was the duty of
women to bring up their sons 'with a Jihad mentality' and boys
should train as soldiers for Islam when they were age fifteen.

Is it sensible for you to be soldiers without Kalashnikov
training? So when you are on holiday from school or college, you must have Jihad training – this is your holiday.

Even if you are hit by a Cruise missile, the pain will
feel like that of a mosquito bite . . .

Religious martyrs are not dead. Do not cry for them.[96]

The way a society recalls and honours the dead of war inevitably reflects the beliefs of that society in an afterlife. Faith systems that teach that the dead will be judged and rewarded or punished in the life beyond according to their deeds in this life teach that death is not the end of existence. The souls of those who die in battle will live on and if they died in a righteous cause they will be rewarded for their sacrifices.

In medieval Europe men who had lived violent and wicked lives could ensure a place in heaven for themselves by devoting themselves to fighting in a crusade. To die in battle as a Christian soldier against a heathen or infidel foe would serve to wipe out all previous sins.

The early Church had been largely pacifistic following the example of Jesus who, when arrested in the Garden of Gethsemane before the Crucifixion, did not fight back. Indeed he rebuked Peter for drawing his sword. Despite the Church's integration in Roman culture, it continued to discourage the use of arms. In the early Middle Ages a man who had killed another, even with good cause, could not be ordained a priest. Lay warriors were expected to do penance.

> During the eleventh century the crusades changed those attitudes. The career of knight was Christianized . . . Bearing arms under a legitimate ruler for a good cause was not merely tolerated, but even came to be sanctioned by blessings and liturgical ceremonies.[97]

The Knights Templar and other similar orders offered a life that combined the religious and the military. Members were obliged not only to follow a pattern of prayer and devotion, but to train as soldiers. Bearing arms became a sacred duty with, so it was believed, eternal rewards. There was Christian soldiering to be done, to wrest control of the holy sites from the infidels in Jerusalem and to protect pilgrims en route to the Holy Land. As previously mentioned, iconography drawn from images of knights and crusaders can be found in many war memorials, especially on mainland Europe. In Britain the sword placed on the coffin of the unknown warrior before it was laid in its tomb in Westminster Abbey was a crusader sword chosen by the King from the Royal Collection.

Before the First World War there was no contradiction perceived between patriotism and Christianity. When in 1908 the diplomat Cecil Spring-Rice wrote the poem, 'I Vow to Thee, My Country' he intended no irony. The consistency between Christianity and loyalty to the Empire, which would come to be derided in later years, was widely accepted. When young men enthusiastically joined up to fight in 1914 it was to serve 'God, King and Country'. The composer Gustav Holst, whose music was adopted to turn Spring-Rice's poem into a hymn, was unhappy with the way his tune had been hijacked, yet today the words and music are inseparable.

> I vow to thee my country, all earthly things above.
> Entire and whole and perfect, the service of my love;
> The love that asks no question, the love that stands the test,
> That lays upon the altar the dearest and the best;
> The love that never falters, the love that pays the price,
> The love that makes undaunted the final sacrifice.
> I heard my country calling, away across the sea,
> Across the waste of waters she calls and calls to me.
> Her sword is girded at her side, her helmet on her head,
> And round her feet are lying the dying and the dead.
> I hear the noise of battle, the thunder of her guns,
> I haste to thee my mother, a son among thy sons.

At this point the hymn changes gear as the symbolism of the first lines is transferred from motherland to Paradise.

> And there's another country, I've heard of long ago,
> Most dear to them that love her, most great to them that know;
> We may not count her armies, we may not see her King;
> Her fortress is a faithful heart, her pride is suffering;
> And soul by soul and silently her shining bounds increase.
> And her ways are ways of gentleness, and all her paths are peace.

Americans sing 'God Bless America' and the words of Irving Berlin's song also express the belief that patriotism has divine approval:

> . . . we raise our voices in a solemn prayer.
> God bless America,
> Land that I love.
> Stand beside her, and guide her . . .

The dovetailing of Christianity and patriotism in the West is to be expected, given the fact that throughout history faith and warfare have coexisted in strange synchronicity and empathy. Warfare has provided much Christian symbolism. This can be dated back to St Paul, who in his letter to the Ephesians created a spiritual analogy from the uniform of a Roman soldier.

> Wherefore take unto you the whole armour of God, that ye may be able to withstand in the evil day, and having done all, to stand.
> Stand therefore, having your loins girt about with truth, and having on the breastplate of righteousness;
> And your feet shod with the preparation of the gospel of peace;
> Above all, taking the shield of faith, wherewith ye shall be able to quench all the fiery darts of the wicked.
> And take the helmet of salvation, and the sword of the Spirit, which is the word of God.[98]

More recently, 'Onward Christian Soldiers' and 'Fight the Good Fight with All Thy Might' have become two popular Christian hymns. The nineteenth-century missionary and charitable organization The Salvation Army was set up on military lines. Its professional ministers wear uniforms and are given ranks: Major, Colonel and, at the head, General. Similarly, religion is given an official recognition within the Western armed forces. Many denominations provide Army chaplains, or 'padres', who find themselves right at the heart of the action. They not only serve as welfare officers and medical assistants, but are often the officers who have to field ethical questions.

The First World War chaplain Frederick Scott recalled in his memoirs:

> many and many a time when the war from our point of view has going badly, and men would ask me, 'How about the war, Sir?' or, 'Are we winning the war, Sir?' I would reply. 'Boys, unless the devil has got into heaven we are going to win. If he has, the German Emperor will have a good friend there. But he hasn't, and any nation which tramples on the rights and liberties of humanity, glories in it, makes it a matter of national boasting; and cuts medals to commemorate the sinking of unprotected ships – any nation which does that is bound to lose the war, no matter how badly things may look at the present time.' It was nothing but that unflinching faith in the power of right which kept our men so steadfast. Right is after all only another name for the will of God. Men who knew no theology, who professed no creed, who even pretended to great indifference about the venture of eternity, were unalterably fixed in their faith in the power of right.[99]

And for those who had an interest in matters eternal, faith provided the ultimate comfort: the promise of an afterlife, that death on the battlefield is not the end, but a new beginning.

A society with no belief in any spiritual dimension or possibility of life beyond regards victims of war differently from one that believes the dead are destined to experience an afterlife where their sacrificial deeds on the battlefield are rewarded. Under the Soviet regime the Russian dead could be said to have sacrificed themselves for the greater good of the country or the party. Huge monuments were raised in steel, stone and concrete showing archetypal Soviet heroes who had died for Mother Russia. But these monuments contained no religious symbolism. They were starkly atheistic. Party loyalty was lauded, as was patriotism, although monuments glorifying Russia appeared grotesquely inappropriate when raised in some of the non-Russian states of the USSR. Grieving relatives holding memories, medals and photographs were offered no further comfort than that their men had died as exemplary patriots and comrades. Families were barely allowed the privilege of private grief. And if, for political reasons, it was deemed that a war had been a mistake, even public grief was curtailed. Troops who had died in the course of the Soviet invasion of Afghanistan in 1979 received scant commemoration. As casualties mounted, the government did not wish to admit the scale of military loss.

As Catherine Merridale observed, 'depending upon circumstances and its own perception of *raison d'Etat*, the Soviet state was skilled at destroying the material basis of collective memory as it was eager to commemorate the selected fallen of Mother Russia in concrete and stone'.[100] It could be said to have been official policy to destroy individual identity at death. Instead of burial, which the Russian Orthodox Church required, cremation became the preferred state option for corpse disposal. The traditional Russian Orthodox funeral rites regarded the corpse as representing a person on a journey. The spirit of the dead person, it was traditionally believed, did not leave his or her relatives at once. 'The commemorative services which were held forty days and a year after death were survivals from an older tradition of appeasing the courts of Heaven and even exorcising the earth-bound spirits of the dead.'[101]

The Soviet state deliberately obstructed the process of remembrance by which families 'constructed dignified narratives to explain the necessity and value of the losses'.[102] And yet, despite the history of the controlling hand of the Soviet state on Remembrance, and the raising of godless monuments, Remembrance as an activity has survived. Personal memory of war and suffering survives. Great-grandmothers can tell their children of the suffering and deprivation of war from their own recollections. In many cities that were once under Soviet control and are now independent from the Russian state, daily rituals of Remembrance survive. School children march to war memorials to salute the dead they never knew. They honour the dead of history. Nowhere, even in the official post-Soviet age, is there any suggestion that the heroes live on other than in the fading memories of the old people who had once known them. There is no Valhalla or Paradise for the fallen.

Forms of Remembrance in the West make no collective claim that those who die have been rewarded in an afterlife. The families of each casualty will be comforted by their own beliefs. A Christian family will believe that the soldier will be judged and saved or damned by God. Some forms of Christianity will teach that salvation or damnation is predestined and that whatever good the fallen soldier might have done in his life will not have earned him a place in heaven. The circumstances of death, whether on the battlefield or at home, make no difference to his eternal destiny.

Other faiths might take a different perspective. Some Muslims believe that death for a righteous cause will lead to rewards. But whether death in a just war is believed to foreshadow reward in an afterlife, or whether a secular view is taken that death in war brings posthumous patriotic glory, what matters is that to die in battle is not seen as purposeless. In the grieving aftermath of war, somehow purpose has to be found. Rousing men to fight is, for the politicians, the easy bit. Explaining it afterwards can be much harder.

The poetry and symbolism of Remembrance in Britain does not explicitly say that the dead from wars past are rewarded in heaven. The dead are 'glorious' and 'the fallen' are honoured through ceremonies that link Christian liturgy, with its promise of eternal life, and civil Remembrance. At the Festival of Remembrance everyone is permitted, though not required, to think of the dead as having gone to their rewards in a life beyond. The words of the hymn chosen to be sung by the audience, massed bands and uniformed servicemen and -women at the end of the festival can be understood in two different ways. It is both a hymn about God reaching across the time zones of the world, and one that speaks of the temporary nature of life on earth and the eternal thereafter.

It begins with a reference that can be taken to refer either to sunset or death:

The day Thou gavest, Lord, is ended,
The darkness falls at Thy behest;
To Thee our morning hymns ascended,
Thy praise shall sanctify our rest.

The third verse speaks of God in the present:

As o'er each continent and island
The dawn leads on another day,
The voice of prayer is never silent,
Nor dies the strain of praise away.

The last verse talks of the future and eternity:

So be it, Lord; Thy throne shall never,
Like earth's proud empires, pass away:
Thy kingdom stands, and grows forever,
Till all Thy creatures own Thy sway.

7

THE POPPY, THEN AND NOW

THE MOST WIDELY RECOGNIZED SYMBOL OF REMEMBRANCE IS the poppy, and yet its iconic importance is relatively recent and dates back less than 100 years, to the period immediately following the First World War. Before then the flower had a very different set of attributes attached to it. Moreover, in the course of its relatively brief history as the flower of Remembrance-tide, the message it has conveyed has not remained constant. It appears to have gradually evolved, and arguably it no longer has the same meaning to the modern generation as it did to those who first wore it.

Papaver rhoeas, as it is known to botanists, goes by several names: field poppy, red weed, American Legion poppy, corn rose and, since the First World War, the Flanders or Remembrance poppy.

It is said that its seed springs to life when the soil in which it has rested through the winter is disturbed. It is thus the wild flower associated with ploughing and often the first flower to return to a site after a battle. When conditions are right the flowers grow in such profusion that, viewed from a distance, they appear to have turned the land blood-red. It can be a spectacular sight.

In May 1915 war raged across northern Europe. It was a mechanized war of unprecedented scale that had reached a state of stalemate. Two mighty opposing armies bombarded each other with high-explosive shells and sacrificed thousands of lives in futile advances to capture small increments of boggy debris- and body-littered ground.

On the fourteenth day of that month a Canadian military doctor based on the front line at Festubert in the Artois region of

France described the scene around him in a letter to his mother. It was written shortly after a period of intense shelling during which, in under two hours, over 200 rounds of 4- or 5-inch shells had landed within 200 yards of him. John McCrae could see the ground about him

> strewn with bits of clothing, pouches, equipment, broken rifles – and here and there an unburied body with black swollen face, and the flies buzzing around. The whole ground is seamed in all directions by trenches and scattered defences, wire, sandbags and dugouts in bewildering disorder.

In another letter home McCrae described a road he could see at the very height of the action.

> I saw all the tragedies of war enacted there. A wagon, or a bunch of horses, or a stray man, or a couple of men, would get there just in time for a shell. One would see the absolute knock-out, and the obviously lightly wounded crawling off on hands and knees; or worse yet, at night, one would hear the tragedy – 'that horse scream' – or the man's moan. Do you wonder that the road got on our nerves? Seventeen days of Hades! At the end of the first day if anyone had told us we had to spend seventeen days there, we would have folded our hands and said it could not be done.

At the beginning of May, near Ypres in Flanders, McCrae had buried a friend and colleague who had been killed in one of the many hellish bombardments. In the absence of an Army chaplain, the doctor had himself recited the church burial service as best he could from memory. The shattered remains of the young man, placed in sandbags and shaped to resemble a human body, were wrapped in an Army blanket and lowered into a grave. 'A soldier's death!' McCrae wrote in his diary. Afterwards McCrae had sat on the steps of an ambulance, taken a pad of paper and hastily scribbled a poem. Then it was back to action.

The Germans attacked, preceded by gas clouds. Fighting went on for an hour and a half, during which the guns hammered heavily with some loss to us . . . The infantry line was very heavy, and we fired incessantly, keeping on into the night. Despite the heavy fire I got to sleep at 12, and slept until daylight which comes at 3.

The poem, as McCrae's biographer Dianne Graves suggests, was a response to 'the inevitable and growing conflict between John's instincts as a soldier and his compassion as a doctor' which must have given him cause to wonder if the loss of his friend was a price worth paying for what the war hoped to achieve.

Around him wild poppies, which had germinated in the churned-up ground, were blowing in the breeze. This is what he wrote:

In Flanders fields the poppies blow
Between the crosses, row on row,
That mark our place; and in the sky
The larks, still bravely singing, fly
Scarce heard amid the guns below.

We are the Dead. Short days ago
We lived, felt dawn, saw sunset glow,
Loved, and were loved, and now we lie
In Flanders fields.

Take up our quarrel with the foe:
To you from failing hands we throw
The torch; be yours to hold it high.
If ye break faith with us who die
We shall not sleep, though poppies grow
In Flanders fields.

McCrae, although a published poet, had no plans at that stage for his latest work to be seen in print. Writing the poem was a cathartic act. His mind was dwelling on the death of the young Lieutenant Alexis Helmer, whose body he had so recently consigned to the earth.

'His face was very tired but calm as he wrote', noted Sgt Major Cyril Allinson. 'He looked around from time to time, his eyes straying to Helmer's grave. The poem was almost an exact description of the scene in front of us both.'[103]

McCrae first showed the poem to fellow soldiers, including Allinson, who was immediately struck by its power, pathos and passion. He tried to learn it by heart. For some months McCrae did nothing more with the poem other than, from time to time, revising and honing the lines until he was satisfied enough to send it to *The Spectator* in London. It was rejected. He reworked it in the autumn of 1915 and with the encouragement of colleagues submitted it to another publication, *Punch*. It was published anonymously on 8 December that same year. As Graves notes, the poem gained immediate popularity. Within days it was being passed from man to man at the front. One Canadian Army chaplain would read it aloud to men he met.

The poem may well have been heard by seventeen-year-old Private Cecil Roughton, who was serving with the Royal Warwickshire Regiment. He picked a poppy in Arras in May 1916 which he posted home to his family in Moseley, near Birmingham. The handwritten note accompanying it read, 'Souvenir from a front line trench near arras May 1916. C. Roughton 1923'. Private Roughton survived the trenches and died in 1977, aged 81. His poppy, however, not only survived the war, but outlived the young man who picked it. On its arrival in Britain in 1916 it was pressed and preserved. Eventually it was given to the Royal British Legion.

'In just fifteen lines', Graves writes, 'John McCrae had captured the prevailing mood at the front . . . Before long 'In Flanders Fields' would become one of the war's best-known poems.' More than that, the image of the blood-red poppy emerging as the first sign of new life in a field of death was to become one of the most potent symbols of the post-war era. The poppy became the natural link between the mystery of death, which has disturbed and fascinated mankind since time immemorial, and the battlefield slaughter of the new industrial age. It was a multi-faceted symbol. The Flanders Fields poppy is blood-red. It grows as a sign of new life where everything else has been destroyed. It demonstrates the power of the natural world to survive the worst destruction the industrial world can invent. In Christian terms, and 100 years ago the language of Christianity was more widely understood than today, the poppy told of the hope of Resurrection.

'This poem was literally born of fire and blood during the hottest phase of the Second Battle of Ypres', McCrae's commanding officer, Major-General E.W.B. Morrison, later wrote.

> My headquarters were in a trench on the top of the bank of Ypres Canal, and John had his dressing station in a hole dug in the foot of the bank. During periods in the battle men who were shot actually rolled down the bank in to his dressing station. Along from us a few hundred yards was the headquarters of the regiment, and many times during the sixteen days of battle, he and I watched them burying their dead whenever there was a lull. Thus the crosses, row on row, grew into a good-sized cemetery. Just as he describes, we often heard in the mornings the larks singing high in the air, between the crash of the shell and the reports of the guns in the battery just beside us. I have a letter from him in which he mentions having written the poem to pass away the time between the arrival of batches of wounded, and partly as an experiment with several varieties of poetic metre.

It was very much a poem of the moment. By May 1915 the true horror of trench warfare was dawning on everyone and yet the war was still in its first year. The idealistic motives for fighting had not decayed into cynicism or despair. Indeed on 7 May an event took place that reinvigorated anti-German feeling and, amidst the despair of drawn-out warfare, reminded troops of the reasons behind the war. The sinking of the trans-Atlantic passenger liner RMS *Lusitania* by a German U-boat off the Old Head of Kinsale, Ireland, is credited by historians as the event which ultimately led to the USA joining the war. It was an unprovoked attack by the German U-20 in which one of the most prestigious liners of its day was sunk in barely 20 minutes. Despite the speed of the sinking, a few lifeboats were launched and 764 passengers and crew were rescued and landed at Queenstown, but 1,195 crew and passengers were lost. The list of casualties included many Americans and the loss of the ship focused American public opinion on the issue of joining the war, which eventually happened in 1917. News of the sinking spread quickly. Newspapers published in London carrying the news reached the trenches within a couple of days. As a Canadian who had himself crossed the Atlantic in wartime conditions, the news would have struck McCrae forcibly. But for the news, his exhortation to 'take up the quarrel with the foe' might have been more tempered. That summer of 1915 was certainly filled with a renewed upsurge in anti-German feeling and a boost in recruitment to the forces. It was also accompanied by an unpleasant wave of xenophobia which resulted in street mobs attacking British shops and businesses that had German-sounding names.

In addition to this new but short-lived burst of jingoism and enthusiasm for the fight, the notion of the fight being for a 'noble cause' remained alive, although as the months of the war wore on cynicism gradually replaced idealism. McCrae's friend Andrew Macphail made this observation on the poem in a published tribute: 'the dead, still conscious, fallen in a noble cause, see their graves overblown in a riot of poppy bloom.'[104] Looking back at the First World War with the hindsight of over 90 years, the overwhelming impression is one of horrific pointlessness. Yet it started as an heroic adventure. Soldiering was an honourable profession and the call to arms in Britain and its Empire in 1914 was to fight for 'God, King and Country' in a righteous war in which good was pitted against evil. Men of all social classes volunteered, eager to play their part in a war that would, so they were assured, be over by Christmas. The writer Rudyard Kipling, whose pen had on many occasions memorably captured the spirit of the Empire, was at the forefront of the recruitment drive.

By the end of the war, four years later, the survivors saw the conflict for what it had really been and many began to question whether it had been worthwhile. The only justification for having taken part, some thought, was that it might turn out to be the war to end all wars. Through experiencing and suffering one huge all-embracing conflict, mankind might finally come to see the futility of fighting. Full-scale warfare in an industrial age was so horrendous that in the peace to come, surely all nations would vow that such a thing should never happen again.

Kipling himself was devastated by grief. He had lost his son and spent much time after the war searching for his grave. A poem he had composed 20 years earlier took on a new meaning and, in contrast to the confidence of his pre-war utterances, became a solemn hymn of contrition, sorrow and regret. This is the second verse:

> The tumult and the shouting dies,
> The Captains and the Kings depart.
> Still stands Thine ancient sacrifice,
> An humble and a contrite heart.
> Lord God of Hosts, be with us yet,
> Lest we forget – lest we forget!

In the second verse he refers to two biblical civilizations, once great cultural and political powers, which have now faded from memory. In the poem they might be seen to represent the two warring empires of 1914–18.

> Lo, all our pomp of yesterday
> Is one with Nineveh and Tyre!
> Judge of the Nations, spare us yet,
> Lest we forget – lest we forget!

And he ends with direct reference to the weapons of war that had devastated a generation:

> For heathen heart that puts her trust
> In reeking tube and iron shard –
> All valiant dust that builds on dust,
> And guarding calls not Thee to guard.
> For frantic boast and foolish word,
> Thy Mercy on Thy People, Lord!

Kipling, always the man to find the pithy words to capture the popular mood of the day, also wrote: 'If any question why we died, Tell them, because our fathers lied.'[105]

In the early stages of the war Kipling had spoken for the jingoistic enthusiasts. He himself was so caught up in the fervour of the time that he had no compunction in pulling strings to get his son John a commission in the Irish Guards, despite his having been turned down on the grounds of poor eyesight. His feelings of guilt at the end of the war, knowing that he had to bear a responsibility for his son's death, haunted him for the rest of his life.

He was not alone. Many who died had been cajoled into joining by parents, wives and girlfriends. Indeed those who didn't volunteer were mocked as cowards. A man seen out of uniform might be handed a white feather by members of the Order of the White Feather as a symbol of disdain. The organization was founded in 1914 and aimed to stigmatize those suspected of being military malingerers. Their shaming policy was so effective at coercing men to enlist that the government became alarmed. Valuable civilian workers were being targeted and so they were given lapel badges reading 'King and Country' to show that they too were serving the war effort. The socialist and pacifist Fenner Brockway joked that over the course of the war he had been given enough white feathers to make a fan.

Sometimes the distributors made mistakes and handed feathers to young men in civilian clothes who were in fact troops on leave. Private Norman Demuth was given one by a woman on a London bus. He took it and used it as a pipe cleaner before handing it back. 'We didn't get these in the trenches', he said. Other passengers on the bus were much amused at the woman's error and barracked her until the bus stopped and she could alight.

In May 1915, when 'In Flanders Fields' was written, it was still the first year of a war that was to drag on for another three-and-a-half years. The naive euphoria of 1914 had not yet transmuted into the attitudes and emotions of 1918. McCrae and others retained their idealism and sense of purpose. Despite the hardships they endured, they remained convinced they were doing the right thing by fighting for King and Empire. Initially

McCrae had been caught up in the enthusiasm of the moment. From the ship crossing the Atlantic from Canada to Europe, he wrote to his mother

> all is excitement over the war . . . surely good old Emperor Billy has got his head in the noose at last; it is now he or us, good and well . . . my services are at the disposal of the country if she needs them. I am afraid my holiday trip in knocked 'galley west'.

McCrae was an experienced military doctor and viewed it as his duty to volunteer. He did not approach the war, as many contemporary volunteers appeared to, as an adventure. Many of them signed up to support their country as if they were cheering on their local sports team. McCrae knew war involved suffering: he had seen action in South Africa fourteen years earlier. He had no illusions. As his biographer said,

> He knew the war could destroy his future and possibly his life, but the tremendous sense of duty he felt was shared by many of his generation. It was not that they felt especially strong anti-German or pro-French sentiments, it was more the result of their high sense of purpose and honour.[106]

There had been no pressure on him to volunteer. Even on arrival in Europe he could have turned back without any recriminations, but he wrote home, 'I would not feel comfortable over it. I am available either as combatant or medical if they need me. I do not go to it very light-heartedly, but I think it is up to me.'

After action in South Africa, the young McCrae had told his sister that he enjoyed soldiering. The challenges and the sense of purpose appealed to him. By 1915, however, any sense of enjoyment, let alone glamour, attached to military service had vanished, for day after day he and his comrades witnessed events of unprecedented horror.

Canon Scott, McCrae's colleague as a Canadian Army chaplain, wrote:

After a war experience of four years, one is almost ashamed to look back upon those early days . . . The hideous thing was then only in its infancy . . . The human mind had not then made, as it afterwards did, the sole object of its energy the destruction of human life. Yet with a deepening knowledge of the instruments of death has come, I trust, a more revolting sense of the horrors and futility of war. The romance and the chivalry of the profession of arms has gone forever. Let us hope that in the years to come the human mind will bend all its energies to right the wrongs and avert the contentions that result in bloodshed.[107]

McCrae's poem thus reflected both the tragedy of warfare and the hope that the just cause for which he believed he was fighting, inspired by his sense of honour and duty, should not be abandoned. In one sense he expressed more than simply a hope. The poem contains an implied threat. McCrae gives the dead words to speak to the living. 'If ye break faith with us who die', say the ghosts of the young men, 'We shall not sleep, though poppies grow / In Flanders fields.' The implication is that the world may return to normal after the war. Nature will restore its kingdom, but we will not rest in peace. If you fail us, by giving up the struggle and by capitulating to the enemy now, after all we have given, we will pursue you and haunt you to the end of time.

John McCrae did not survive the war. He died in January 1918, ten months before the war's end. His death came from pneumonia and meningitis rather than battle wounds. He lived long enough to know of the impact his fifteen lines had made on the world, but died before their enduring legacy was known. He died three years before the sale of the first Remembrance poppy. He had only witnessed the sight of the poppies rejuvenating the battlefield on one occasion. After the spring of 1915 his promotion meant that he worked away from the front line.

One important aspect of the symbolism of the Remembrance poppy is that it represents the idea that the living 'keep faith' with those who have died. What McCrae meant by this line in 1915 is self-evident. It was an exhortation to the troops in the field not to give up, to pursue the fight against the enemy for a victory that would give posthumous purpose to the lives of those who had been killed. Had McCrae written the poem in 1918, after three more years of suffering and death, would he have felt the same way? Had he survived the war, might he have wanted to rewrite the poem or pen a sequel? At the time of his death in 1918, what were his feelings about the sacrifices made? Had they been worthwhile? Or suppose that he had known in 1915 what was to come – three more years of suffering to no discernible purpose – would he have still written 'Take up our quarrel with the foe: / To you from failing hands we throw / The torch; be yours to hold it high'?

There are some suggestions that the war years of 1915 to 1918 changed McCrae. He spent less time at the front and more time treating casualties behind the lines, but nevertheless he continued to witness the relentless casualties of war as men came under his care. He was a popular figure and a tireless worker, yet the war inevitably took its toll. 'John did not seem at all like the "In Flanders Fields" person of former days, but was silent, asthmatic and moody', noted one colleague of him in early 1918.

McCrae wrote a poem in 1917 following the third Battle of Ypres which he called 'The Anxious Dead'. The title hints at a change in emphasis. No longer were the ghosts of the battlefield issuing such confident demands. 'These fought their fight in time of bitter fear, and died not knowing how the day had gone.'

McCrae's message appears hesitant and less certain. There is an ambivalence which perhaps, as the renowned author of 'In Flanders Fields', he could not allow himself openly to admit. He could not be seen by his public to backtrack from those popular sentiments. So in the third verse he returns to the themes of 1915:

Tell them, O guns, that we have heard their call,
That we have sworn, and will not turn aside,
That we will onward 'til we win or fall,
That we will keep the faith for which they died.

The final verse, however, does not repeat the threat of ghostly return. After two further years of warfare at the front, he portrays the dead as more understanding, more sympathetic to the living.

> Bid them be patient, and some day anon,
> They shall feel earth enwrapt in silence deep;
> Shall greet, in wonderment, the quiet dawn,
> And in content may turn them to their sleep.

The dead will sleep when the guns are silenced, McCrae appears to be saying. Who wins or who loses the battle is now less important. Peace is the goal.

Some writers have noted 'In Flanders Fields' also expresses a perspective on the war that is ambivalent. It is divided into two distinct sections, one part apparently giving a very different impression to the other. The first nine lines, the source of the enduring poppy image of Remembrance, are lyrical and thoughtful, written in sadness to purge the sorrow of the moment. Andrew Macphail called it a poem in three phases. The first was deadly calm, the second was an expression of regret, but the third was 'without preliminary crescendo, breaking out into passionate adjuration in vivid metaphor, a poignant appeal which is at once a blessing and a curse. The closing line is a satisfying return to the first phase – and the thing is done.'[108]

To some readers that final verse, which arrives without preamble or crescendo, presents a radical change of mood. 'It is grievously out of contact with the symbolism of the first part', as Paul Fussell puts it in his book *The Great War and Modern Memory*. 'We finally see, and with a shock, what the last six lines really are: they are a propaganda argument, words like vicious and stupid would not seem to go too far, against a negotiated peace.'[109]

A harsh indictment, but the poem needs to be placed in historical context. The poem was written in 1915, only a fifth of the way through the war. The mood changed as the war progressed. As each week passed, the voice of the recruitment campaign sounded more and more hollow. So why, if the mood and morale of the fighting troops changed, did the poem retain its popularity? Why, after the war, did it still resonate with the public?

To answer those questions, one has to consider the national mood in Britain after the Armistice had been signed. It contained elements of relief, guilt, trauma and regret. The 1914 propaganda message that the war was to be a short-lived military adventure, quickly settled and over by Christmas, had long been exposed as either lies or delusional. But at the same time few who had been through the war wanted to believe it had all been a shocking waste of time, money and life. The spirit of 1915 was the compromise instinctively reached. That spirit captured the moment when the initial enthusiasm for war was tipping towards the later feelings of desolation and purposelessness. That was the mood captured in McCrae's poem.

The poppy may be understood as an appropriate symbol of Remembrance as it captures its essential ambivalence. The sacrifice of those who go to war in a good cause needs to be honoured, while the deeds they were trained to perform on the battlefield must to be abhorred.

How the poppy of the poem came to be adopted as the symbol of Remembrance is a different story to the writing of the poem and takes place in circumstances far removed from the battlefields of Europe. In 1918 Moina Belle Michael, who was at the time working as a secretary in New York, read the poem in a copy of the American *Ladies' Home Journal*. Four years earlier, at the start of the war, Michael had been in Europe. She had travelled across Belgium, France and Germany on her way to Italy and had seen Europe in its last weeks of peace. 'On the brink of the cataclysm', she wrote later, 'we were unconscious of the impending danger'. In Cologne she had seen some of the Kaiser's troops in helmets, spurs and heavy boots. Her study leave ended with her party having to leave Europe and return across the Atlantic. It took sixteen days to cross the ocean with the *Calgarian*, on which she was travelling, alert for mines and submarines.

Back in the safety of Georgia, Michael's fascination with the war in Europe was intense. Aware of the fighting taking place in the towns and countryside she had so recently visited, she followed the news reports with great interest. When America declared war on Germany in 1917, she volunteered her services and took a job in

New York with the YMCA, which at the time was one of the welfare organizations helping troops and their families.

On 9 November, just two days before the war was due to end, everyone was awaiting final confirmation of the ceasefire. Michael was working as a secretary at Hamilton Hall, Columbia University, in New York City, where the Twenty-fifth Conference of the Overseas YMCA was being held. In her autobiography, she described her moment of inspiration.

> A young soldier . . . placed a copy of the November *Ladies' Home Journal* on my desk at Headquarters. About 10:30 o'clock, when everyone was on duty elsewhere, I found time to read it and discovered the marked page which carried Colonel John McCrae's poem, 'We Shall Not Sleep', later named 'In Flanders Fields'. It was vividly picturized – most strikingly illustrated in color.
>
> I read the poem, which I had read many times previously, and studied its graphic picturization. The last verse transfixed me – 'To you from failing hands we throw the Torch; be yours to hold it high. If ye break faith with us who die, we shall not sleep, though poppies grow in Flanders Fields'.
>
> This was for me a full spiritual experience. It seemed as though the silent voices again were vocal, whispering, in sighs of anxiety unto anguish, 'To you from failing hands we throw the Torch; *be yours* to hold it high. If *ye* break faith with us who die we shall not sleep, though poppies grow in Flanders Fields'.
>
> Alone, again, in a high moment of white resolve I pledged to KEEP THE FAITH and always to wear a red poppy of Flanders Fields as a sign of remembrance and the emblem of 'keeping the faith with all who died'.
>
> In hectic times as were those times, great emotional impacts may be obliterated by succeeding greater ones. So I felt impelled to make note of my pledge. I reached for a used yellow envelope, turned the blank side up and hastily scribbled my pledge to keep the faith with all who died.

At that moment three men, as a committee from the Twenty-fifth Conference, appeared at my desk to bring a check for ten dollars from the Twenty-fifth Conference in appreciation of my efforts to make a home-like Hostess House of their headquarters. I had furnished the flowers before that time from by own purse, and I was not even a 'dollar a year man'. It was a pleasant surprise to find this appreciation, and, looking up from my intense reverie of dedication, I replied: 'How strange. I shall buy red poppies – twenty-five red poppies. I shall always wear red poppies – poppies of Flanders Fields! Do you know why?' Then I showed them the illustrated poem of Colonel John McCrae. The Committee was duly impressed and requested the permission to take the material with them back to the Conference room, 'Old number Three, Hamilton Hall'.

The Conference was equally pleased and after adjournment the men came down asking for red poppies to wear. This is the first group-effort asking for poppies to wear in memory of all who died in Flanders Fields.

I had no poppies at our headquarters, but promised I would get them that afternoon down in the city. It never occurred to me the difficulty I would have in finding artificial poppies of Flanders Fields in the novelty shops of New York City.

That Saturday afternoon, before Armistice, November 9, 1918, I went down poppy hunting in New York City. After visiting several novelty shops that featured artificial flowers and failing to find red poppies, I went to Wanamaker's. After searching in the flower collections I found a large red poppy, which I bought for my desk bud-vase and two dozen small silk red four-petaled poppies, fashioned after the wild poppies of Flanders. Having made the purchase I told the pretty little Jewess, who served me, why I was searching for single petalled red poppies. She was quite sympathetic, for her brother was then sleeping among the poppies behind the battle lines of France in a few-months' old soldier's grave. This personal contact with such a personal reaction further convinced me that this choice of a remembrance emblem for those sleeping in Flanders Fields was no accident but a logical one.

Michael's idea rapidly caught on as word of her initiative quickly spread to and via colleagues.

When I returned to duty at our headquarters for the evening hours the men came crowding again for poppies to wear. I had pinned one on my cloak collar, and gave out the others until the last of the twenty-five red poppies was pinned on a lapel of a Y.M.C.A. secretary of the Twenty-fifth Conference, who would soon be on his way to France to do his bit. I wore my poppy until I reached home in February, when I made some fresh ones.

Since this was the first group ever to ask for poppies to wear in memory of our soldier dead, and since this group gave me the money with which to buy them, I have always considered that I, then and there, consummated the first sale of the Flanders Fields Memorial Poppy. [110]

The positive reaction she received gave her the encouragement to spread the idea to other organizations. Within four months she had galvanized the enthusiastic support of the American press for her idea that the poppy should become the symbol of Remembrance.

The American Legion had been founded in 1919 as an organization of US military veterans to help men returning from the war in Europe. Moina Michael lobbied the organization to adopt the poppy as a symbol of Remembrance. Her first success was to persuade the local veterans in Georgia to endorse her idea and in September 1920 the National American Legion Convention agreed on the use of the Flanders Fields Memorial Poppy as the United States' national emblem of Remembrance.

By coincidence, also attending the national convention, was Anne Guerin, who quite independently had been promoting the sale of poppies made by widows and children of the American and French Children's League. Guerin too had been inspired by Mc-Crae's poem and had read many of the replies to it, including Michael's 'We Shall Keep The Faith'.

Her reply, like others, is written in the style of the original, in many ways a pastiche of it. She focuses not on the thoughtful and regretful first part, but the last section following the abrupt change of mood.

> Take up our quarrel with the foe:
> To you from failing hands we throw
> The torch; be yours to hold it high.
> If ye break faith with us who die
> We shall not sleep, though poppies grow
> In Flanders fields.

Michael, no doubt referring to her increasingly successful campaign to adopt the poppy as a symbol of Remembrance, claims, 'We caught the torch you threw'. And a few lines on she says that the red poppy should be worn

> . . . in honour of our dead. Fear not that ye have died
>   for naught:
> We've learned the lesson that ye taught.

Explaining her interest and motivation, Guerin wrote that the red poppy would be the international emblem that 'would allow the American and French Children's League to carry on the work of Justice, Humanity and Remembrance.' She became known in America as the 'Poppy Lady of France'. It was Guerin who made the first approach to the British Legion when in August 1921, shortly after it was founded, she went to its new offices to look for sales for her poppies.

The Legion had formally started life in May with the amalgamation of four national organizations of ex-servicemen. Its main purpose was straightforward: to care for those who had suffered as a result of service in the armed forces in the Great War, whether through their own service or through that of a husband, father or son, and whatever form that suffering took.

A year earlier an American newspaper had called on every patriotic man and woman to wear a poppy to show that the 'brave dead had not died in vain', but wearing a poppy in Britain was quite an unfamiliar idea. It was however quickly taken up and in November 1921 a sum of £106,000 was raised from poppy sales.

Canada, too, McCrae's home nation, also caught on to the idea of buying and wearing poppies. By 1922 poppy sales on the western side of the Atlantic had reached the millions and Michael and Guerin were in correspondence discussing the advancement of their mutual interest. The next step in the development of the poppy story came when the idea arose that poppies could not only be sold to benefit ex-servicemen, but made by ex-servicemen. A Major George Howson approached Earl Haig and the British Legion. He envisaged an industry eventually employing 150 disabled men. He found a site off London's Old Kent Road and by the summer of 1922 had a work force of over 40 men.

Douglas, the First Earl Haig, was the British military commander responsible for many of the tactics and military policies of the First World War. By some he was dubbed 'Butcher Haig' as so many men died under his command. He was also the commander who signed the death warrants of the many men executed by the Army for desertion or cowardice. Many of those men shot at dawn were suffering from shell shock, a condition known today as post-traumatic stress disorder (PTSD). When Haig left the Army he made some amends by dedicating the rest of his life to the welfare of his former troops. He was a founding member of the British Legion and for many years the sale of poppies was organized by the Haig Fund. The small black button in the centre of each poppy sold had the words 'Haig Fund' inscribed on it.

By Armistice Day 1922 there were millions of poppies for sale. Posters advertising them began to appear around the country. At the same time many communities in Britain were setting up their local war memorials on which the names of those who had died were recorded. The sale and wearing of poppies and the November observances at the war memorials became interlinked. The pattern of Remembrance became quickly established and by 1925 the poppy factory had to be expanded and was relocated to Richmond, Surrey. It was in 1928 that Major Howson and some of his employees gathered in Westminster with a tray of poppies, starting the long-running tradition of street sales.

The message of the poppy also reached the Southern Hemisphere. Australia adopted the practice of wearing a poppy on Armistice Day in November. Today Armistice Day in Australia is, as in Britain, renamed Remembrance Day and poppies continue to be worn. Poppy wreaths are also laid on 25 April, Anzac Day. In New Zealand the first Poppy Day was held in 1922. Poppies sent by Guerin's organization had been dispatched, but had not arrived in time for sale in the November, so it was decided to sell them in the spring to coincide with the Anzac anniversary. Poppies, it was noted, also bloomed in Gallipoli, on the battlefield where so many Australians and New Zealanders had died in the spring of 1915.

Proceeds from New Zealand's first Poppy Day were divided between the French and American Childrens' League and the New Zealand association which supported military veterans of the First World War. Today the sale of poppies on the Friday before Anzac Day provides the main income for the RSA, The Royal New Zealand Returned and Services' Association.

Today, whether in Britain, New Zealand or wherever the poppy has become the symbol of Remembrance, the injunction is that the poppy is to be worn with pride. In the 1920s the mood was different in that the memories of warfare touched everyone directly. The memories of slaughter and bereavement remained raw. The first poppies were worn in grief, with sorrow and as a sign of dedication to peace and the pledge that a war like the one just endured must never happen again. As Guerin put it, the sale of her poppies was to raise funds to carry on the work of 'Justice, Humanity and Remembrance'.

Perhaps the most touching answer to McCrae's poem was written long after McCrae's death by his colleague during the war, Frederick George Scott. Scott, a well-established poet before the war, was an Anglican minister McCrae had known in Canada.

Scott served as chaplain to the First Canadian Division during the First World War. He survived the war and his memoir, *The Great War As I Saw It*, is often cited as one of the important personal memoirs of the war from a Canadian perspective.

As a fellow Canadian from a similar background, and a friend of McCrae, Scott's motives for joining the war and his attitude towards it would have undoubtedly been very similar to those of his medical colleague. He too witnessed the Second Battle of Ypres that had prompted McCrae to write his celebrated poem. He ministered to the dying and witnessed many agonizing ends to young lives. In his memoirs, *The Great War as I Saw It*, he spoke of a talk he had given to the wounded. His words, while not as eloquent as those of McCrae's poem, are equally evocative of the mood of the time.

> I told them what great things were being done that night and what a noble part they had played in holding back the German advance and how all the world would honour them in after time. Then I said, 'Boys, let us have a prayer for our comrades up in that roar of a battle at the front'.[III]

Twenty years later, as war approached in Europe yet again, Archdeacon Scott attended the unveiling of the Canadian National Vimy Memorial in France. By that time the poppy was the widely recognized symbol it is today and was carved into the new monument.

He wrote his own response to McCrae's poem under the title 'Rememberance [sic]'. It starts as an echo of his friend's verse, but by the end the mood has changed.

> And those who sleep are not forgot . . .
> The price for peace our heroes gave,
> Pray God from future wars may save,
> Lest other heroes find a grave
> Like Flanders Fields.

Scott ponders the torch, thrown symbolically to the living by the stricken hands of the dead, and prays thus:

God grant shall light a better land,
And all the world united stand
By Flanders Fields.

There is no way of knowing how John McCrae would have
viewed the Remembrance traditions which his poem had inspired
and the way the poppy motif came to be used. Frederick Scott's
response may be the best clue we have. He clearly saw the imagery of the torch that future generation would pick up, not as a
call to jingoism and militarism, but as a reminder that war was
the evil option.

The response in poetry of those who had never known war
took the sentimental line; creating an idea of heroism far removed
from the experience of those who had known the war first-hand.
Moina Michael did not witness the fighting; nor did she suffer the
loss of a son, brother or husband in the conflict. Her view of the
poppy as a symbol was focused and unconfused.

Other Americans who responded to McCrae's poem did so to
justify the war as one fought to conserve 'freedom'. They too were
writing as people who had not, unlike Scott, McCrae, Owen and
others, experienced the full horror of the four years.

The American poet R. W. Lilliard was one such poet, who con-
cluded his response with the words:

Fear not that ye have died for naught;
The torch ye threw to us we caught,
Ten million hands will hold it high,
And freedom's light shall never die!

Another reply to McCrae's poem has become part of the literary
tradition. It was written by John Mitchell, described in *Legion
Magazine* as 'a now obscure poet who may owe his immortality to
having been selected by Hazel Felleman for her 1936 anthology *The
Best Loved Poems Of The American People*'.[112]

The torch your falling hands let go
Was caught by us, again held high . . .

Oh! Rest in peace, we quickly go
To you who bravely died, and know
In other fields was heard the cry,
For freedom's cause, of you who lie,
So still asleep where poppies grow,
In Flanders Fields.

However, no simple reading of McCrae's original poem, or any response to it, can convey the true complexity of the poppy symbol. To wear a poppy and afford the paper flower a single, unsophisticated explanation is to do the poem, the flower and the memory of the fallen a great disservice. The symbolism of the poppy cannot be reduced to a simple sentiment. It is multi-layered and complex.

McCrae was not the only soldier to notice the poppies of the battlefields and write about them. Cecil Lewis described a walk behind the lines:

Among the devastated cottages, the tumbled twisted trees, the desecrated cemeteries, opening, candid, to the blue heaven, the poppies were growing! Clumps of crimson poppies, thrusting out from the lips of craters, straggling in between the hummocks, undaunted by the desolation, heedless of human fury and stupidity, Flanders poppies basking in the sun.

Two aspects of the poppy were especially appropriate to war poets looking for imagery with which to express both their sorrow and hope. First was the fact that the poppy was blood-red in colour. This symbolized both the bodily suffering of the victims of war and the wounds of Christ, who died, so the dominant faith of Europe teaches, to redeem humankind from their sins. Second, the poppy was observed to be the first flower to return to the battlefields after the fighting, poets felt it represented a hope that the world could return to normality again. The role of nature at work, regenerating itself amidst the human-wrought destruction, was one that intrigued many writers. To see nature in this way was a reminder that despite the abnormality of war, seedtime and harvest, growth and decay, continued. To those of a religious mind it was a way of thinking of God remaining unchanged in his love, while humans indulged in hatred. To a Christian world it represented resurrection from the dead, echoing the Easter story.

But not all poets saw the flower in the same way. Isaac Rosenberg's poem 'Break of Day in the Trenches' puts the flower back into a context of trench realism, adding a touch of irony.

> The darkness crumbles way –
> Only a living thing leaps my hand
> A queer sardonic rat –
> As I pull the parapet's poppy
> To stick behind my ear.

Before the First World War, the poppy had its place in literature, but its image was of a very different flower to that of the Flanders trenches. The art critic John Ruskin wrote of the poppy as 'like a burning coal fallen from Heaven's altars'.[113] He also likened the petals to painted glass, glowing brightly as the sun shone through it: 'always it is flame, and warms the wind like a blown ruby'.[114] It was a flower with mystical properties which refracted sunlight and was life-affirming, not a representative of grief and a reminder of death.

To Victorians and Edwardians it was an effeminate bloom with connotations of the homoerotic. W. S. Gilbert mocked the camp associations with the flower in the operetta *Patience*:

> If you walk down Piccadilly with a poppy or a lily
>   in your medieval hand,
>   Everyone will say
>   As you walk your flowery way,
> What a most particularly pure young man this pure
>   young man must be.

By contrast, seven centuries earlier, at the time of the Mongol leader Genghis Khan, poppies were associated in legend with human sacrifice. Following the brutal annihilation of his enemies, it was noted that poppies were the first flowers to emerge from the fields of carnage.

The poppy is also a flower of oblivion. A close relative of the Flanders poppy is *Papaver somniferum*, the source of opium, a narcotic that dulls the senses and lures takers into its web of dependence. Andrew Macphail described the poppy as the emblem of sleep. The dead referred to in McCrae's poem desire to sleep, he wrote,

> but yet curiously take an interest in passing events. They regret that they have not been permitted to live out their life to its normal end. They call on the living to finish their task, else they shall not sink into that complete repose which they desire, in spite of the balm of the poppy.[115]

There was some surprise expressed in 2011 when, on a British delegation to China at Remembrance-tide, it was suggested to Prime Minister David Cameron that he should not wear a Remembrance poppy. To the host nation the poppy was viewed as a symbol of China's humiliation at the hands of Europe in the opium wars.

One of the ironies of the poppy as a twenty-first century symbol is that soldiers killed in action in Afghanistan are recalled by the wearing of a poppy, even though they died in a conflict partly justified as a campaign to rid the world of the menace of the flower and its role in the production of heroin.

Paul Fussell wrote of the transformation of the poppy as one of the neatest turns in popular symbolism, noting how the British Legion paper poppies can be conceived of as

> emblems at once of oblivion and remembrance: a traditional happy oblivion of their agony by the dead, and at the same time an unprecedented mass remembrance of their painful loss by the living. These little paper simulacra come from pastoral elegy, pass through Victorian male sentimental poetry, flesh themselves out in the actual

blossoms of Flanders, and come back to be worn as button holes on Remembrance Day.[116]

Like memories, the paper poppies only slowly decompose, and like memories they are incapable of reproducing themselves and creating new life. Most of the paper poppies worn are discarded after 11 November. The wreaths laid at war memorials survive longer, but within days begin to appear bedraggled. After a while, according to local practice, they are removed unceremoniously, usually by council workmen.

In the twenty-first century the poppy has transformed again into a commodity. It is marketed; it is endorsed by celebrities; it has become one of Britain's best-known brands, winning for itself a strong market share in competition with other military charities and wider good causes. It is the most valuable brand in the world, according to Paul Mellor, a director of the London-based marketing design agency Mellor & Scott.

> How many brands can truly say they have no competitor? Even heavyweight brands such as Microsoft, Coca Cola and Nike have competitors, yet the Poppy Appeal dominates charitable activity on and around Remembrance Day.
>
> How many brands are able to say that they have one singular graphical identity that encompasses everything to which the brand stands for?
>
> How many brands have the power to make millions of people buy and then proudly wear the same accessory as everyone else? No brand in the world has that kind of power. The poppy offers the very opposite to the exclusivity that most brands wish to communicate.
>
> It has the value that all marketeers aspire to have; unquestioned importance. Every brand owner believes his or her brand is of critical importance to a consumer's life. There are far too many fancy metrics by which designers and marketeers score the importance of a brand, but I think the absolute score of importance is how much consumers love the brand and its values.

The poppy appeal is inclusive, durable, courageous, humble and inspirational.[117]

As the poppy brand flourishes, there are some who feel that it is degrading to the purpose and spirit of the poppy for it to be considered in marketing terms. In recent times there has been evidence of a growing disquiet over the commercialization of the Poppy Appeal. Questions were asked as to whether it was right that what became known as 'bling poppies' should be sold as an alternative to the standard paper poppy. The disquiet was one many serving men and women shared and the issue was raised in a report on British Forces News. The bling poppies were shown on the telecast being made, not by the Royal British Legion in its workshops giving employment to veterans, but by private entrepreneurs who promised to donate profits to the legion. The bling poppies, in effect items of jewellery in red enamel or sparkling crystal, became 'must have' fashion items after being worn by several celebrities, including *X-Factor* judge Danni Minogue and the girl group The Saturdays. Bling poppies were also spotted for sale on online auctions, with none of the profits going to charity.

Poppy 'commemorative items', as they are officially described, are sold directly by The Royal British Legion. Poppy bracelet charms can be had for £10 and the Buckley Poppy Brooch for £9.99. In its 2011 advertising the brooch was marketed as 'last year's favourite', now slightly larger and 'stunning with its red crystals and 18-carat gold plating'. The legion also promised to send a free copy of 'Shoulder to Shoulder with all who serve' with every order. Items for sale at the poppy shop website included a poppy novel, a poppy shopping bag and a book of Remembrance recipes.

Very much at the forefront of the commercialization of the Poppy campaign has been the public relations industry. Consciences pricked perhaps by criticism of the commercialism, a debate has taken place within the PR industry. It was initiated on a PR media blog by practitioner Jon Clements, who had read the letter from Ben Griffin and the other veterans questioning the term 'hero' and the way it was used within the poppy appeal.[118]

'Brands that could be considered sacrosanct are not immune from criticism – and sometimes from the most unexpected quarters', Clements noted.

But do the veterans have a point? Does launching a campaign around a serious and sombre subject with girl group, The Saturdays, diminish its solemnity? Does it devalue the message that those who died in battle were the victims of human folly and we shouldn't forget the stupidity of war?

But the risk the Poppy Appeal runs by looking trendy is nothing new. Eyebrows were raised in 1997 when the Spice Girls – at the height of Girl Power mania – were used to make the campaign more appealing to young people in light of falling revenues. But . . . the risky move paid off.

It's a balance the British Legion needs to strike; between being seen to muddy the message about war and being able to fund ongoing help for our military victims of conflict. And as the last remaining veterans from World War 2, and their tales of all-encompassing conflict touching millions, pass away, the more remote we become from the topic of war.

The Poppy Appeal is taking a pragmatic approach that clearly doesn't please everyone. But if that means getting the judges of the currently most watched TV programme X Factor to wear poppies – prompting questions on Twitter as to what they are – the British Legion is making the best job of a sensitive situation. There were also poppy logos, or avatars, made available for tweeters to use.

Reader Ann Wright responded:

I feel very close to this issue, as I worked for many years on the Remembrance Sunday programme for the BBC, and have interviewed many veterans. It is a difficult one, and I've felt uneasy about the use of poppy avatars as rather commercial, something I know that most veterans would abhor. However, we have to be realistic about society and what presses it's buttons nowadays, so if that means reaching out to a younger generation by whatever means possible, then RBL should do so.

Clements responded

It's a tough one . . . On one hand, the ease with which you can upload a poppy to your Twitter avatar doesn't necessarily involve a lot of thought about why it's there. On the other hand, there's a younger generation who won't ever know a father or grandfather who had anything to do with war and their experience of conflict will be limited to TV news coverage or *Call of Duty* games. Getting them to remember something annually that couldn't be further from their experience needs new ways of working.

Another PR blogger calling himself Jerry added his voice.

I belong to the generation that had grandfathers and fathers in the Second World War. I have a Poppy on my twitter avatar, to show that I remember the sacrifice former generations made so I could live the wonderful life I have. I made a donation to the poppy appeal, to a bored scout outside my local supermarket. Anything that reminds anyone, whatever the generation, of the sacrifices made during such terrible conflicts is a good thing. I do not feel it glorifies wars or conflicts, just as a pink ribbon does not glorify Breast Cancer, it expresses empathy, and sympathy. I remember the fuss about the Spice Girls, but it worked. Like any 'business' marketing has to evolve to appeal to a new generation and new ways of thinking.

The qualms expressed by Methodist minister Revd Dr Angela Shier-Jones took a different line, in keeping with the values of her professional calling. She told her Surrey congregation that she would be buying a poppy, but would not always be wearing it. She explained on her website The Kneeler,

> I struggle with the idea of Remembrance Sunday with its mixed up messages of faith and nationalism giving people the mistaken impression that this is a Christian country and that only Christians fought in the war and when we are effectively still at war in a country that is a Muslim country, participating in what is clearly for some a predominantly religious war (even if we don't see the Taliban in that way) – then my unease multiplies. Islamaphobia is a sin – Jesus taught us to love our neighbour.
>
> I have bought a poppy – but this year I have chosen not to wear it when I am wearing a clerical collar, I just can't bring myself to reinforce the association of Christianity with nationalism, or war, especially not when I am so conscious of the rise of fascism, racism and religious intolerance.
>
> I also can't, as a minister, bring myself to only pray for 'our' fallen heroes. You have taught us that we should pray for our enemies, not those we love. When we are prepared to remember the lives we have taken, as well as those we have lost, and remember the cost in terms of religious, economic and political freedoms won and lost – I will be a lot happier about 'remembrance' day. But I think I would still want to break the link between Remembrance Day and the Lord's Day.

The message, process and tradition of Remembrance is more nuanced and deeper than any advertising and PR campaign can convey; especially if the campaign is being aimed at a generation without the background knowledge or experiences of their grandparents. The younger generation lives in the age where every commodity of life is branded and marketed. As children they bought toys which were the product of marketing campaigns, film tie-ins and public relations hype. Their choice of food was similarly determined: which breakfast cereal, fizzy drink, snack bar or fast food would they choose? Clothes, mobile phones, music, television channels, holiday destinations, everything and anything that can be branded has been branded. And branding is more than the marketing and advertising of a consumer product; it involves giving the product an image: an added intangible value. It may add status or self-esteem to the user and a feelgood factor to the purchaser.

The poppy has now become one of Britain's most familiar brands. In a commercial world dominated by marketing, the Royal British Legion has had to turn to the professionals to promote the core values of Remembrance using the poppy logo and techniques of modern advertising. It is a year-long campaign that peaks in October and early November when 45 million poppies are sold. They come in many shapes and forms, from the most commonly seen lapel poppy for which a modest donation is expected, through to wreaths, stickers, badges and poppies for the front bumpers of cars.

As well as the bracelet charms and other poppy items previously highlighted, The Royal British Legion also markets Golden Bath-oil with poppy seed and ladies' poppy watches. A poppy golf-umbrella can be bought online for £23.25 and a fashion umbrella for £18.50. For those seeking to spend a bit less, a poppy teabag-tidy can be bought for £4.80.

A DVD of the annual Albert Hall Festival is described as a 'must-have gift for any supporters of the British Armed Forces community'. In 2011 the Official Poppy Appeal Single being sold was described as 'the poignant "I've Gotta Get a Message to You", performed by The Soldiers with Bee Gees legend Robin Gibb'. The Soldiers who sing with the ex-Bee Gee are Sergeant Major Gary Chilton, Staff Sergeant Richie Maddocks and Lance Corporal Ryan Idzi, all serving members of the armed services.

Merchandizing, however, is just one aspect of the poppy brand campaign. To maximize the potential of the brand, the Royal British Legion is advised by leading marketing consultants The Gate. The Gate's slogan is 'Ideas that Work' and in promoting their expertise to potential clients they boast of their 'enticing design, hard-hitting copy, innovative use of media – each can add the emotional edge that separates great brands from the also-rans.' The Gate's main clients come from the financial sector and include The Royal Bank of Scotland, Schroders and Aviva. With the Royal British Legion they rise to the challenge of adding 'the emotional edge' to the poppy appeal. This they certainly did when the 2010 campaign got under way. One poster featured an amputee, another a forces' widow. Accompanying the image of a wounded veteran shown strapping on a prosthetic leg were the words, 'It only takes a second to put on a poppy.' 'It's not as painful to put on a poppy' were the words which went with a photograph of a widow at her husband's grave. In addition to the poster campaign, The Gate's strategy was both to maximize use of new media and utilize traditional outlets such as radio and television. The campaign lasted two weeks. In addition to its creative input, The Gate also masterminded the buying of advertising slots for maximum impact and value for money.

The most unusual publicity ploy, or gimmick, was the idea in 2010 of Joe Sinclair, Creative Director at Burson-Marsteller UK. He produced a 'music' video that attempted, via a British Legion-backed Facebook campaign, to reach number one in the music charts on Remembrance Sunday, 14 November. The video was not a musical contribution, but featured the two minutes' silence. It featured ex-servicemen and -women who had received help from The Royal British Legion together with Radiohead vocalist Thom Yorke, rapper Plan B and DJ and guitarist Mark Ronson. When it was released however, the silence got no further than number 20 and Rihanna kept her top spot, with Take That and Cheryl Cole also well ahead.

In the wider world of marketing and advertising, commercial interests often associate themselves with good causes in the hope that some of the goodwill will rub off on them. There is wide awareness of the power of the poppy brand and major companies are keen to associate themselves with it. Around Remembrance-tide in 2009 an advertisement for Hovis appeared showing sticks of brown-bread toast being dipped into a boiled egg with the slogan, 'Here's To Our Soldiers'. It was a cooperation between the Royal British Legion and the company to boost the profile of both. The double meaning of 'soldier' was at the core of the campaign and appealed to the nostalgia element in both brands. The campaign was described by the website Thirdsector as 'a perfect way to boost the profile of both of them. The charity would benefit from the advertising and promotional machine of Hovis, while the bread brand's reputation would be enhanced by its association with a highly respected charity.' Hovis pledged 4p for every loaf sold, aiming to raise £100,000. The specific marketing aim of the campaign was to increase awareness of the Hovis and Royal British Legion brands, particularly among women aged 45 and over. Sales of Hovis products rose by 10 per cent during the campaign, and the target of raising £100,000 in on-pack promotional sales was exceeded by £30,000. The brand cooperation was judged a success and was only marred by a price war between Hovis and Tesco that threatened to undermine Hovis's sales. Tesco eventually donated £40,00 to the charity to offset any loss. In 2010 the poppy campaign was linked with Hovis again, this time with Hovis's multiseed bread, seed that included 'those from the poppy'.

In 2011 the supermarket Waitrose had a recipe book for sale with a Remembrance theme. It showed pictures of cupcakes adorned with a large red confectionery poppy. The book was also available via a website entitled Flossiecrums.com. The initiative for 'the family-friendly baking book' came from the Royal British Legion and was less a money-making venture than one intended to introduce the idea of Remembrance to young children.

Because of the seasonal nature of the poppy business, there are some public relations pitfalls to avoid. One PR consultant, with the business motto 'creating reputations', has felt the need to advise his clients on the 'dos and don'ts' of poppy-wearing.

You should be wearing one if you are photographed at an event or even the Remembrance Parades that will take place later this month – being seen without one is actually bad PR! However, if you are getting shots taken to submit with a press release, or to promote a forthcoming event or simple portraiture that could be used beyond November, then take some with and most important some without.

In simple terms imagine your release was held over and was being considered for publication later on, if you were wearing a poppy there is a good chance that a news editor would not use your story as it will look out of date – because of the poppy.

Back in the summer I spent an hour on Photoshop erasing poppies from the lapels of business folk who had been snapped back in November last year and wanted to use the same photograph again – but recognised the red tribute did not lend itself to this.[119]

In commercial terms, the promotion, advertising and marketing of the poppy brand can be judged a success. As each year passes, the Royal British Legion announces new income records. The poppy appeal is the most widely recognized charity appeal of the year. Even with competition from a new rival, 'Help for Heroes', which also raises money to help ex-service personnel, the Legion retains its market lead. Indeed the Help for Heroes campaign might be seen to raise awareness of shared issues. In 2011 it asked that all its supporters buy a poppy and wear it with pride. Help for Heroes was launched in 2007 and within two years had raised almost £30 million. This compares with approaching £40 million raised annually by the Royal British Legion. In 2009 Chris Simpkins said that the new charity had given other forces charities a wake-up call with its effective fundraising techniques. The Help for Heroes founder said that established forces charities had been 'doing a great job but were perhaps not focused on modern soldiers' needs'.

From a wild flower growing over the graves of men killed in battle, to a successful marketing and commercial brand, the Remembrance poppy has travelled a long way. What would John McCrae make of the poppy brand? Would Moina Michael or Anne Guerin recognize the flower? Is the poppy today, in its symbolism, public image and purpose, the same as the poppy worn in the years immediately after the 1914–18 war? Or has it changed so much that it has become something quite different?

Was journalist Robert Fiske expressing a commonly held view when he wrote this in *The Independent* in November 2011?

As a young boy, I went to Ypres with my Dad, stayed at the 'Old Tom Hotel' (it is still there, on the same side of the square as the Cloth Hall) and met many other 'old soldiers', all now dead. I remember that they wanted to remember their dead comrades. But above all, they wanted an end to war. But now I see these pathetic creatures with their little sand-pit poppies – I notice that our masters in the House of Commons do the same – and I despise them. Heaven be thanked that the soldiers of the Great War cannot return today to discover how their sacrifice has been turned into a fashion appendage.[120]

No sooner had Robert Fiske's comments been published than other journalists and commentators leapt on the phrase. To those for whom the poppy is a 'sacred' symbol, through to those who feel it is a political emblem associated with jingoistic patriotism, there was a feeling that Fiske had made a valid point. A. P. Schrader, who blogs on the site politicsontoast and is generally considered to be very conservative in his outlook, wrote:

> Poppies are worn ostentatiously for work or social reasons as a vainglorious opportunity to exhibit one's 'caring' and 'patriotic' credentials. As attached as I am to the Poppy Appeal and Remembrance Sunday (the closest we have, really, to anything approaching a 'Britishness Day'), there is something incredibly vulgar and depressing in the way this potent national symbol has been hijacked and debased by a certain creed of holier-than-thou busibodies . . . I find it difficult to suppress the innate dislike this officious 'poppy policing' engenders in me. The subsequent excoriation of all those whom the self-appointed 'poppy police' judge to have 'disrespected' the poppy is becoming an increasingly tedious feature of an otherwise noble and dignified occasion. Frankly, the magnitude of the debt of honour we owe to our men and women in uniform deserves better than this self-indulgent, self-aggrandising, *faux* outrage.

The story of how the poppy came to represent Remembrance is well known. It reaches back to the dark days of trench warfare.

The account of those events has become a modern myth in the sense that it is a story full of meaning conveying a deeper truth. And, as with any myth, the truth it conveys is more important than its absolute historical accuracy. That is not to say that the story commonly told today and passed on to the young is inaccurate. It is based on solid fact, but the way in which the story is told, and which facts are emphasized and which are omitted, help to shape its familiar symbolism.

What is not in question is that the origin of the poppy story can be traced back to a poem. But in that fact lies the problem, for much of the imagery and symbolism of the poppy is poetic and cannot be nailed down. It is profound, beautiful and elusive. The poppy myth is both universal and individual and the poppy means different things to different wearers.

The poppy appeal judges its success in financial terms and in this respect does well. The Royal British Legion continues to perform an important role. It also monitors public awareness of the brand. Year on year, even though the world wars fade from memory, the poppy's image does not diminish. But in one respect the poppy's story is of failure. Wars continue to be waged. The wearing of the poppy has not served as a powerful enough warning against war, in the way that the First World War generation had hoped.

8

A HISTORY OF THE HERO

THE NAME OF EVERY BRITISH SERVICEMAN KILLED IN THE
First World War is recorded somewhere in Britain. Names appear
in small batches on village memorials. There are longer lists in
town churches and huge scrolls of names in alphabetical order on
the great memorials at the battlegrounds.

Names appear on individual graves too. At the cemeteries
managed by the Commonwealth War Graves Commission there
are rows and rows of near-identical stones, in neat, precise lines,
each one marking the resting place of one person. Some give a name,
rank, brief regimental or service information and age. Most carry
a carving of a cross, although some will show the Star of David if
the serviceman or -woman was Jewish, or Koranic script if they
were a Muslim. Other nations have their war graves too, and across
the plains of northern France war cemeteries are a common landmark. Some are small, with just a few hundred graves; others have
tens of thousands. Each country has a unique grave design, making it relatively easy to tell the British from the French or German.

The role of the Commission is to pay tribute to the 1.7 million
men and women of the Commonwealth forces who died in the two
world wars. To date it has constructed 2,500 war cemeteries and
plots, erecting headstones over graves and, in the many instances
where the remains were never recovered, inscribing the names of
the dead on permanent memorials. Over 1 million casualties are
now commemorated at military and civil sites in some 150 countries. If anyone is omitted, it is only through administrative over-
sight, not intent. Even the names of those who died ignominiously,

shot at dawn for cowardice, are gradually being added to the rolls of honour, since it is now realized that in the vast majority of cases these men were not cowards, but victims of 'shell-shock', or to give it its current medical term, post-traumatic stress disorder.

The War Graves Commission was established by Royal Charter in 1917. In the context of the history of armed conflict, the listing and honouring of every casualty is a relatively modern practice. History books give the names of the leaders and generals involved in the great battles of yesteryear: William the Conqueror was the victor of the Battle of Hastings; King Henry V inspired his troops at Agincourt; Prince Rupert led the charge at the Civil War Battle of Edgehill; the Duke of Marlborough commanded the troops at Blenheim; General Wolfe masterminded the attack on Quebec; Wellington won the Battle of Waterloo. Some leaders died in action, others went on to new and greater victories, but for most of history it has been the leaders who have taken the glory. There is no list of names of the archers who defeated the French at Agincourt, the foot soldiers who marched with the Saxons against the Normans in 1066, or the musketeers and pikemen of Edgehill.

Before the mid-nineteenth century the only names recorded were those of generals and heroes. Only if someone of lowly rank performed an extraordinary deed, around which an inspiring or moving story could be woven, did his name survive. The only rare exceptions are found in cultures where a national story is recorded in literary or oral form. Thus in both the Old Testament and the Norse Sagas, found alongside the names of heroes are the names of just a few of the 'bit players'.

By contrast, today everyone in uniform is dubbed a hero. In Britain every victim of a foreign war is personally commended by the Prime Minister in the House of Commons. To understand Remembrance in the twenty-first century, one has to look at the significant change in emphasis over the last 150 years; away from the celebration of the few and famous, to the cult of the many, indeed of everyone.

Wars have been fought for centuries, millennia even. History is told through tales of conflict. The Greeks, the Romans, the Vikings, the Normans, the Mongols – empires and civilizations have defined themselves by their military conquests and prowess. Centuries before the advent of artillery and explosions, men went to war with swords, cavalry and spears; long after battles were finished, they were relived through stories of leaders and heroes. The history books do not dwell on the pain and the brutality of fighting, but on the 'great deeds' and heroism of the hour. If the death of a man in battle can be retold as a story of selflessness and courage, it not only brings a purpose to his death, but can encourage future generations to emulate his bravery.

These stories have taken many forms over the years. The epic poem 'Horatius' by Thomas Babington Macaulay, for instance, mythologizes a celebrated sixth-century Roman battle and a hero standing alone facing a seemingly overwhelming enemy.

> Then out spake brave Horatius,
> The Captain of the gate:
> To every man upon this earth
> Death cometh soon or late.
> And how can man die better
> Than facing fearful odds,
> For the ashes of his fathers,
> And the temples of his Gods.[121]

Even military disasters, such as the ill-fated Charge of the Light Brigade during the Crimean War, can be turned into stories of heroism. The poem celebrating the event by Alfred, Lord Tennyson, honoured the men who did not flinch from obeying orders and doing their duty, even though they knew the orders to be flawed and that 'someone had blundered'.

> Cannon to right of them,
> Cannon to left of them,
> Cannon behind them
> Volley'd and thunder'd;
> Storm'd at with shot and shell,
> While horse and hero fell,
> They that had fought so well

Came thro' the jaws of Death
Back from the mouth of Hell,
All that was left of them,
Left of six hundred.

When can their glory fade?
O the wild charge they made!
All the world wondered.
Honor the charge they made,
Honor the Light Brigade,
Noble six hundred.

Stories of heroism are told both formally by poets and informally through folk tales. They are not reportage and make no claim to be; there is no need for the events described to be verifiable facts. The stories capture the spirit of a time. They are re-creations with a noble purpose. Historians have questioned Tennyson's accuracy in depicting the events at Balaclava in 1854. He was not an eyewitness. But no one questions the power of his words to convey a message.

One heroic story of the First World War that was told to inspire the German people was subjected to close scrutiny and found to be largely fabricated. The version of the story of the Battle of Langemarck that was widely told and believed was that an army of young people stormed the enemy trenches singing the nationalistic song 'Deutschland, Deutschland über alles'. 'This was patriotic youth in action sacrificing themselves in order to attain victory, fired by a famous patriotic song as testimony of their youthful ardor', wrote George Mosse, 'Those who fell symbolized what German youth ought to be.'[122]

The reality, however, was rather different. Most of those who fell in battle were older conscripts. The battle was not fought at Langemarck, but at a less Germanic-sounding location 5 km west at Bixchote. The soldiers, he acknowledges, might have sung as a way of keeping in contact in the fog. 'Yet it seems unlikely they sang very much, given their circumstances: under strong fire which came from an unknown direction, stranded in some god-forsaken field, surrounded by death and confusion.' If they had sung a

German song it might have been to identify themselves as German so as not to be killed by their own side. 'The evidence clearly speaks against the claim that the song was an expression of enthusiasm for battle.'

The story, which originated in an army bulletin, and was intended to disguise defeat and the reckless waste of life, 'in reality created a popular myth' of manly youths sacrificing themselves for the fatherland, suggests Mosse. The battle was recalled as a time when youths became men. Much of the poetry and prose about Langemarck emphasized this transformation, says Mosse. Hitler claimed to have been at the battle and to have heard the sound of the patriotic song reaching him 'just as death was reaping its harvest on his own ranks'. The legend was transmitted with full force into the Third Reich. 'Manhood was cast in the warrior image, symbolizing youth grown to maturity . . . Now they could be seen as Greek heroes who were to grace many a war monument.'[123]

All nations are capable of taking grains of truth and fabricating stories of heroism from them. Military engagements are normally confused and brutal affairs with no one recording an accurate account of every cut and thrust. Even impartial war reporters on the scene can only attest to one narrow view of the action: their own. One common way for a story to begin is with a medal citation. Medals for valour are rarely awarded collectively to regiments, companies or platoons; they are almost invariably individually assigned. When the Victoria Cross was introduced as the ultimate British award for bravery it was often the case that a regiment was awarded the accolade, but an individual had to be chosen from amongst the number of men to receive it. The story is told of the award of Victoria Crosses to the 93rd Highlanders after the Siege of Lucknow in 1857. A young officer, Frederick William Traill-Burroughs, was much aggrieved that he was not a recipient of the medal. He was, he claimed, the first man through the breach in the wall: a plausible claim as the breach was not large and Burroughs was a small man. But he was not popular among his fellow officers and his claim was not substantiated.

Although the Victoria Crosses awarded were to the regiment as a whole, each of the six men presented with the medal had their own part in the action written up as a story of individual heroism. Of Private David Mackay, the *London Gazette* of 1858 recorded his

> great personal gallantry in capturing an enemy colour after a most obstinate resistance, at the Secunderabagh, Lucknow, on the 16th of November 1857. He was severely wounded afterwards at the capture of the Shah Nujjif. Elected by the private soldiers of the Regiment.

Of James Munro it was said in his *London Gazette* citation that his VC was awarded

> for devoted gallantry, at Secunderabagh, on the 16th November, 1857, in having promptly rushed to the rescue of Captain E. Walsh, of the same corps, when wounded, and in danger of his life, whom he carried to a place of comparative safety, to which place the Serjeant was brought in, very shortly afterwards, badly wounded.

The introduction of the Victoria Cross in 1856 came at a time when for the first time the ordinary soldier's contribution to warfare was being officially recognized. It was introduced in response to the Crimean War, Britain's first major military action since the defeat of Napoleon at Waterloo in 1815. Before then the British Army and Navy had very few formal ways of acknowledging conspicuous gallantry. A man might be mentioned in dispatches or awarded a promotion if his deeds were noted by a commanding officer, but the now familiar system of awarding crosses and medals did not exist. Indeed the ordinary fighting man's contribution to battles and victories was largely unsung.

Another innovation was that when the Victoria Cross was introduced, it was stipulated that it be awarded irrespective of rank. In doing so the British came in line with the French, whose Legion of Honour disregarded social standing when recognizing bravery. Thus any man in arms could become a hero.

It was at this time too that the war memorials were first raised giving lists of names of the ordinary men who fought, their names listed by rank or alphabetically. Sometimes, in Britain, decorations are given by initial (for example, the Military Cross is 'MC') after the name, but the key feature is that everyone who died having enlisted is named, irrespective of their individual contribution to the outcome of the war. Some will not have died on the field of battle, but from disease or an accident when training. But as long as they were under orders and in uniform at the time of their death their name is given as one of 'the fallen'. The only exceptions are those who were shot, supposedly for cowardice: more recently some of them have had their honour restored. An example of this is Reginald Tite, shot by firing squad in 1916 after twice deserting his post. With the backing of local MP Nicholas Soames and the Royal British Legion, his name now appears on the East Grinstead Roll of Remembrance in Sussex.

War memorials dating back to before the nineteenth century do exist, but they are rare. The earliest listed by the UK National Inventory of War Memorials is from the tenth century and is to be found in Forres, Scotland. Sueno's Stone has scenes of fighting, decapitation and piles of dead carved into it. What it commemorates is unclear, but it is thought to be one of three possible events: Kenneth McAlpin's victory over Pictish nobles; a confrontation between Picts and Norsemen; or the death of King Dubh at the Battle of Forres in AD 966. Certainly the stone makes no attempt to list the names of the dead.

There are several examples in Britain of stones or plaques marking battle sites, some of which are memorials from the time, though most were raised several centuries after the events recorded. Around mainland Europe there are similar monuments marking battlefields. One of the most frequently visited by British visitors to northern France is that near Agincourt marking the place where the English defeated the French on St Crispin's Day, 25 October 1415, during the Hundred Years War.

As previously mentioned, there is no list of names of those of either side who died at Agincourt. Finding a roll of honour, or list of individual names of ordinary soldiers, dated earlier than the nineteenth century is almost impossible. However a copy of a rare, possibly unique, sixteenth-century list can be found at St Oswald's

Church, Arncliffe, Yorkshire. On it are recorded the names of local men who fought at the Battle of Flodden Field in 1513. The Arncliffe list contains 35 names and, like a First World War memorial, has a number of repeated surnames. There are seven with the family name of Knolle and four Franklins. Each man is also given his rank, or rather his battle skill. John Knolle and three others are 'able horse and harnish'd (armoured)'. The others have the word 'bowe' or 'bille' after their name. The battle was a victory for the English led by the Earl of Surrey over the Scots. It was a sizeable confrontation of armies and the casualty figure was large, numbering in thousands. A figure of 17,000 is given on the memorial to the English commander in Thetford parish church in Norfolk.

Going further back in British history, at Carisbrooke Castle Museum there is a modern memorial to 440 men who died at the Battle of St Aubin in 1488. Two of the men who took part are named: Sir Edward Woodville, the commander, and Diccon Cheke, the sole survivor who returned with the news of a massacre.

One form of medieval war memorial was that of a church built on the site of a battle, usually by the winner. The Battle of Hastings was celebrated by the victorious Normans with the construction of an abbey. The church at Battlefield, Shropshire, also celebrates a victory, but is reputed to have a grimmer history. It is said to stand on the mass grave of 9,000 dead from the Battle of Shrewsbury of 1403. There is no list of names of the ordinary bowmen and infantry soldiers. The victor, Henry IV, is however recalled in the form of a statue on the outside of the building and his knights have their shields recorded in the roof timbers. The Cinque Port of Sandwich in Kent also has a church celebrating a victory. This one was a naval battle over the French in 1217.

The earliest example of an individual victim of war being named on a memorial in the UK inventory is that of Richard Percival, who died on a crusade with Richard the Lionheart in 1202. It is to be found at the church dedicated to St Peter and St Paul in Weston in Gordano, Somerset.

The whole question of when and why war memorials came to list the names of all ranks was the subject of an article in the *Daily Telegraph* in November 2010 by the columnist Simon Heffer.

Our people have fought wars since the earliest record of our history, but it has only been in the last century or so that we have chosen to remember our dead rather than our battles and our victories. Nelson's column and the Wellington memorial in London commemorate great leaders; but the men who died at Trafalgar have no memorial, any more than do those who died in the Peninsular War or at Waterloo.

At all our battles until the Crimean War – whether Agincourt, Bosworth, Naseby or that defeat of Napoleon in a field outside Brussels – the dead were simply gathered up and chucked into pits. Death was an occupational hazard of war and, in the culture as it then was, required no special public recognition. Triumphs were different: which is not just why we have Waterloo station and Trafalgar Square, but why the French have the Gare d'Austerlitz and the Arc de Triomphe.

Life was not necessarily much nastier, more brutish or shorter out of uniform than in it, which perhaps explains the lack of respect for the dead. But by the middle of the 19th century, civilian life had changed. People lived longer and had a higher standard of living. Human life had a higher price put on it; and war became about more than, at best, glory and triumph. Some of the Crimean war dead have marked graves, though they are mainly those who died of a cholera epidemic in Istanbul.

The oldest memorial I recall seeing was not really a war memorial at all. It was a tablet set in the wall of the pretty little cathedral in Bridgetown, Barbados, commemorating the men who died in an epidemic of disease while garrisoned on the island in the 1820s. The next, chronologically, was an austere obelisk outside the cathedral in St Paul, Minnesota, to local men who died fighting for the North in the American Civil War.[124]

Shakespeare reinforces Simon Heffer's description of the lot of the common soldier who died in battle in the days before repatriation of bodies with military honours and the raising of war memorials on which the names of all who died were recorded. In Montjoy's words to the king after the battle:

> I come to thee for charitable licence,
> That we may wander o'er this bloody field
> To look our dead, and then to bury them;
> To sort our nobles from our common men. (IV, 7)

In Britain there are no 'rolls of honour' recorded by the UK inventory earlier than the nineteenth century, and the few listed come from very late in the century and cannot be counted as community memorials. They are military, or quasi-military monuments; one such gives names of old boys of the United Services College at Westward Ho!, Devon; another is the roll at the Manchester Regimental Museum at Ashton under Lyne; a third example lists the members of the Northumberland Fusiliers who died in Egypt and the Sudan between 1882 and 1899. It is to be found in the regimental museum at Alnwick Castle. It is a framed and glazed illuminated document handwritten within decorative flames. In each corner is a painting of a soldier in historic regimental dress.

Perhaps one reason for the new interest in the individuality of the common soldier was the growing awareness amongst an educated and informed middle class of the realities of war and what the ordinary combatant went through. The American Civil and Crimean Wars were the first conflicts to be photographed. They were the first reported upon by the press using independent eyewitness accounts. Dispatches from the Crimea reached *The Times* in London via early telegraph and graphic descriptions of the hardships endured by the troops were published. No longer did the public rely solely on official military reports and the imagination of poets for their picture of war. They could read accounts for themselves and relate what they read to the men they knew suffering the privations described.

Contrast the official dispatch announcing the victory at the Battle of Trafalgar of the British over the French and Spanish navies in 1805 with the reports from the Crimean War printed in *The Times* some 50 years later. Vice Admiral Collingwood wrote:

> After such a victory it may appear unnecessary to enter into encomiums on the particular parts taken by the several Commanders; the conclusion says more on the subject than I have language to express; the spirit which animated all was the same; when all exerted themselves zealously in their country's service, all deserve that their high merits should stand recorded; and never was high merit more conspicuous than in the battle I have described.
>
> A circumstance occurred during the action, which so strongly marks the invincible spirit of British seamen, when engaging the enemies of their country, that I cannot resist the pleasure I have in making it known to their Lordships; the *Temeraire* was boarded by accident, or design, by a French ship on one side, and a Spaniard on the other; the contest was vigorous, but, in the end, the combined ensigns were torn from the poop, and the British hoisted in their places.
>
> Such a battle could not be fought without sustaining a great loss of men. I have not only to lament in common with the British Navy, and the British Nation, in the fall of the Commander in Chief, the loss of a Hero, whose name will be immortal, and his memory ever dear to his country; but my heart is rent with the most poignant grief for the death of a friend, to whom, by many years intimacy, and a perfect knowledge of the virtues of his mind, which inspired ideas superior to the common race of men, I was bound by the strongest ties of affection; a grief to which even the glorious occasion in which he fell, does not bring the consolation which perhaps it ought; his Lordship received a musket ball in his left breast, about the middle of the action, and sent an officer to me immediately with his last farewell; and soon after expired.
>
> I have also to lament the loss of those excellent officers, Captains Duff, of the *Mars*, and Cooke, of the

Bellerophon; I have yet heard of no others. I fear the numbers that have fallen will be found very great.

William Russell wrote with far less formality and a great deal more grit after the Battle of Alma in 1854.

The number of dead and wounded Russians lying around the breastwork when I visited it was enormous. Those of the brave Guardsmen, 7th, 23rd, Highlanders and 95th, poor fellows in front of it, showed how fierce had been the assault. Just at the close of the action an officer of ours gave a wounded Russian some spirits from his flask to drink: the scoundrel in return shot him in the back as he turned to leave him, and was of course bayoneted immediately. During the action a wounded Russian being on the ground cut with his sword at the English soldiers; they quickly placed him beyond reach of annoying their comrades in the rear.

Russell's reports, as well as highlighting the actions of ordinary, individual soldiers, included direct criticisms of the commanders and officers. In one section of his Alma report he creates an anti-hero. He describes the ghastly sight of seeing men lying dead and observes: 'how horrible that such an awful sacrifice should be entirely owing to the obstinacy and ambition of one man.'

He also mocks the leaders of the Russian forces. In one passage he employs sarcasm:

Yet we hear today that Prince Menschikoff and Gortachakoff, who were here yesterday, in person, making the utmost use of their heels, have today had the impudence to cause salutes to be fired in Sebastopol, the ships to be dressed, and perhaps have sung their last Te Deum for their ignominious flight![125]

Since the pioneering reporting of William Russell, the war correspondent has become an established, and often glamorous, role within journalism. Today the war correspondent does not only report in written form; he or she may be a radio or television reporter sending dispatches from battlefield to living room.

As war correspondents only have a narrow view of the action on the ground, by necessity they have to focus on describing what they see people doing in their immediate vicinity. This can make a report very influential, especially if what they describe is not what the authorities want the public to hear. The BBC correspondent Kate Adie's description of the American bombing raid on Libya in April 1986, which followed a terrorist attack on a nightclub used by American service personnel in Germany, was criticized by the government of the day, but widely praised by her peers.

It included images of casualties and eyewitness accounts of bombs falling on Tripoli. The Americans' intended target was pos-sibly the Libyan security headquarters. They missed. Instead a medical clinic and ordinary flats and houses took the hit. The then Conservative Party Chairman Norman Tebbit complained that the BBC's reporting portrayed the raids, supported by the British and only made possible through American use of British air bases, as 'bullying'.

One method governments use to keep control of what is reported at times of war is by giving approved reporters special access to source material. The correspondents who are embedded are given privileged but controlled access to the action by the military authorities. They are in combat kit. They live alongside the fighting men and depend on them for transport, food and their own safety. They often form a close bond with the combatants around them and should one be killed, their reports of the action become personal.

The history of war reporting shows that the more the real action is described by journalists who are not under the control of the authorities, the less governments and rulers are able to manage the news to focus on the triumphant aspects of military action. Wellington and Nelson were the heroes of the wars of the early nineteenth century. By the time of the Crimean War the com-manders came to be seen as men with feet of clay. The image that has gone down in history of Lords Raglan and Cardigan is of blundering old aristocrats whose mistakes resulted in unnecessary loss of life. By the time of the First World War, many commanders were viewed with open disdain. 'Lions led by donkeys', to borrow the phrase made famous by military historian Alan Clark, was the view of the troops (the lions) and of their commanders (the donkeys) encamped safely behind the lines.

The impact of the old and the new comes through in the parliamentary debates of the time. In 1855 Admiral Walcott addressed the House of Commons during a debate on the Crimean War. He was a man steeped in naval and military tradition, or so one might deduce from his position and rank, who was nevertheless aware of changing times and attitudes. He spoke of the need for the country to go to war.

> Our honour is at stake, we must redeem it. Our place in the nations is at issue, we must maintain it. The sword we had drawn untarnished, we must sheath without a stain. Sorrow and suffering are inseparable from war, but let not the mourners say their dead fell in vain, and that incompetence and timid counsels had inflicted more wounds than the weapons of the Czar. When I look on that battlefield; there standing soldier, sailor, and marine, enduring the scanty food and water, the harassing march, the perpetual alarm, the wearisome watch, the sharpness and cold, the tentless camp, the toil and dangers of the trenches – shell, shot, and sortie – men susceptible of one common nature, animated by the same hope, repugnant to the same pain, and loving life as we do, yet risking all and daring all for the honour and glory of their country – extinction in a moment, eternity in an instant, yet never dismayed, ever hopeful of success, and never faltering in loyalty – I do indeed glory in my native country and that brave brotherhood. And when I recollect how much depends on this continued constancy, how many precious lives are bound up in theirs, I never kneel me down, and other hon. Members I doubt not do the same, but I evoke the blessing of God upon their heads and arms. Our

prayers are offered up that they may return to this country covered with glory and the high sense of duty done.

One of the features of the First World War was that the action took place very close to home. The two previous wars had been fought overseas, many days' sailing away, in the Crimea and South Africa. The battlefields of 1914–18 were a short Channel crossing away. The sound of heavy artillery could be heard from England. Officers and men on leave could return home and enjoy brief respites of ordinary life, bringing with them first-hand accounts of what they had seen and experienced. 'A ridiculous proximity' is how Paul Fussell describes the nearness of the action. He quotes one officer who in 1917 said he had 'breakfasted in the trenches and dined in his club in London.' 'The absurdity of it all became an obsession. One soldier spoke for everyone when he wrote home, "England is so absurdly near."'[126]

By 1914 there had been no fighting on British soil for over 150 years. Wars had been 'adventures' that had happened abroad. The battle honours on the colours of Britain's regiments named places on mainland Europe, Russia and South Africa. Modern war reporting and faster communications had brought news of fighting in those places back to the homeland in graphic form, but nothing compared with the immediacy of the reports from the front. The human cost of war could not be disguised. By the time of the Second World War, the conflict had moved even closer to home. Civilians were at the front: the home front. The Blitz and its attacks on London and Britain's major cities delivered the realities of war to almost everyone.

Other countries had different experiences of the effect of mass communication and the development of mechanized warfare on public perceptions of war. In 1914, in both Europe and America, there were people still alive who had memories of wars being fought on their own soil. They were wars in which civilians had been closely involved. War was not a distant event, but an immediate reality. During the American Civil War families were sometimes divided amongst themselves. As in Europe, there were times when towns and villages were overrun by marching armies looking for food and supplies, who often took what they wanted for themselves. This was nothing new; it had always been thus when armies were on the move. Men and horses had to be fed and before the days of mechanization it was impossible to carry everything required or set up reliable supply lines.

Over the last 150 years the nature of warfare has changed and with those changes have come new ways of perceiving and honouring those taking part. One aspect of Remembrance that has perhaps changed less is that countries honour their heroes more after a victory than a defeat. In 1902 a peace agreement was signed to bring the Boer War to an end. It was a nominal victory, won at a very high price. In June 1902 Lord Tweedmouth's address to the House of Lords typified the attitude of the ruling classes.

> I am sure that the first feeling in the minds of all of us is one of intense gratitude to the higher Power that this war has been brought to a close . . . I fervently hope that all remembrances of an unpleasant character in this war will pass away, and that the only remembrances that will remain in the minds of those who have taken part in the war will be remembrances of the good deeds and the valour which the trial of war has brought out on either side.[127]

As has been observed, war memorials are, with a few exceptions, largely a twentieth-century innovation. Their introduction coincided with developments in the speed of reporting news. With the opportunity to show photographs, the mechanization of the process of battlefield slaughter and also, as Simon Heffer suggests, the fact that people lived longer and enjoyed higher standards of living, a higher price was placed on human life. As the twentieth century progressed the vast majority of babies born survived childhood and those who did could reasonably expect to live to old age. Therefore for young men to die in their thousands in war was an aberration.

Three other factors must also be mentioned. The first is the growth of democracy, whereby every citizen is given a stake in the responsibility for war. Once men fought as a feudal obligation, or because they were 'pressed' into service by the monarch. In modern times, in the West, servicemen and -women go to war at the initiation of a government for which they have had the opportunity to vote. The US government is 'of the people, by the people, for the people', and however much individuals might oppose government policy, that policy is enacted on their behalf and with their authority. As the American Declaration of Independence of 1776 states:

> All men are created equal, that they are endowed by their Creator with certain unalienable Rights, that among these are Life, Liberty and the pursuit of Happiness . . . That to secure these rights, Governments are instituted among Men, deriving their just powers from the consent of the governed.

Democracy is an expression of the second factor: the growth of individualism. In the West no man or woman is identified by tribe or ownership. The human rights of a person are not in the gift of anyone else, whether overlord or tribal leader. Human rights are 'self-evident'. The first four articles of the Universal Declaration of Human Rights state:

> 1. All human beings are born free and equal in dignity and rights. They are endowed with reason and conscience and should act towards one another in a spirit of brotherhood.
> 2. Everyone is entitled to all the rights and freedoms set forth in this Declaration, without distinction of any kind, such as race, colour, sex, language, religion, political or other opinion, national or social origin, property, birth or other status. Furthermore, no distinction shall be made on the basis of the political, jurisdictional or international status of the country or territory to which a person belongs, whether it be independent, trust, non-self-governing or under any other limitation of sovereignty.
> 3. Everyone has the right to life, liberty and security of person.

4. No one shall be held in slavery or servitude; slavery and the slave trade shall be prohibited in all their forms.

The third factor can loosely be called secularism. There remains religious belief in society, but there is no longer universally shared religion. Many people are atheists, others nominal Christians, whilst there are also growing numbers of fundamentalists. In the context of secularism, the wide acceptance of evolution has contributed to people having a different self-identity from that of their forebears. No longer is it commonly acknowledged in society that mankind was a one-off creation of a God. Mankind has evolved over millions of years and, it is said, a product of chance and not purpose. Humans thus have no divine purpose and like any other animal are destined to die and to have their material remains recycled.

Religion provided a source of comfort to people living in ancient societies where death was commonplace. Religion taught that this life had a purpose and was but a brief preparation for a life eternal. Yet as Western culture has grown more secular, the importance of life here and now takes on a far greater significance. For a humanist, life here and now is the only life available. There is no second chance and if a man is killed young it is seen as a wasted life. His potential is unrealized. The only way anything of him survives is in memory. Unless his name is recorded in a public place of Remembrance, it is as if he had never been, and what he was able to achieve in his time on this earth is of no importance. He may be remembered by his family, but his contribution to his community, society and country is in some way nullified unless his name is given some public recognition. As the writer of the Book of Ecclestiasticus wrote over 2,000 years ago,

> There be of them, that have left a name behind them, that their praises might be reported.
> And some there be, which have no memorial; who are perished, as though they had never been; and are become as though they had never been born.[128]

A name on a war memorial provides a hope of some form of immortality, for a name is more than an identity tag or an Army number. In ancient times it was believed that one needed to know a name in order to give a blessing or issue a curse. To know someone's name in life is to know something of that person's identity. A name identifies someone as an individual and not just a member of the human species. Thus to record a name for posterity is to grant a kind of immortality. In an age where there is no agreement on what happens after death, recording a name is an acceptable compromise to both those who believe in an afterlife and those who do not.

In many Western cultures, Remembrance rituals include an explicitly religious element, but it is interesting to note that church leaders often avoid any overt reference to religious belief in life after death.

Following the two minutes' silence in London every year and the laying of wreaths, the Bishop of London leads an inter-denominational Christian service. He leads the outdoor congregation in prayer. The Lord's Prayer is said collectively, a hymn is sung and a blessing given. Yet in the two other prayers offered on behalf of those present, there is no mention of anything of the Christian hope for eternal life. There is not a word about the core Christian doctrine of Christ's conquering of death through the resurrection.

The first is this:

> O Almighty God, grant, we beseech thee, that we who here do honour to the memory of those who have died in the service of their country and of the Crown, may be so inspired by the spirit of their love and fortitude that, forgetting all selfish and unworthy motives, we may live only to thy glory and to the service of mankind through Jesus Christ our Lord.

And the second is the prayer of St Ignatius Loyola:

> Teach us, good Lord, to serve thee as thou deservest;
> to give and not to count the cost;

to fight and not to heed the wounds;
to toil and not to seek for rest;
to labour and not to ask for any reward, save that of
knowing that we do thy will.[129]

Despite the lack of any direct reference to an afterlife at the Cenotaph, British acts of Remembrance are notably more religious in tone than those in many other European countries. In a speech in the House of Lords, the former British foreign secretary Lord Hurd shared a telling story.

I remember going to France on the occasion of the D-day memorial celebrations, in 1994, and attending some of the British service commemorations that took place . . . along the beaches that day. The then French Foreign Minister, Alain Juppé, courteously came with me. Afterwards, I asked him how our services differed from those which would have occurred on a French occasion. He said at once, 'You have much more religion in your form of service. You have hymns and a blessing.'

The Cenotaph service, the naming of the fallen, the wearing of poppies and the new forms of Remembrance are actions and rituals which contain compromises. In the absence of a single set of universally agreed religious teaching about the purpose of life, modern secularism coexists with faith and borrows imagery from many sources, including Christianity. The question of what exactly happens after death remains unaddressed. There is no equivalence to those promises of reward after death in battle that were, and still are, common in many other cultures. Where do dead heroes go? In the pluralistic West there is no official line and folk faith is beginning to fill the vacuum. And yet to give purpose to Remembrance, the observances cannot be left hanging in limbo as an empty secular rite. Enough must be said or implied at the Cenotaph and Albert Hall festival to allow everyone taking part to do so both as one of the community and as an individual with his or her own beliefs or faith. The British are good at ambiguity and the

Church of England, as the established church, is well practised in the art. Listeners are not told how to interpret the words spoken or gestures made. Anyone can put the construction they wish on the words they hear. The words spoken at the Cenotaph do not raise the dead to heroic status, but they do not dissuade people from thinking that way.

In Britain and America in recent times, a new cult of the modern hero has grown. It puts emphasis on the uniqueness of every individual, and the heroic qualities of everyone and anyone who volunteers for military service. In Britain, the newly introduced Armed Forces Day in June lends official support to this view. Parades and celebrations are held to 'pay tribute to our heroes past and present', to quote the 2012 Armed Forces Day publicity. There is an unacknowledged classical input to this notion, in that heroes are the mortals touched by the gods. It is a grassroots response to the contemporary nature of war, which to nations of the West is small-scale, but high-profile. Folk traditions, such as those seen at Wootton Bassett, have grown up in response to the deaths in these conflicts. These traditions have had no input from organized religion.

The British charity Help for Heroes is a product of this age and uses the celebration of heroism to raise money to help servicemen and -women who have been injured or traumatized in current conflicts. The assumption is made that all who opt to become professional soldiers, sailors or airmen and -women are heroes. It is implied that the act of signing up and volunteering is heroic. That the war the heroes are sent to fight might be illegal, immoral, foolish or unjustified is immaterial. That the soldier may be wounded in an accident or by friendly fire, as opposed to in the thick of battle with an enemy, is also by the way. Anyone who wears the uniform and is prepared to fight is a hero by this definition – even, presumably, the three NCOs who beat up a colleague for the offence of wearing the wrong shoes in the mess. They were allowed to remain in the forces after their drink-fuelled acts of violence, while their victim, who had survived Afghanistan, Iraq, Bosnia, Kosovo and Northern Ireland, suffered such severe head injuries and memory loss that they ended his seventeen-year Army career.

The question 'Who is a hero?' has prompted a heated debate within the social network site Facebook. In 2012 a website called 'Soldiers are not Heroes' was set up 'as a means for people to inter-act about the military . . . a uniform does not make a man [*sic*] a hero'. An attempt was made to ban the site from the network. On 11 June the group 'Soldiers Are Heroes' posted the slogan 'People sleep peacefully in their beds at night only because rough men stand ready to do violence on their behalf '.

Help for Heroes focuses on those wounded in current wars.

> It's about the 'blokes', our men and women of the Armed Forces. It's about Derek, a rugby player who has lost both his legs, it's about Carl whose jaw is wired up so he has been drinking through a straw. It's about Richard who was handed a mobile phone as he lay on the stretcher so he could say goodbye to his wife. It's about Ben, it's about Steven and Andy and Mark, it's about them all. They are just blokes but they are our blokes; they are our heroes. We want to help our heroes.

The former Foreign Secretary Lord Owen noted

> I think the charity Help for Heroes has been an outstand-ing success, and at a time when, to put it neutrally, we have not been very well led through two major wars in Afghani-stan and Iraq either militarily or politically. It is amazing that the British people did seem to find their voice and in interesting new ways such as Wootton Bassett and Help for Heroes. That does not mean of course that everyone who serves in the Armed Services is a hero, but it does mean that they deserve and have our respect.[130]

The charity strikes a populist chord. If the Royal British Legion is seen as 'official' and concerned with wars of the past, Help for Heroes is for the ordinary soldier, the Tommy of today. It appears to have grown in strength and popularity as political support for the wars in which British troops are engaged wanes.

Instead of finding justification for these conflicts in national policy or public myth, the individual fighting man and woman are given the central role. Their sacrifices are worthwhile because they themselves are brave and selfless. The cause for which they fight or die is not important; their individual bravery and sacrifice are what bring them honour. This idea turns on its head the official notion that what a soldier does is fight for Queen and country, or to defend freedom – that a soldier forgoes his or her individuality for a wider good. The modern cult of the hero stresses that the individual soldier is essentially heroic whatever cause he or she might be called upon to fight for by politicians.

In the television broadcast *America: A Tribute to Heroes*, aired shortly after the events of 9/11, the singer Mariah Carey took this view to its logical conclusion. In the contemporary hero cult there is a hero in every heart, she claimed. Potentially, everyone is a hero. The hero who comes along to give you strength to face adversity, to help you cast your fears aside and enable you to survive, is found, not by looking for outside help, but by drawing on your inner resources. The truth to be discovered is that heroism lies in you.

The sentiment is the very antithesis of the hero cult of totalitarianism. Under the Nazis the fighting man had no status as an individual. His identity was not important except insofar as he was a member of the tribe, the nation or race. His heroism lay only in what he did to further the wider cause, as a bit player in the propagation of the heroic national myth. By contrast, in twenty-first century Britain the dead soldier being carried in a hearse through Wootton Bassett is a named warrior, afforded a public tribute whatever his or her rank and service record. Currently, in Britain, tribute is paid by name in Parliament to every serviceman or -woman who dies in Afghanistan. His or her photograph will be placed on a heroes' website. He or she is not a cog in a fighting machine. While the politicians might have sent him to die in a futile or pointless war, he died, heroically doing what was expected of him. Wootton Bassett has been renamed Royal Wootton Bassett in recognition of the town's role in honouring the returning the bodies of service personnel who had died abroad. The town was on the route taken by the hearses carrying the repatriated bodies that had landed at nearby RAF Lyneham. Townsfolk stood quietly to attention along the streets as the cortèges came through. This happened over four years and in honour of 345 individuals. The last occasion was in September 2011, and the custom only came to an end when the RAF base used for repatriation was changed.

The Guardian newspaper recorded that

The pattern was a familiar one. The bikers turned up first and parked next to the war memorial . . . Regulars who had travelled from far afield grabbed a cup of tea and a sandwich before making sure of their places. The locals came last, arriving by car, foot and mobility scooter to take part in a ceremony to mark the passing on of a sad honour.

As the sun set on Wootton Bassett, the Wiltshire town that, over the past four years, has become a focus for the nation's grief at the loss of the lives of service personnel in Iraq and Afghanistan, the union flag fluttering next to the war memorial was lowered.

It was carefully folded and left overnight on the altar of St Bartholomew's church before being handed over to the people of Carterton across the border in Oxfordshire, the town which will, from now on, bear witness to the return of coffins carrying men and women killed while on active service abroad.

'I'm sure the people of Carterton will do them proud,' said Ken Scott, 95, who made it his job to collect and preserve the messages, cards and photographs left at the memorial by bereaved families and friends.

'It doesn't matter whether they come back through Wootton Bassett or wherever. What does matter is that those poor boys and girls are honoured.'

Since 2007, the bodies of service personnel have been repatriated via RAF Lyneham and taken on to a hospital in Oxford via Wootton Bassett's high street.

To honour the dead, the people of Bassett, as everyone here calls it, took to pausing in their everyday life when a cortege passed. Over the months and years they were joined by an ever-growing number of bereaved families, veterans' groups and ordinary people (including a fair few leather-clad bikers), some of whom travelled many miles to pay tribute.

By 2009, at the height of the conflict in Afghanistan, thousands of people were lining the streets of this modest little town.

The Wootton Bassett phenomenon has been extraordinary. It began almost by chance when a former mayor, Percy Miles, was out shopping with his wife in the spring of 2007. Someone from the town council ran out to tell him that a cortege was coming through. Nothing had been planned but he dashed home, put on his mayoral robes and stood to attention as the body was driven through.

'I was amazed it became such a huge thing. Bassett has done wonders over the years,' said Miles. 'I didn't go to all of them because it hurt too much and I won't go to Brize Norton for the same reason. I get too emotional. I feel strongly we shouldn't be out in Afghanistan in the first place.'[131]

Herein, in the words of the former mayor, perhaps lies the clue as to why the Wootton Bassett phenomenon occurred. It was to pay 'respects', but also acted as a public admonishment to the politicians. It was a way of saying 'we don't agree with the war'. Our troops are volunteers who train and serve to defend the nation. They are our sons, daughters, husbands and wives, brothers and sisters who have nobly and courageously agreed to defend our freedoms and take up arms on our behalf, yet you, the politicians, are sending them abroad on futile or illegal missions. You do not even have the wit to provide them with the right equipment and should they return home wounded in body or mind you wash your hands of responsibility. Nevertheless, they do no flinch, but do their duty. This is why each one who dies has earned our respect.

The notion of a hero makes no distinction in rank. Privates and generals alike are celebrated. It was one of the distinguishing features of the British Legion when it was founded that help was given according to need and not rank and that there should be no separate section of the organization for the officer class.

The First World War raised the social standing of the ordinary combatant. Previously privates and the lower ranks were of low standing. Often they were drawn from what were perceived as the dregs of society, or had volunteered in desperation to find a job and food to eat. One survey of recruits in 1839 observed that those aged over 25 who enlisted were 'habitually dissipated and profligate characters, broken-down gentlemen, discharged soldiers, deserters etc.'[132]

By the time of the First World War, social change was having an effect. The ordinary man had a vote. Rates of literacy had risen sharply and there was a popular press. The impression that the privileged officers who were organizing the war were a bunch of incompetents gained pace too.

Kipling's poem in praise of the Tommy of the British Army struck a chord.

> You talk o' better food for us, an' schools, an' fires, an' all:
> We'll wait for extry rations if you treat us rational.
> Don't mess about the cook-room slops, but prove it to our face
> The Widow's Uniform is not the soldier-man's disgrace.
> For it's Tommy this, an' Tommy that, an' 'Chuck him out,
>   the brute!'
> But it's 'Saviour of 'is country' when the guns begin to shoot;
> An' it's Tommy this, an' Tommy that, an' anything you please;
> An' Tommy ain't a bloomin' fool – you bet that Tommy sees!

The raising of everyone in uniform to the status of hero and the cult of the Tommy can, in some circumstances, help focus Remembrance on the ordinary soldier. This helps to emphasize the human dimension of war and that armies are made up of men and not fighting machines. Some towns and villages have a tradition by which all the individual names on their local war memorial are read aloud on Remembrance Sunday. Often the surnames are still commonly found in the community. One effect of this, however, is to widen the gap between 'our boys' and 'the enemy'. The more our troops are seen as real people, the less human in comparison the enemy becomes.

The logical consequence of this perception of the value of every individual member of the forces can be seen in the technological innovations of war. Unmanned aerial vehicles (UAVs), also known as 'drones', are regularly used to attack sites in Pakistan and Afghanistan. As American casualties are reduced to a minimum, the enemy's humanity becomes correspondingly reduced. They become as expendable as digital targets in a computer game.

The drones may be flown by pilots thousands of miles from the target or programmed to function autonomously without any direct human control. The American military drones honing in on targets in Afghanistan, Pakistan and Iraq are controlled from Creech Air Force Base in Nevada. It is believed that the CIA has drones in the same area of conflict controlled from their headquarters in Langley, Virginia. They were initially developed for surveillance, but later generations can now drop explosives.

Drones are increasing the remote and robotic nature of modern hi-tech warfare. They are encouraging a 'Play-Station mentality' amongst the troops where killing is simply watching the movement of figures or vehicles on the ground, pushing a button and seeing them engulfed in an explosion plume. There is a huge margin of error, often because of faulty intelligence, and civilian casualties are mounting. There is no measure for the terror and psychological damage being done to the millions of children and adults who are in the constant sights of these predators.[133]

The future of warfare might be like something out of science fiction and be entirely virtual. Cadres of highly competent video game players will be the front-line troops, causing massive damage from a distance and never facing danger themselves. The adrenaline rush of playing these lethal games would provide these armchair troops with a new motive for going to war. But even in the present world it has to be stated that there are people who enjoy war. There are many people in Britain who lived through the Second World War who look back on the period with nostalgia. It was a time when society gave everyone a role to play. Everyone was important, whether as combatants, serving as fire watchers or air raid wardens, making munitions or 'keeping the home fires burning'. After the war some never again achieved a position of such significance in the community. Their brief taste of excitement and importance faded into memory as they returned to insignificant humdrum lives.

There will be some for whom Remembrance provides a reminder of those times. Every November they will relive the war years in mind and memory. The human mind has the gift of hiding the hurtful and promoting welcome memories.

An article in *Amnesty International Magazine* explored the unacknowledged pleasures some people derive from taking part in war. The author Chris Hedges, one of the *New York Times* team that won the 2002 Pulitzer Prize for reporting on global terrorism, owned up to his emotional attachment to warfare.

War and conflict have marked most of my adult life. I have been in ambushes on desolate stretches of Central American roads, locked in unnerving firefights in the marshes in southern Iraq, imprisoned in the Sudan, beaten by Saudi military police, deported from Libya and Iran, captured and held for a week by Iraqi Republican Guards, strafed by Russian Mig-21s in central Bosnia, shot at by Serb snipers and shelled with deafening rounds of artillery in Sarajevo that threw out thousands of deadly bits of iron fragments. I have seen too much of violent death. I have tasted too much of my own fear. I have painful memories that lie buried most of the time. It is never easy when they surface.

And yet there is a part of me that remains nostalgic for war's simplicity and high. The enduring attraction of war is this: Even with its destruction and carnage it gives us what we all long for in life. It gives us purpose, meaning, a reason for living. Only when we are in the midst of conflict does the shallowness and vapidness of our lives become apparent. Trivia dominates our conversations and increasingly our news. And war is an enticing elixir. It gives us resolve, a cause. It allows us to be noble. And those that have the least meaning in their lives-the impoverished refugees in Gaza, the disenfranchised North African immigrants in France, even the lost legions of youth that live in the splendid indolence and safety of the industrialized world-are all susceptible to war's appeal.

Chris Hedges identified three aspects of war that made it an attractive option: war seen as a culture in and of itself; war as the embodiment of heroic myth; and war as a crusade.

I learned early on that war forms its own culture. The rush of battle is a potent and often lethal addiction, for war is a drug, one I ingested for many years. It is peddled by myth makers – historians, war correspondents, filmmakers novelists and the state – all of whom endow it with qualities it often does possess: excitement, exoticism, power, chances to rise above our small stations in life, and a bizarre and fantastic universe that has a grotesque and dark beauty. It dominates culture, distorts memory, corrupts language and infects everything around it, even humor, which becomes preoccupied with the grim perversities of smut and death. Fundamental questions about the meaning, or meaninglessness, of our place on the planet are laid bare when we watch those around us sink to the lowest depths. War exposes the capacity for evil that lurks just below the surface within all of us.

And so it takes little in wartime to turn ordinary men into killers. Most give themselves willingly to the seduction of unlimited power to destroy, and all feel the peer pressure. Few, once in bottle, can find the strength to resist.

The historian Christopher Browning noted the willingness to kill in *Ordinary Men*, his study of Reserve Police

Battalion 101 in Poland during World War II. On the morning of 12 July 1942, the battalion was ordered to shoot 1800 Jews in the village of Jozefow in a day-long action. The men in the unit had to round up the Jews, march them into the forest and one by one order them to lie down in a row. The victims, including women, infants, children and the elderly, were shot dead at close range.

Battalion members were offered the option to refuse, an option only about a dozen men took, although more asked to be relieved once the killing began. Those who did not want to continue, Browning says, were disgusted rather than plagued by conscience. When the men returned to the barracks they 'were depressed, angered, embittered and shaken.' They drank heavily. They were told not to talk about the event, 'but they needed no encouragement in that direction.'

Turning to war as myth, Hedges admitted how his own profession was at fault. They failed to report conflict fully.

The most recent U.S. conflicts have insulated the public and U.S. troops from both the disgust and pangs of conscience. The Gulf War – waged from bombers high above the fray and reported by carefully controlled journalists – made war fashionable again. It was a cause the nation willingly embraced. It exorcised the ghosts of Vietnam. It gave us heroes and the heady belief in our own military superiority and technology. It almost made war fun. And the chief culprit was, as in many conflicts, not the military but the press. Television reporters happily disseminated the spoon-fed images that served the propaganda effort of the military and the state. These images did little to convey the reality of war. Pool reporters, those guided around in groups by the military, wrote once again about 'our boys' eating packaged army food, practicing for chemical weapons attacks and bathing out of buckets in the desert. It was war as spectacle, war, if we are honest, as entertainment. The images and stories were designed to make us feel good about our nation, about ourselves. The families and soldiers being blown to bits by iron fragmentation bombs just over the border in Iraq were faceless and nameless phantoms.

The moment I stepped off an Army C-130 military transport in Dhahran, Saudi Arabia, to cover the Persian Gulf War, I was escorted to a room with several dozen other reporters and photographers. I was told to sign a paper that said I would abide by the severe restrictions placed on the press. The restrictions authorized 'pool reporters' to be escorted by the military on field trips. Most of the press sat in hotel rooms and rewrote the bland copy filed by the pool or used the pool video and photos. I violated this agreement the next morning when I went into the field without authorization. The rest of the war, most of which I spent dodging Military Police and trying to talk my way into units, was a forlorn and lonely struggle against the heavy press control.

The notion that the press was used in the war is incorrect. The press wanted to be used. It saw itself as part of the war effort. Most reporters sent to cover a war don't really want to go near the fighting. They do not tell this to their editors and indeed will moan and complain about restrictions. The handful who actually head out into the field have a bitter enmity with the hotel room warriors. But even those who do go out are guilty of distortion – maybe more so. For they not only believe the myth, feed off of the drug, but also embrace the cause. They may do it with more skepticism. They certainly expose more lies and misconceptions. But they believe. We all believe. When you stop believing you stop going to war.

I knew a Muslim soldier, a father, who fought on the front lines around Sarajevo. His unit, in one of the rare attempts to take back a few streets controlled by the Serbs, pushed across Serb lines. They did not get very far. The fighting was heavy. As he moved down the street, he heard a door swing open and fired a burst from his AK-47 assault rifle. A 12-year-old girl dropped dead. He saw in the body of the unknown girl lying prostrate in front of him the image of his own 12-year-old daughter. He broke down. He had to be helped back to the city. He was lost for the rest of the war, shuttered inside his apartment, nervous, morose and broken. This experience is far more typical of warfare than the Rambo heroics we are fed by the state and the entertainment industry. The cost of killing is all the more bitter because of the deep disillusionment that war usually brings.

But that disillusionment is not immediate, as Hedges wrote when looking at the third aspect of war – as crusade.

The disillusionment comes later. Each generation again responds to war as innocents. Each generation discovers its own disillusionment-often at a terrible price.

'We believed we were there for a high moral purpose,' wrote Philip Caputo in his book on Vietnam, *Rumor of War*. 'But somehow our idealism was lost, our morals corrupted, and the purpose forgotten.'

Once again the United States stands poised on the threshold of war. 'We go forward', President George W. Bush assures us, 'to defend freedom and all that is good and just in the world.' He is not shy about warning other states that they either stand with us in the war on terrorism or will be counted as aligned with those that defy us. This too is a crusade.

But the war on terrorism is different in that we Americans find ourselves in the dangerous position of going to war not against a state but a phantom. The crusade we have embarked upon in the war on terrorism is targeting an elusive and protean enemy. The battle we have begun is never-ending. But it may be too late to wind back the heady rhetoric. We have embarked on a campaign as quixotic as the one mounted to destroy us. As it continues, as terrorist attacks intrude on our lives, as we feel less and less secure, the acceptance of all methods to lash out at real and perceived enemies will distort and deform our democracy.

And yet, the campaign's attraction seems irresistible. War makes the world understandable, a black-and-white tableau of them and us. It suspends thought, especially self-critical thought. All bow before the supreme effort. We are one. Most of us willingly accept war as long as we can fold it into a belief system that paints the ensuing suffering as necessary for a higher good; for human beings seek not only happiness but also meaning. And tragically, war is sometimes the most powerful way in human society to achieve meaning.[134]

One way to reduce the temptation to go to war is for nations, leaders, opinion-formers and the media to reduce the appeal of war. It is to look for ways to ensure that those who go to war do not rise in the esteem of others and themselves. It is to find alternative stories to tell about war that negate the heroic myths. It is to calm the language of crusades. It is counter the tendency of war to become a culture of its own with its abnormal moral codes of behaviour.

Remembrance can only have a role to play in achieving these aims if it ceases to create heroic myths and to give participants a raised sense of self-esteem. But for many veterans, Remembrance Day is the only day in the year when they can wear their medals and march through the streets, with heads held high and be proud of the deeds of their youth; or, at least, the deeds as recalled as reconstructions in their minds. No change to Remembrance should steal this moment from them, but yet society must be aware of the downside of such displays of pride in the nation's military past.

9

REMEMBRANCE IN THE
TWENTY-FIRST CENTURY

FEW THINGS ARE AS GUARANTEED TO ENRAGE POPULAR OPINION in any nation as public displays of disrespect to national symbols of identity. In many countries, to dishonour the flag leads to arrest and imprisonment. In the USA there has been much debate as to whether desecrating the flag should be a crime, and in many states it is already a punishable offence. It is the case in most countries that anyone found guilty by a court of vandalizing a national monument attracts a far sharper punishment than might have been received for trashing any other form of public or private property.

Britain might take a more tolerant attitude to flags, as the Union Flag has been hijacked both by fashion designers and right-wing political parties without legal reprisals, but is very protective of its most potent symbol of national identity, its Remembrance traditions. As previously mentioned, there was a fierce outcry when a group of militant Muslims took the opportunity of the two minutes' silence to voice a protest. An even greater sense of outrage was expressed when Charlie Gilmour, a Cambridge University undergraduate and the adopted son of Pink Floyd guitarist David Gilmour, was arrested for swinging from a flag on the Cenotaph during a student street protest in December 2010. It was the most memorable and infamous image of a day of protest which also involved an attack on a car carrying Prince Charles and the Duchess of Cornwall.

When Gilmour was given a sixteen-month prison sentence he received little media or public sympathy for the disrespect he had shown to the focal national monument of Remembrance. His lawyers and parents argued that his actions had been completely out of character and the sentence was 'unduly harsh', but the appeal court judges were unmoved. They ruled that the penalty could not be described as 'manifestly excessive or wrong in principle'.

Charlie Gilmour was said to be 'out of his mind' on LSD, whisky and Valium when, to quote the *Daily Mail*, 'he indulged in outrageous and deeply offensive behaviour'. He was jailed after admitting a charge of violent disorder. As well as swinging on the Union Flag at the Cenotaph, he also hurled a bin at a car with the Royal Party, jumped on the bonnet of the car carrying protection officers and twice kicked a window of an Oxford Street store. Gilmour said in personal mitigation that he had not realized that it was the Cenotaph flag on which he was swinging. His claim of ignorance produced a public reaction of incredulity. How could a privileged, well-educated young man not be aware of the signifi-cance of what he was doing and where? The appeal judges called his action 'deeply offensive' and said that he was acting in an 'exhibitionist manner' and that he was at times 'over-excited, out of control, and raising the temperature in a manner which could only be dangerous in the context of a large and angry crowd.' (After serving his sentence, Gilmour heard in March 2012 that he would be allowed to resume his studies at Cambridge.)

Gilmour has not been the only student to appear in court for desecrating a war memorial. In 2009, in the course of a seven-hour drinking binge in Sheffield, nineteen-year-old Philip Laing, a sports technology student from Hallam University, urinated on the city's memorial to the dead of the First World War. In court the student was told that a prison sentence had been an option given serious consideration, but the judge said he had 'never seen anyone before him who was more contrite' and Laing was given 250 hours of community service. The judge told him,

The image of your urinating over the wreath of poppies at the city war memorial was a truly shocking one. That is no understatement. There you are, a young man of 19, urinating on the war memorial erected to honour the memory of so many other young men. You have understandably had the wrath and indignation of the public heaped upon you and your family.

War memorials across Britain have also suffered from acts of destructive vandalism as well as student disrespect. In February 2009 a concrete slab was thrown at a memorial in Stamford, Lincolnshire. A month later graffiti was scrawled over a memorial in Oxford. That same month a swastika was sprayed in bright blue paint over the names of the dead on a memorial in Fleetwood, Lancashire. Spray paint was in action again in April in Cardiff; in July a Merseyside Garden of Remembrance was wrecked; in August there were acts of destruction reported from Allenton in Derbyshire, Briton Ferry, South Wales and North Rigton, Yorkshire. The list is unrelenting. Yet perhaps even more offensive to the British public than either the sight of drink and drug-fuelled students desecrating the nation's Remembrance shrines, or acts of mindless vandalism, has been the systematic and deliberate vandalism of war memorials for financial gain.

In October 2011, a bronze plaque was stolen from a war memorial in Twickenham, Middlesex. In Tidworth in Wiltshire thieves stole the bronze statue of a Second World War soldier from a memorial. When CCTV footage was later reviewed two men were seen taking the statue from its plinth and driving away with it – presumably to melt down and sell the metal for cash. On 29 September 2011 a police patrol came across three men in the grounds of the War Memorial Park in Low Road, Conisbrough, Yorkshire. When the officers gave chase on foot the trio fled, discarding a bronze plaque on which the names of the town's war dead were engraved. Similar crimes have been reported from Walsall, Portsmouth, Southampton, Prestbury in Gloucestershire and many other sites around Britain. Thefts have been so numerous that many war memorials have been marked with ultraviolet marks to enable the metal to be identified if stolen. The spate of thefts have coincided with the rise in the price of scrap metal. Thieves have been targeting any metal they can 'recycle', whether from churches or war memorials. Frances Moreton, director of the War Memorials Trust, confirmed the rise in instances of theft in line with the rise in metal prices.

We used to hear of one theft a week at the start of the year, it rose to two or three over the summer . . . There have been cases of stuff being put of for sale on the internet but increasingly it is the case of metal being stolen because of its scrap value.

In October 2011 the Trust was dealing with 300 cases a month; this was believed to be an underestimation of the scale of the problem, as many cases of theft and vandalism went unreported.

At one point, both war memorials and churches would have been protected by a universally shared sense that to target either would have been socially unacceptable or blasphemous. To steal from a church would have risked divine punishment. Sacred places and objects had an almost superstitious protection. Today few such inhibitions are prevalent, although some scrap metal merchants have, to their credit, refused to accept stolen memorials and the thieves have had to accept lower prices from unofficial and unscrupulous dealers. Churches are regularly stripped of roof lead and to many criminals today a war memorial is of little more than passing historic interest, if that. Arrests suggest that the thieves are young and thus none of the names recorded can mean anything to them. They have no sense of the grief attached to the memorials when they were first raised, financed by local subscription. The sense of community that existed then, and a social cohesiveness which resulted from shared spiritual and cultural values, no longer applies. The passing years have distanced the current generation from the values and shared experiences of their grandparents. This is no excuse for loutish or criminal behaviour, but perhaps offers a partial explanation. Court reports suggest that those apprehended and charged with vandalism to war memorials are aged generally between fourteen and eighteen. A fifteen-year-old girl was believed to have sprayed the Wolverhampton War Memorial with graffiti in 2010; a sixteen-year-old was arrested following the painting of a swastika on the memorial in Southampton in 2011. When police were investigating the damage to the Prestbury memorial they took a CCTV image around local school and colleges.

If Remembrance is a distant and difficult concept for those born a generation after the end of the Second World War, then how much more distant must it seem to their children? So much has changed in over 60 years that many young people must find it hard to engage with the generation that cherishes and values the memorials. What then do children of the 1990s make of the rituals associated with Remembrance? If, passing by a memorial on Remembrance Sunday, they notice the marching columns and hear the bugle calls, what does it mean to them? Many of them must be baffled by what they see going on. To them the time-honoured Remembrance traditions must look very strange. The flags, poppy wreaths, military music and the declamations must seem very odd. In the same way that for those who have not been brought up to go to church, going to a religious service can be an alien and alien-ating experience, the rituals of Remembrance must seem worry-ingly off-putting. They may appear like the peculiar ceremonials of a members-only club, a kind of open-air Freemasonry. Nothing in the ritual, as it is performed by old men in berets, carrying flags and wearing their medals, suggests that it exists as an ongoing reminder of the evils of war.

The Royal British Legion is aware of the need to be involved in education and provides school with classroom material, teach-ing guides and model assemblies. One of the suggested poems to be used is 'Remember' by the nineteenth-century poet Christina Rossetti.

Remember me when I am gone away,
Gone far away into the silent land;
When you can no more hold me by the hand,
Nor I half turn to go, yet turning stay.
Remember me when no more day by day
You tell me of our future that you plann'd:
Only remember me; you understand
It will be late to counsel then or pray.
Yet if you should forget me for a while
And afterwards remember, do not grieve:
For if the darkness and corruption leave

A vestige of the thoughts that once I had,
Better by far you should forget and smile
Than that you should remember and be sad.

It is a poem written well before the First World War. It focuses on
the relationship between the living and the dead without any
reference to war, violence or premature death. It is appropriate for
a school assembly in autumn, at the time when all the dead are recalled. It has no special relevance to war dead, either the 'glorious
sacrifice' or 'pointless waste' of death on the battlefield. In other
material provided by the Legion the wars of the last 100 years are,
of course, examined and the standard account of the origins and
purpose of Remembrance is given. The material focuses on the
poppy as a symbol and retells the British national story of the
twentieth century, very much in a sanitized version. It does not
dodge the issues of disability and genocide that are the inevitable
consequence of war, but fails to convey the true nature of the
suffering. It fails to analyse the causes of conflict or reflect on
the ethics of war. As the Rossetti poem indicates, the tone is often
sentimental and the portrayal of service personnel as brave,
glorious, heroic and sacrificial gives a one-sided image of the combatant's lot.

Remembrance literature designed for young people in many
other countries has a similar feel. One school resource handbook
provided by The US Department of Veterans Affairs and the
Veterans Day National Committee to schools in 2006 said in its
preamble: 'It is our hope that by thanking America's veterans and
their families for their service and sacrifice, we can reward them
with the honor they so richly deserve.' The book included a section
on showing respect to the flag.

The Pledge of Allegiance to the Flag should be given by
standing at attention facing the flag with the right hand
over the heart.
    On Memorial Day, the flag should be flown at half-
staff from sunrise until noon. Always hoist the U.S. flag
briskly. Lower it slowly and ceremoniously.

> Never show disrespect to the U.S. flag, place anything on it, draw on it or use it as anything but as a flag. Never display the U.S. flag with the stars at the bottom, except as a distress signal.

What impact does the standard portrayal of Remembrance have on the generation of British, European and American young people that have no first-hand experience of the evils of war? Even more than their parents, this younger generation has, in the West, enjoyed a lifetime of protection from risk and danger. It is a generation that interacts with computer screens and much of its image of war comes from the electronic media. Nothing in the Remembrance ceremonial counters their image of war as exciting and heroic. Whether portrayed in film or video game, war, as seen by the computer and television generation, does not involve pain or blood. It is high-tech excitement.

There is a genre of video game that is particular popular with young men. 'From the beaches of Normandy to the jungles of Vietnam and the wars of the 22nd century, nothing gets you closer to the action', reads the promotional text for the game *Battlefield 3*.

> With more than 20 million copies sold worldwide, the Battlefield series is the premier tactical shooter. Consistently hailed by critics as one of the best online experiences in gaming, Battlefield allows you to fire realistic weaponry, pilot genuine vehicles and participate in real-world conflicts against friend and foe alike. Whether it's the classic Battlefield 1942, the irreverent Battlefield: Bad Company or the upcoming, groundbreaking Battlefield 3, Battlefield is the king of action-packed shooters and online combat. Since 2002, no series has put you closer to the front lines of combat in a more authentic way. Join us on the Battlefield.

The action of the game focuses on noise, explosions and the excitement of battle. There is no fear, danger, smell or grief.

Here is a review of another popular game, *Soldiers of Anarchy*:

> Sometimes you get tired of saving the World by controlling vast amounts of air, sea, and land power, and you just want to go back to the good old days when you were an NCO in charge of a squad. Enter Soldiers of Anarchy. You're the leader of a small group of survivors of an apocalyptic inferno. After months of isolation, you decide to venture out from your safe-haven to discover what has happened to the World around you. Small unit tactics are definitely a player here. To succeed, you must make the right choices at the right time. An interesting feature makes it advisable not to waste your troops. The longer an individual troop stays alive, the more experienced he/she becomes, and are able to perform more specialized missions.[135]

Arguably it is better that a generation of young men vents its anger and energy via a virtual game than on the real battlefields of war. Yet in playing a dehumanized war game, might they become more willing to condone war as a real-life strategy? Could they view 'our heroes' in Afghanistan as another version of their computer fantasies?

Even news reports of real and current wars focus on the technology and not the killing. Missiles are shown being launched, but not impacting. There are reports of Scud and Cruise missiles and Exocet rockets, television shots of computer-controlled warheads honing in on their targets. If explosions are seen, they are from the safe distance of the hotels where the international press corp is staying. The more explosions, the greater the drama in the 'live' television reports.

If there is little in the way Remembrance is seen or portrayed that conveys the reality of war, there is nothing that conveys that other, hidden agenda of Remembrance: atonement. For veterans the annual rituals are a reminder, and perhaps not a welcome one, of the deeds they performed as soldiers of which they are not proud. The times when they crossed normal moral boundaries. Soldiers in all armies do things which, years later, they profoundly regret. Are there American veterans standing smartly to attention, wearing their Vietnam medals, who in their youth took macabre souvenirs? On the day they recall their fallen comrades, do they also have flashbacks to the time when they mutilated bodies to have ears, breasts or penises to show their comrades? Remembrance refers to 'glorious dead', but not to the guilt-ridden living. Guilt is a common emotion brought back from conflict by veterans; the guilt that comrades died and they survived; the guilt that in the heat of battle they could have done something different to have protected a colleague; guilt for having killed another human being. Even guilt, in a minority of cases, for complicity in acts that clearly overstepped accepted notions of moral behaviour.

Herold Noel was as a tank refueller with the 3rd Infantry, 7th Cavalry, sent as part of the US Army to Iraq during the Second Gulf War. When he returned home in August 2003 he could not believe that he had survived.

> When I came back, it was unreal to me because I was supposed to be dead . . . When I first got back, I couldn't believe I was alive. I couldn't believe I was looking at people. I couldn't believe I was hugging my kids. I couldn't even touch my kids at a point, because I had seen kids die over there. I was looking at a little girl in Iraq who got her head blown off, and I'm looking at my daughter. The girl was the same age as my daughter.[136]

There are probably thousands of men like Herold Noel. Ordinary, decent, sensitive men who joined the military, saw action and returned to civilian life with such vivid memories of what they witnessed that they will never be erased.

In 1919 there were millions of ex-servicemen in that category, with painful, abiding recollections of the unspeakable scenes they had witnessed. Alongside them, on the first Armistice Day, there were millions of civilians in shock and mourning. Their grief may also have been tainted with guilt and regret. Their last memory of their husbands might not have been of a romantic farewell, but a row. Why had he joined up? Was not his first duty to his wife and family and not his country? And how did the wife feel who had cheated on her husband in his absence? What unresolved anger and guilt existed beneath the tears of sorrow shed on Armistice Day? And how did those feel who, like Kipling, had encouraged their sons to go to war and yet stayed at home themselves?

In the twenty-first century it is very different. The generation without a personal commitment, or understanding, of grief or guilt is asked to acknowledge 'the fallen' in an abstract, idealized form. In the 1970s there was an expectation that Remembrance would fade away as the older generation died. In recent times new wars have produced new casualties. Not in such vast numbers to touch every family in the nation, but nevertheless in sufficient numbers to revive an interest in the rituals of Remembrance. The few who serve are now all raised to the rank of hero in public perception. Their deeds are glorified and sentimentalized by a generation that mostly has no knowledge of the pain and cost of war.

Remembrance has to be marketed to grab attention in a world crowded with commercial messages. The poppy, that once sorrowful symbol of grief and a rededication to peace, is branded as an icon of pride in the military. The image has to be focused in such a way as to raise the most money for the legion's ongoing work. To do this image-makers and marketing experts have to know which emotional strings to pull. The rapid rise to prominence of Help for Heroes, which appeals to the same constituency as the Poppy Appeal, suggests which marketing image works best. The image it has chosen to portray is that of the organization for the hero squaddies. It positions itself as the service organization that understands best the needs of today's soldier serving in Afghanistan. Its online bookshop reflects the interests of supporters, and offers for sale macho titles such as *Everyone a Hero*, *Bullet Proof*, *Soft Target*, *Man Down* and *Real Heroes: Courage under Fire*. The bookshop offers a mix of fiction and true stories about heroes, often told by heroes. The Help for Heroes fundraising has been strongly supported by Britain's leading mass-circulation red-top tabloid. In 2009 *The Sun* claimed that its support had helped raise £30 million in the charity's first two years. *The Sun* has had a close association with Help for Heroes since the charity was founded in 2007 and one of the paper's columnists, Jeremy Clarkson, the controversial *Top Gear* presenter of famed illiberal opinions, was a founding patron. *The Sun* has also financed a television advertisement to help fundraise.

The Poppy Appeal remains as market leader. It is the brand most closely associated by the older generation with the traditions of Remembrance. It has the advantage that its main fundraising push comes in the autumn and coincides with the ancient season of the dead. In marketing terms, any item that is associated with a special time of year sells well in season, whether Easter eggs, pumpkins or Christmas puddings.

Following a century in which the two most devastating wars of history were fought, Remembrance observations have become established as the contemporary expression of the traditional autumnal season of the dead. Yet as time passes and the veterans of war die, a new generation emerges which does not know the grief and trauma of war. They add new meaning to Remembrance and the occasion also becomes an opportunity to affirm national identity. It is also the time when the new generation identifies with the armed services and raises all members of the services to heroic status. The spirit of the occasion has also changed in line with the expectations, demands and norms of a consumer society.

The Remembrance rituals have hardly changed over 90 years, although the meaning attached to them has. If alterations are made to the rituals they should be to reaffirm some of the original ideals of Remembrance that have altered over time. In particular, Remembrance should remind the present and future generations of the horrors of war and the widespread grief and sorrow it causes. Fundamental to this is the restoration of the prime and original meaning of Remembrance and the wearing of the poppy, as a public commitment to peace.

To those who have suffered from war, to the survivors of the Second World War, to the families and widows of servicemen who have died, to the veterans of recent wars nursing the mental and physical wounds of war and seeing their comrades killed, Remembrance brings comfort. For this reason alone it must continue. It also brings an opportunity for private atonement, the largely un-recognised function of the rituals.

But few of those who derive comfort from Remembrance would object to changes that would reduce the chances of others needing to fight and suffer. It has been argued since the 1920s that the militarism associated with Remembrance is inappropriate. If there is any chance, however remote, that it is seen to glorify, sanitise or glamorize war, then there must be a case for change. There should be no hint that Remembrance serves to hallow or condone the baser instincts of human kind that derive excitement from war. It is of genuine and pressing concern to many that the spectacle, choreography and music of remembrance might tend to rouse the wrong emotions. They should not induce pride in the profession of arms. It would be better if they induced a sense of reflection and shame that nations still go to war.

When the ancient and primal season of the dead becomes confused with the cultural and national rituals of honouring, hallowing, sanctifying, justifying and even sentimentalizing the dead of past and present wars, then a key element of Remembrance, as originally envisaged and practiced 90 years ago, gets overlooked.

That element is to remind future generations that despite national affronts, jingoistic excitement, the promise of glory and adventure and the feelings of duty, fear and insecurity that result in wars, war itself, although sometimes sadly necessary, is essentially vile, horrible, demeaning and degrading to the human spirit. It can be hoped that by enacting certain sensitive changes to the observances, Remembrance might be restored to its original purpose.

It would be a tragedy for the nation and an insult to the war dead if Remembrance were to become a divisive issue. Early signs of a divide are already apparent and changes to the observances might heal a crack in the social fabric before it becomes a chasm. Is Remembrance about standing shoulder to shoulder with our troops, 'our heroes', or is it about recalling the horrors of war and re-dedicating the nation to peace? To some it is the former, to others the latter. Can it be about both? During the two minutes' silence, everyone has their own thoughts, but in the public rituals, Remembrance must be poignant, neutral and all-inclusive.

POSTSCRIPT: SOME
PRACTICAL CHANGES

THE FIRST CHANGE PROPOSED IS ONE THAT MIGHT BE UNI-versally welcomed by the public, but strongly resisted by those with their own special interest and agenda at Remembrance-tide. The practice of the party political leaders, and others holding political office, laying wreaths at the Cenotaph should be discontinued. A clear distinction should be made between those whose failures or ambitions result in wars and those whose duty it is to risk being killed in conflict. In countries where the head of state is also the head of government, making this separation will be harder than in countries where the two offices are clearly delineated. In Britain the separation is easily made as the monarch stays irreproachably out of political decision-making. Therefore in Britain the laying of wreaths by the politicians could be discontinued without any major alteration being made to the Cenotaph ceremony. The politicians might protest at such a move. To be at the Cenotaph is viewed as one of the honours of office and who should be seen there looking serious and important for the cameras is a matter of significance to the political class.

Lord Owen, former Foreign Secretary and party leader says that he remembers

> with some pride when I laid wreath as Foreign secretary and it has only been a very rare occasion since then that I have been unable to watch the ceremony on TV.
>
> I was glad I played a part in the negotiations that I had with Margaret Thatcher over the representation of the

SDP at the Cenotaph which was initially refused in 1983. But eventually a formula was established in 1984, with the agreement of the Queen and the Speaker of the House of Commons, following discussions with party leaders. This stipulates that only the leaders at Westminster of parties that win (and take up) six or more seats at the preceding General Election should lay wreaths.

I was glad when that formula was slightly amended so that, should the joint Parliamentary Group of the SNP and Plaid Cymru at Westminster pass the six seat threshold, the leader of one party would be entitled to lay a wreath on behalf of both, with the wreath-layer alternating each year. There have been no subsequent changes to this formula and I currently see no reason for further changes.[137]

That is not to say that jockeying behind the scenes between serving politicians are a thing of the past. There continue to be undignified squabbles over the details of the event; particularly about who should lay wreaths and in what order.

If there were no politicians at the Cenotaph, there would be no opportunity for party political points to be scored. Much more important, deliberately excluding them from any prominent position would be a reminder to all members of the political class that they are the people whose failures and enthusiasms, delusions and opportunism, result in troops being killed.

A second area of possible change to Remembrance Day involves the music chosen for the occasion. The key question to be asked is: is the military music associated with Remembrance appropriate to a day both of recollection of past sacrifice and rededication to peace, in the present and the future?

There is a chapter in Richard Holmes's *Soldiers* entitled 'Tunes of Glory' which examines the role of music in military life. Initially music had a functional purpose in communicating orders. Before the days of electronic communication, bugle calls and drum beats conveyed messages. Music too had a role in the bonding process, the cementing of comradeship and *esprit de corps*. Thus regiments have their own tunes. Some tunes are instantly recognizable, like 'The British Grenadiers'; others may only be connected to the regiment by those in the know. The gallop march of the Royal Horse Artillery is a version of the tune 'Bonny Dundee' and the Royal Corps of Signals marches to 'Begone Dull Care'. In many cases regiments adapted folk tunes from the district where they recruited. Many regiments today maintain their own bands and in Britain, the Royal Military School of Music at Kneller Hall near Twickenham has trained musicians for over 150 years. It trains all soldiers joining the Corps of Army Music. Tuition is delivered by some of Britain's leading instrumental and academic professors, many of whom play in leading symphony orchestras or teach in the London music colleges.

Scottish regiments maintained pipers whose role in battle was to inspire and rally the troops. The legendary Bill Millin piped the invasion D-Day forces ashore. He played unflinchingly as men fell all around him.

Millin began his apparently suicidal serenade immediately upon jumping from the ramp of the landing craft into the icy water. As the Cameron tartan of his kilt floated to the surface he struck up with Hieland Laddie. He continued even as the man behind him was hit, dropped into the sea and sank.

Once ashore Millin did not run, but walked up and down the beach, blasting out a series of tunes. Bodies of the fallen were drifting to and fro in the surf. Soldiers were trying to dig in and, when they heard the pipes, many of them waved and cheered – although one came up to Millin and called him a 'mad bastard'.

For many other soldiers, however, the piper provided a unique boost to morale. 'I shall never forget hearing the skirl of Bill Millin's pipes,' said one, Tom Duncan, many years later. 'It is hard to describe the impact it had. It gave us a great lift and increased our determination. As well as the pride we felt, it reminded us of home and why we were there fighting for our lives and those of our loved ones.'[138]

After the 1994 Defence Review, the number of British military bands was reduced from 69 to 29 and this number has been reduced yet further since. Although there are fewer bands than there once were, military music continues to play an important part in inspiring troops. Binyon, the Remembrance Day poet, made several references to music in war. He described music in the midst of desolation and how the young men went with songs to battle.[139]

Music evokes and expresses emotion in a way nothing else does. It can inspire and rally troops, or it can comfort the bereaved and speak of peace. What style of music should therefore be encouraged, and what should be avoided, at a Remembrance-tide focusing on peace?

The Remembrance-tide musical instrument is the bugle. It is an instrument of military origin, having once been employed to communicate orders. Today it is exclusively used to evoke a military mood. If a bugle sound is heard from the orchestra pit during an opera it is invariably a sign that troops are about to march on stage. 'The Last Post' is the call most instantly recognized as that of Remembrance Day. Originally its sounding in camp marked the end of the day, or if heard after battle, it signified that the fighting was over and the wounded and those disorientated by the fighting could follow the sound to find their way back to a place of safety. When sounded at Remembrance-tide it symbolically, in the minds of some, summons the spirits of the Fallen to the Cenotaph. To suggest that the sounding of the 'Last Post' be discontinued might be a change too far and result in resistance to all change from traditionalists. For now, perhaps the playing of a shortened version of the 'Last Post' could be suggested and bugle playing restricted to that one call.

Ideally music played at Remembrance-tide should not be that which rouses marshal or jingoistic feelings. That would be to betray the hopes of 1919. By and large the music played at the Cenotaph on Remembrance Sunday does not do that. The music chosen might serve to sanitize war and the words to hymns might sentamentalize death, but the music is suitable muted and sombre in tone. The music chosen for the Festival of Remembrance, however, needs to be re-examined. At one point members of the three services march down the steps and into the central arena of the Royal Albert Hall to what a BBC presenter in 2009 called 'rousing music'. The Navy marches to 'Hearts of Oak' and the Royal Marines to 'A Life on the Ocean Wave'. The audience claps in time to the music. The audience attends the festival to be entertained as much as to remember, and that entertainment comes from creating an atmosphere of sugary jingoism. The Festival can be traced back to the 1920s and the first performance of John Foulds' composition for massed choir and orchestra, 'A World Requiem', although by the twenty-first century, the Festival had taken on a very different tone. In 2011 it featured celebrity singers, Cliff Richard, Alfie Boe and Katherine Jenkins as well as military bands and displays of marching. If there is a strong case to be made for the Cenotaph rituals to be revised and updated, there is an even stronger argument for the Festival of Remembrance to be overhauled, if not ended altogether. Perhaps the Royal British Legion could set a date for the final Festival to take place in 2021, the organization's centenary. In the meantime, the Festival could be gradually downplayed in national significance with the presence of the Queen, the Prime Minister and the Leader of the Opposition no longer required. The BBC might also consider broadcasting only highlights and eventually phasing out its coverage. To those involved, and regular viewers, the festival might be a popular annual outing or harmless piece of evening's entertainment, but to many others it appears to panders to all the worst aspects of Remembrance sentimentality and the glorification and sanitization of war. It condones the half-truth that all wars waged by Britain can be justified as being fought to protect our freedom.

When a child enters the Albert Hall arena and declares that his poppy is given 'to say thank you from children to those who gave their lives so that we can live and be free', it would be far more honest to show images on the screens of children killed and injured by British troops in the course of their freedom battles. Children are not killed deliberately, but they do die as the inevitable consequence of adults' conflicts.

If the Royal Albert Hall Festival came to an end, so too would other similar music and marching festivals held around the country featuring uniformed organizations. There may be resistance to the phasing out of the Festival, in that it resonates with a particular generation with memories of the war. 'I am not in favour of any substantive changes in the Festival of Remembrance', says Lord Owen.

> I was born in 1938 but the Second World War still has vivid memories, and the 6 o'clock news on the radio was when my mother listened for any hint of what was happening where my father was fighting in the Royal Army Medical Corps, either in France with the Expeditionary Force or later at Alamein and then with even more vivid memories of when he was in Italy.[140]

For many of an older generation, the festival combines nostalgia with Remembrance. To many, nostalgia is an emotion to be savoured and enjoyed. It is a harmless pleasure. If it can be shown that the passing of the Festival of Remembrance would contribute towards a return of Remembrance to its original purpose, then nostalgia would have to be forgone. To insist on maintaining the Festival for nostalgic reasons would be a gross indulgence.

Another reform that could be considered concerns the wearing of uniforms at Remembrance-tide. What message is being conveyed when members of the armed services wear ceremonial bearskins, a form of headgear that has not been worn on the battlefield since the nineteenth century? These trappings, along with scarlet uniforms, are only maintained for ceremonial duties such as Royal Guard duty. They are the acceptable face of soldiering: romantic, traditional, immaculate, dashing. They might have a role in attracting tourists, but it is not what soldiers wear in the field. The suggestion is that serving military personnel should be seen on parade at the cenotaph in their real clothes, the specialist protective combat kit, for instance, worn in Helmand province. This symbolic change would remind onlookers that the bearing of arms may be a necessary profession, but it should not be glamorized.

It carries dangers and responsibilities. In the same vein, members of the Royal Family would be advised not to appear in uniform unless currently serving in the forces. The Queen does not wear a uniform, although she would be entitled to do so as holder of numerous honorary positions. Her family should follow her example, even those who are retired members of the services. Only her two grandsons who are currently active members of the services would wear uniform, and then appear as their colleagues in their working clothes.

Another change to the Remembrance Day observations to be considered concerns marching. It might be acceptable for a regiment to march through its home town to applause on returning from a tour of duty, but is marching appropriate at a ceremony dedicated to peace? I would propose there be no formal marching by either active or former service men and women who take part. They should be invited to walk solemnly and in a dignified manner past the Cenotaph, not in military formation. Some veterans seem to revel in showing off an exaggerated swinging of the arms as if they were on the parade grounds of their youth. Troops and veterans should be encouraged too to walk in the company of the civilians bereaved by war, widows and families, not separated into marching columns by service or regiment. Veterans from former enemy countries could be invited to accompany the walk past. If the French president and German chancellor can meet at the Arc de Triomphe on 11 November, then Argentinian, German, Italian and Japanese veterans can be invited to walk with the Cenotaph column.

To mark the two minutes' silence it should be sufficient to start on the sound of Big Ben striking the first beat of eleven o'clock and finish with the 'Last Post' or some other appropriate music and not, as currently happens, with the sound of a cannon. This would be a small change to the tradition which would remove another one of its military trappings.

These proposals, however, are not all negative suggestions of things to change or abolish. Alterations to the Remembrance Day observances could include the introduction of three new traditions.

The first would be to adopt a suitable way of recalling the civilians who have died in Britain's wars: both civilians overseas and in Britain. It would need to be a form of Remembrance that reaches out beyond the confines of war memorials dedicated to the military dead. One suggestion could be for bell ringers at churches around the country to be asked to ring a half-muffled peal for at least an hour on 11 November. This form of ringing heard, for instance, from Westminster Abbey, after important funerals, is a traditional mark of respect for the dead. The six, eight or twelve bells are rung in sequence and then a muffled echo of them is heard before they ring again. The effect is achieved when one side of the clapper of each bell is covered, creating an evocative blend of ringing and muffled notes. Where a church has only a single bell, it could be tolled for that hour, slowly, as it might be for a funeral.

The second proposal is to include an additional short set of lines to follow the declamation of Binyon's famous lines that begin, 'they shall not grow old . . .'. These would be lines to offer a balance to Binyon's sentiments and could be those of his contemporary, the poet A. E. Housman.

> Here dead we lie
> Because we did not choose
> To live and shame the land
> From which we sprung.
>
> Life, to be sure,
> Is nothing much to lose,
> But young men think it is,
> And we were young.

Housman's words repeat many of Binyon's thoughts, but less sentimentally. They suggest not the myth of eternal youth that comes with dying in battle, but the sense of disappointment at wasted potential. It is a subtle reminder too that politicians and the public should never regard the troops as expendable commodities, sacrificed for a greater national good, but always as individuals.

The irony and anger of the line 'Life, to be sure, is nothing much to lose' would counter Binyon's sunset prose.

In 'Anthem for a Doomed Youth', there are bitter lines from Wilfred Owen that would make for a far sharper statement. But might it be heartless to veterans who cherish Remembrance, as they understand it, to force them to listen to reminders of a harsh reality they knew to well? It would however be a dereliction of duty by this generation to those of the future to allow the words of Binyon to continue being said entirely unquestioned. And if, at the Cenotaph and the nation's war memorials, words of atonement are to be added to those of Remembrance, those of Wilfred Gibson (1872–1962) from his poem 'Back' might be suitable.

He expresses the thoughts of the returned soldier looking back. Was it really me, he wonders? Who was the person who went abroad to war . . .

> And with my head and hands
> Killed men in foreign lands?

Could it have been the same man who now stays at home in peace and lives by the rules of civilized society? But sadly, he realizes, he must 'bear the blame, because he bore my name.'

The third proposal is more substantial than either of the above. It involves creating a direct correction between the wearers of poppies and the men whose deaths are celebrated and honoured by the poppies. This would be done by linking each poppy sold with an individual and his story.

Suppose each poppy sold had a number printed on the back, any number from one to a thousand. It would be a matter of chance which number the buyer would find. At the same time a website would be created on which there would be 1,000 names listed corresponding to the numbers on the poppy. Each name would be of a member of the forces who had died in uniform over the last 100 years. Overwhelmingly the names would be of the fallen of the First and Second World War, but more recent servicemen and -women would be included. By each name there would be a photograph and a biography, including names of family. Information would be given about how the individual died and when. It might have been in battle, such as going over the top at the Somme. Perhaps it was of disease; or an accident in training; a victim of friendly fire. In style and presentation it might be based on the highly successful 'Missing of the Somme' exhibition presented at the Great War Museum in Peronne, France, in 2012.

Every person who bought a poppy would thus have a direct link with an individual by name and learn something about that person in life and death. Get poppy 413 and look up 413 on the website and discover, say, the history of a young man who joined a Pals' Regiment with his work colleagues, was badly injured in a gas attack in 1917 and died several painful weeks later, leaving a widow and two young children. A poppy with number 982 would tell a different story of, perhaps, a Royal Navy gunner drowned when the ship on which he was serving in 1943 was sunk by a submarine in the Atlantic Ocean. Number 52 might tell the story of a Spitfire mechanic killed when German aircraft bombed a Battle of Britain airfield. Number 276 on a poppy might correspond with a civil fire fighter killed in a Second World War air raid.

The names would be chosen at random, but all the stories would be true. Instead of wearing a poppy because everyone else does, or as some abstract expression of respect, or out of a general sense of pride for members of the armed forces, or to be patriotic, everyone would have the opportunity to identify with a real person. The personal story revealed might help the wearer of the poppy understand something of the grief felt by the man's family and friends.

There might even be a case, in due course, for including names of enemy combatants on the list; an Argentine conscript who died in the Falklands; a German in Rommel's Afrika Korps who died when the tank in which he was travelling was set on fire; a young Turkish officer who died from wounds sustained at Gallipoli. The short biography would be a reminder that enemies too had families, civilian jobs and identities that were not solely military.

Case histories of participants in the World Wars are already published and the Imperial War Museum in London is an invaluable source. This idea however would encourage every poppy wearer to identify with a real person, their life, experience of war and death. It is a small and, hopefully, non-controversial amendment to the traditions of Remembrance-tide that would help lessen any tendency for Remembrance to be a glorification of war.

To abolish Remembrance Day and the other rituals of Remembrance would be hurtful, meaningless and ungrateful. Changes, however, are long overdue, although in making changes care has to be taken not to hinder any who grieve from finding comfort and purpose in Remembrance.

The aim of any set of changes must be to encourage the younger generation to see warfare more in terms of individual cost and not in misleading broad-brush generalizations of heroism and sacrifice in the cause of freedom. It would be to refocus Remembrance tide, which has moved too far away from its origins. It would not dishonour anyone who has died in the service of their country, but would be a timely reminder of the true cost of war and a check against the glorifying, sanitizing or sentimentalizing of war. It would be a renewed warning to both politicians and the electorate that the use of arms should never be embarked upon lightly.

REFERENCES

1   www.battleofideas.org.uk
2   T. Harrison and P. Williams, *McIndoe's Army: The Story of the Guinea Pig Club and Its Indomitable Members* (London, 1979).
3   Katie Dicker, *Special Days of the Year: Poppy Day* (London, 2007).
4   Laurence Binyon, 'For the Fallen' (1914).
5   Wilfred Owen, 'Anthem for Doomed Youth' (1917).
6   Richard Holmes, *Soldiers: Army Lives and Loyalties from Redcoats to Dusty Warriors* (London, 2011), p. 300.
7   www.hmforces.co.uk/join_The_Forces
8   President George W. Bush on the 'Lessons in Liberty' initiative.
9   Hansard, vol. 145, 22 January 1947, cc41–60.
10 Sir Donald Somervell, Cabinet memorandum (National Archives, 12 July 1945).
11 www.bbc.co.uk/history/historic_figures/keynes_john_maynard
12 Pierre Sorlin, *War and Remembrance in the Twentieth Century*, ed. Jay Winter (Cambridge, 2000), p. 104.
13 Winston Churchill, Speech to Joint Session of Congress, Washington, DC, December 1941.
14 Jonathan Jones, *The Guardian*, 25 October 2011.
15 Juliet Nicolson, *The Great Silence, 1918–20: Living in the Shadow of the Great War* (London, 2009) p. 5.
16 Frederick George Scott, *The Great War As I Saw It* (Toronto, 1922), chapter 35.
17 Nicolson, *The Great Silence*, pp. 38–9.
18 Paul Rubens, 'Your King and Country Want You' (1914).
19 www.ppu.org.uk/whitepoppy
20 George Mosse, *Fallen Soldiers: Reshaping the Memory of the World Wars* (Oxford, 1991), p. 106.
21 BBC News website, 28 May 2006.
22 Politicsontoast.com

23 threethousandversts.blogspot.com/2008/10/poppy-day

24 Dr Abdul Wahid is Chairman of the UK-Executive Committee of Hizb ut-Tahrir.

25 www.eurasiareview.com

26 *Daily Telegraph*, 7 November 2008.

27 Observational survey carried out by author.

28 *The Daily Telegraph*, 11 November 2011.

29 *The Sunday Telegraph*, 13 November 2011.

30 www.parliament.uk/briefing-papers/SN05979.

31 Stefan Goebel, *The Great War and Medieval Memory: Remembrance and Medievalism in Britain and Germany, 1914–1940* (Cambridge, 2007), p. 27.

32 Herbert Baker, 'War Memorials: The Ideal of Beauty', *The Times*, 9 January 1919, p. 9.

33 Pope John Paul II speaking at a general audience 4 August 1999.

34 www.dayofthedead.com

35 www.sweden.se/eng/Home/Lifestyle/Traditions

36 Sinquanon's Journal, Samhain cited on website www.garden digest.com

37 www.pagan-heart.co.uk

38 www.wicca.com

39 *New York Times*, 1 June 2005.

40 Goebel, *The Great War and Medieval Memory*, p. 280.

41 Chris Womersley, *The Sydney Morning Herald*, reproduced in *Spirit of PN*, 3 November 2010.

42 Goebel, *The Great War and Medieval Memory*, p. 251.

43 Sir Donald Somervell, Cabinet memorandum (National Archives, 12 July 1945).

44 Ibid.

45 Gordon Stuart, Church of the Messiah, Birmingham, 9 May 1945.

46 Mosse, *Fallen Soldiers*, pp. 212–13.

47 Correspondence with author, August 2011.

48 Lt.-Col. Dave Grossman, *On Killing: The Psychological Cost of Learning to Kill in War and Society* (New York, 1995), p. 31.

49 David Livingstone Smith, *The Most Dangerous Animal: Human Nature and the Origins of War* (New York, 2007), p. 158.

50 Ibid., p. 157.

51 Goebel, *The Great War and Medieval Memory*, p. 22.

52 Nicolson, *The Great Silence*, p. 330.

53 Richard van Emden, *The Quick and the Dead: Fallen Soldiers and their Families in The Great War* (London, 2011).

54 Hansard, 30 July 1919, vol. 118, cc2112–13.

55 Goebel, *The Great War and Medieval Memory*, p. 34.

56 Hansard, 29 October 1919, vol. 120, cc657–8.
57 www.va.gov/opa/vetsday/vetdayhistory
58 www.nlplanet.com/almanac/liberation-day
59 www.dw-world.de
60 *The Economist*, 11 November 2010.
61 Rupert Brooke, 'The Soldier' (1915).
62 Margaret Thatcher, *The Downing Street Years* (London, 1993), p. 179.
63 *The Sun*, 4 May 1982.
64 Livingstone Smith, *The Most Dangerous Animal*, p. 183.
65 Chris Hedges, *War is a Force that Gives Us Meaning* (New York, 2002), pp. 13–14.
66 Livingstone Smith, *The Most Dangerous Animal*, p. 197.
67 Ibid., p. 210.
68 Joanna Bourke, *An Intimate History of Killing: Face-to-face Killing in Twentieth-century Warfare* (New York, 2000), p. 16.
69 Wilfred Owen, 'Apologia Pro Poemate Meo' (1917).
70 *The Observer*, 23 January 2011.
71 Improvised explosive device.
72 Forward Operating Bases.
73 *The Independent*, 20 July 2009.
74 BBC World Service, 'The Kill Factor', 11 June 2011.
75 Jonathan Jones, *The Guardian*, 25 October 2011.
76 www.westernfrontassociation.com
77 Ibid.
78 Paul Fussell, *The Great War and Modern Memory* (Oxford, 1975), p. 116.
79 www.westernfrontassociation.com
80 *Fortean Times*, May 2003.
81 Mosse, *Fallen Soldiers*, p. 75.
82 picturesofjesus4you.com
83 Ibid.
84 Scott, *The Great War as I Saw It*, pp. 48–9.
85 www.smithmag.net, January 2007
86 Holmes, *Soldiers*, p. xxvi.
87 Ibid., p. xxv.
88 www.forceswatch.net
89 *Band of Brothers*: music by Michael Kamen, lyrics by Frank Musker.
90 *Henry V*, Act IV, Scene iii.
91 Rev. 20:12–14 (King James Version).
92 Matt. 25:31–32 (King James Version).
93 Jay Winter, *Sites of Memory, Sites of Mourning: The Great War in European Cultural History* (Cambridge, 1995), pp. 169–71.

94   Matthew Arnold, 'Balder Dead' (1855).
95   H. A. Guerber, *Myths of the Norsemen: From the Eddas and Sagas* (London, 1908), p. 19.
96   BBC News, 7 March 2003.
97   Joseph Lynch, *The Medieval Church: A Brief History* (London, 1992), p. 208.
98   Eph. 6:13–17.
99   Scott, *The War as I Saw It*, p. 70.
100 Catherine Merridale, 'War, Death and Remembrance in Soviet Russia' in *War and Remembrance in the Twentieth Century*, ed. Jay Winter (Cambridge, 1999), p. 63.
101 Ibid., p. 72.
102 Ibid., p. 73.
103 Dianne Graves, *A Crown of Life: The World of John McCrae* (Tonbridge, 1997).
104 Andrew Macphail, *John Macrae* (Gloucester, 2008).
105 Rudyard Kipling, *Epitaphs of the War, 1914–1918* (1918).
106 Graves, *A Crown of Life*, p. 162.
107 Scott, *The Great War as I Saw It*, p. 41.
108 Macphail, *John McCrae*, p. 4.
109 Fussell, *The Great War and Modern Memory*, p. 250.
110 Moina Michael, *The Miracle Flower: The Story of the Flanders Field Memorial Poppy* (Pittsburgh, PA, 1941) p. 46.
111 Scott, *The Great War as I Saw It*, p. 71.
112 *Legion Magazine*, 21 June 2009.
113 John Ruskin, *Prosperina: Studies of Wayside Flowers*, vol. 1 (1875).
114 Ibid.
115 Macphail, *John McCrae*.
116 Fussell, *The Great War and Modern Memory*, p. 248.
117 Paul Mellor, *Design Week*, 10 November 2011.
118 www.pr-media-blog.co.uk/the-poppy-appeal-brand-under-attack
119 www.morganpr.co.uk
120 *The Independent*, 5 November 2011.
121 Thomas Macaulay, 'Horatius', *The Lays of Ancient Rome* (London, 1842).
122 Mosse, *Fallen Soldiers*, p. 71.
123 Ibid., p. 73.
124 *The Daily Telegraph*, 6 November 2010.
125 *The Times*, 12 October 1854.
126 Fussell, *The Great War and Modern Memory*, p. 64.
127 *Hansard*, 2 June 1902.
128 Eccles. 44:8–9, The Apocrypha.

129 www.culture.gov.uk/images/publications/RS-Order-of-Service.pdf.

130 Lord Owen, correspondence with author.

131 *The Guardian*, 1 September 2011.

132 Richard Holmes, 'Soldiers', p. 272.

133 www.childvictimsofwar.org.uk

134 *Amnesty International NOW magazine*, Winter 2002.

135 usmilitary.about.com/cs/swgames/gr/soa.htm

136 www.smithmag.net, January 2007.

137 Correspondence with author.

138 *Daily Telegraph*, 18 August 2010.

139 Binyon, 'For the Fallen'.

140 Correspondence with author quoted with permission.

INDEX